The State of Global Education: Learning with the World and its People

A battle is being waged in classrooms and capitals around the world over the goals and objectives of the future of global education. While there is growing research in the area of global education, much remains to be uncovered, challenged, and learned through sound empirical research and conceptual explorations. What type of global citizens will schools promote? What types of policies, programs and instructional practices best promote effective global citizenship? Will global education curricula advance an unwavering loyalty to neoliberal ideologies and interests over the strengthening of human rights and the environmental health of our planet? This volume presents a series of research studies and innovative instructional practices centered on advancing global learning opportunities and literacies.

The authors in this volume initiate a much needed conversation on ways students in multiple contexts can and should learn with the world and its people. Part I addresses global education in theory, with a particular focus on development, intercultural competence, and global citizenship. Part II addresses educational programs and practices that foster global learning and action to help build a better future for all citizens of our planet – including experiential education, university initiatives, and conceptual approaches to teaching and learning. This scholarship spans four continents in a multitude of educational contexts – primary, secondary, and tertiary – each with a focus on a different dimension of the possibilities and pitfalls in teaching about and with the world and its people.

Brad M. Maguth is an assistant professor in the Department of Curricular and Instructional Studies and director of the H.K. Barker Center for Economic Education at The University of Akron. Dr. Maguth served as the editor of *New Directions in Social Education Research: The Influence of Technology and Globalization on the Lives of Students* (Information Age Press, 2012).

Jeremy Hilburn, PhD, is an assistant professor at the University of North Carolina Wilmington, his alma mater. His recent scholarly work includes manuscripts in *Urban Review, Journal of Social Studies Research, Social Studies Research and Practice, Theory and Research in Social Studies*, and the Asian American education anthology.

Citizenship, Character and Values Education

Edited by James Arthur and Wing On Lee

1 **The State of Global Education**
   Learning with the World and its People
   Edited by Brad M. Maguth and Jeremy Hilburn

The State of Global Education
Learning with the World and Its People

**Edited by Brad M. Maguth
and Jeremy Hilburn**

NEW YORK AND LONDON

First published 2015
by Routledge
711 Third Avenue, New York, NY 10017

and by Routledge
2 Park Square, Milton Park, Abingdon, Oxon OX14 4RN

Routledge is an imprint of the Taylor & Francis Group, an informa business

© 2015 Taylor & Francis

The right of the editors to be identified as the authors of the editorial material, and of the authors for their individual chapters, has been asserted in accordance with sections 77 and 78 of the Copyright, Designs and Patents Act 1988.

All rights reserved. No part of this book may be reprinted or reproduced or utilised in any form or by any electronic, mechanical, or other means, now known or hereafter invented, including photocopying and recording, or in any information storage or retrieval system, without permission in writing from the publishers.

Trademark notice: Product or corporate names may be trademarks or registered trademarks, and are used only for identification and explanation without intent to infringe.

Library of Congress Cataloging-in-Publication Data

The state of global education : learning with the world and its people / edited by Brad Maguth and Jeremy Hilburn.
    pages cm. — (Citizenship, character and values education)
  Includes bibliographical references and index.
  1. Citizenship—Study and teaching. 2. Education and globalization. 3. Teachers—Training of. I. Maguth, Brad M., 1980–
  LC1091.S73 2015
  370.116—dc23   2014045246

ISBN: 978-0-415-72167-7 (hbk)
ISBN: 978-1-315-86297-2 (ebk)

Typeset in Sabon LT
by Apex CoVantage, LLC

Dedicated to Sheila, Haley, Evan and to my parents
—Jeremy

To those global educators helping their students see the world
—Brad

Contents

External Reviewers — ix
Acknowledgments — xi
Series Foreword — xiii
JAMES ARTHUR AND WING ON LEE

1 Introduction: The State of Global Education: Learning with the World and Its People — 1
BRAD M. MAGUTH AND JEREMY HILBURN

Part I: Global Education in Theory — 11

2 A Pedagogy of Development Education: Lessons for a More Critical Global Education — 13
DOUGLAS BOURN

3 Global Aspects of Citizenship Education: Challenges and Perspectives — 27
ANATOLI RAPOPORT

4 Global Education in Theory: The Centrality of Intercultural Competence — 41
CAPRICE LANTZ AND IAN DAVIES

Part II: Global Education Programs and Practices — 61

Section 1: Experiential Education — 61

5 On the Modern Silk Road: A Case Study of the Limits and Promise of International In-Service Teacher Professional Development — 63
TIMOTHY PATTERSON

6 Teacher Conceptualizations of Global Citizenship:
   Global Immersion Experiences and Implications for
   the Empathy/Threat Dialectic   78
   DEBORA HINDERLITER ORTLOFF AND OLGA N. SHONIA

7 Globalization and Teacher Education: Teaching about
   Globalization through Community-Based Inquiry   92
   GUICHUN ZONG

Section 2: University Initiatives   111

8 Globalization of Elementary Teacher Preparation in the
   United States: A National Snapshot   113
   CYNDI MOTTOLA POOLE AND WILLIAM B. RUSSELL III

9 Discussions within Online Learning Formats: Are Meaningful
   Encounters with Difference Possible?   133
   SARAH A. MATHEWS AND HILARY LANDORF

Section 3: Conceptual Approaches to Teaching and Learning   153

10 Learning from 21st-Century International Schools:
   Global Education That Is Action-Oriented, Globally
   Connected, and Inclusive   155
   ADRIENNE MICHETTI, REBEKAH MADRID, AND KIMBERLY COFINO

11 A Values-Based Pedagogical Stance: Teaching Teachers
   for Global Education in Australia   174
   RUTH REYNOLDS, DEBBIE BRADBERY, JOANNA BROWN, DEBRA DONNELLY,
     KATE FERGUSON-PATRICK, SUZANNE MACQUEEN, AND ANNE ROSS

   Contributors   189
   Author Index   195
   Subject Index   201

External Reviewers

We would like to thank the following external peer reviewers for their constructive, careful, and timely feedback to submitted manuscripts. Their efforts were invaluable to the advancement of this project.

- Linda Bennett, University of Missouri
- Veronica Boix-Mansilla, Harvard University
- Lisa Brown Buchanan, UNC Wilmington
- Ken Carano, Western Oregon University
- Susan Colville-Hall, The University of Akron
- Elizabeth Crawford, UNC Wilmington
- Margaret Crocco, Michigan State University
- Ken Cushner, Kent State University
- Alfred Daviso, The University of Akron
- Matthew Hayden, Drake University
- Kosta Kyriacopoulos, UNC Wilmington
- Hans Schattle, Underwood International College
- Binaya Subedi, The Ohio State University
- Omiunota N. Ukpokodu, University of Missouri–Kansas City
- Other reviewers who wished to remain anonymous

Acknowledgments

We would like to thank all of the contributing authors to this volume for their time and effort in participating in numerous rounds of revisions and for helping to serve as internal-peer reviewers of manuscripts. A special thank-you to Mr. William McSuley for his review efforts and feedback. We are very grateful to James Arthur and Wing On Lee for including this volume in their series *Citizenship, Character and Values Education*. To Lauren M. Verity, our editor at Routledge, we are most appreciative of your support and wisdom, which helped make this book possible.

Finally, a special thank-you to our families and loved ones for all of their support, patience, and encouragement in helping us move forward.

Series Foreword

Our understanding of "citizenship" originates from a privileged concept of citizenship. For example, in the time of Aristotle almost 90 percent of the people in Athens were not entitled to citizenship. Only the privileged, elite, and aristocratic class enjoyed citizenship, and all were male. Although indebted to historical constructs, citizenship today is understood in more inclusive ways. Our historical scan of conceptions of citizenship is one that continuously opens up the boundary of citizenship by including more and more people within a jurisdiction, enabling them to enjoy citizenship and economic choice. This opening up of citizenship has been largely influenced and shaped by our constantly expanding understanding of human rights and equality. This greater recognition of cultural and education rights has influenced our notions of citizenship, so that minority groups are integrated into full citizenship. Citizens are also expected to be educated and literate, so that they can understand, critique, and deliberate on matters of public policy. Today's expectation of active citizenship is essentially about engagement and active participation. For a long period, citizenship was legally recognized by the nation-state and was often coupled with an expectation of nationalism and patriotism, although they are not necessarily always to be understood as compliance with the state.

The emergence of globalization has changed the landscape of citizenship, challenging historical constructs based on the nation-state. Living in a period of unprecedented international migration, people have learned to develop multiple identities. In addition, with the Internet, multinational corporations, globalized cultural exchanges—particularly pop culture—and the growth of the idea of the global village, the world has become interconnected and interdependent. While it is debatable whether the role of the nation-state has become weaker, theorists of citizenship have increasingly identified that we are already living in a post-national citizenship era—one characterized by diversity, a fluid movement of people, and multiple identities. The advent of the 21st century's knowledge economy has also led to the awareness of the need for global skills, such as communication, collaboration, and cooperation.

Global citizenship education is affected by, and affects, the processes of globalization. Global citizenship education is one of the strategic areas of work for UNESCO's Education Programme (2014–2017) and one of the three priorities of the UN secretary-general's Global Education First Initiative (GEFI), launched in September 2012.

Global citizenship education (GCE) equips learners of all ages with those values, knowledge, and skills that are based on, and instill respect for, human rights, social justice, diversity, gender equality, and environmental sustainability, and that empower learners to be responsible global citizens. GCE gives learners the competencies and opportunity to realize their rights and obligations to promote a better world and future for all.

UNESCO's work on GCE is guided by a three-pronged approach:

- Policy dialogue in connection with the post-2015 education agenda
- Providing technical guidance on GCE and promoting transformative pedagogies
- Clearing-house function (UNESCO, 2014)

UNESCO (2013) suggests that education in a globalized world increasingly places emphasis on the importance of values, attitudes, and communication skills as a critical complement to cognitive knowledge and skills. The education community is also paying increasing attention to the relevance of education in understanding and resolving social, political, cultural, and global issues. This includes the role of education in supporting peace, human rights, equity, acceptance of diversity, and sustainable development.

However, despite the opportunities brought about by the concept of global citizenship and global citizenship education, the emergence of the concept of global citizenship brings tensions and conflicts that have causes and impacts beyond national boundaries. Challenges such as sustainable development, including climate change, are demonstrating the need for cooperation and collaboration beyond land, air, and water boundaries. Continuing global challenges call for collective actions at the global level as well as at the local level. These are all the issues that global citizenship education has to tackle.

Our series welcomes this book as an important contribution to the debate about critical global citizenship. It covers many aspects of global education and is written by well-known experts in the field. It also presents new perspectives and offers challenges to educators in preparing students for a global and interconnected future.

This book asks fundamental questions about global citizenship education. As the editors put it: What types of global citizens will schools promote? What types of policies, programs, and instructional practices at the primary, secondary, and tertiary levels best promote effective global citizenship? Will global education curricula advance an unwavering loyalty to the profit motive and corporate interests over the strengthening of human rights and the environmental health of our planet? How many more wars, famines, and other man-made acts of disasters must occur before we empower students with the tools and competencies to facilitate real and meaningful global change?

The authors promote global education research and practice that are founded on advancing a notion of inclusivity. They seek to build rich and meaningful cross-cultural relationships through empathy and understanding, and they leverage the technological resources and assets of the 21st century to collaboratively build a more equitable, socially just, and sustainable planet. The book advocates the need for global learning, which is bound to be a learning attitude to be developed, if we are to take diversity and inclusiveness seriously.

Wing On Lee and James Arthur

REFERENCES

UNESCO. (2013). *Global citizenship education: An emerging perspective. Outcome document of the Technical Consultation on Global Citizenship Education*. Retrieved October 31, 2014, from http://unesdoc.unesco.org/images/0022/002241/224115E.pdf

UNESCO. (2014). Global citizenship education. Retrieved October 31, 2014, from www.unesco.org/new/en/global-citizenship-education

1 Introduction
The State of Global Education: Learning with the World and Its People

Brad M. Maguth and Jeremy Hilburn

As the title of this book suggests, its chapters relate to global education with a focus on learning *with* the world and its people. While there is a growing research base on the topic of global education, there is much that remains to be uncovered, challenged, and learned through sound empirical research studies and conceptual explorations. The ten externally peer reviewed chapters in this volume are authored by well-known researchers in the field, as well as emerging scholars, and they contain new perspectives on global education relevant to national and international primary and secondary schools, universities, teacher education programs, professional development for in-service teachers, and global education scholars. This book aims to initiate a conversation on those issues critical to the next generation of theory, research, programs, and policies, and instructional practices in global education—with a specific focus on the possibilities and pitfalls in teaching about and *with* the world and its people.

In 1976 Robert Hanvey identified those modes of thought, skills, and attitudes that he believed contributed toward the formulation of a global perspective. In his foundational work "An Attainable Global Perspective," Hanvey outlined the following core dimensions: perspective consciousness, state of the planet awareness, cross-cultural awareness, knowledge of global dynamics, and awareness of human choices. His scholarship influenced, and continues to influence, an entire generation of global educators who seek to help their students understand the ways in which individuals are connected to one another (locally, nationally, regionally, and globally) across culture, time, and space through their economic, political, and environmental decisions and actions.

In order to make sense of the historical roots of global education as a precursor to the present volume, we provide a brief glimpse into the objectives and structures of global education as it existed in the 1970s and outline some of the changes in global education contexts and scholarship until the present. The first wave of global education centered on helping youth and citizens become cognizant of the many ways in which they were connected to global organizations, markets, businesses, people, systems, and issues. In a Cold War era, democratic nations were pitted against communist states.

The actions citizens took in their everyday life had an aggregate effect on the overall health and well-being of their nation and the larger world. Politicians lectured to teachers and children the importance of knowing about the rest of the world so the United States and West could defeat and conquer the Soviet threat. Events and actions in places like Vietnam and Moscow reverberated around the world, as all nations were fearful of the realities and consequences of a nuclear confrontation during the Cold War.

As distrust and hostility grew between Cold War enemies, U.S. president John F. Kennedy created the Peace Corp, which sent thousands of young American volunteers abroad in an attempt to bring social and economic progress to underdeveloped nations. These volunteers served as ambassadors of their country abroad and aimed to win the hearts and minds of those they served. With years of cross-cultural experience under their belt, Peace Corp volunteers came back home to share their experiences. In particular, many of these volunteers went into U.S. classrooms to teach the importance of open-mindedness and to discuss the profound role culture plays in shaping thought and action (Merryfield & Wilson, 2005). The focus was on exposing students to different worldviews, and helping students look at the world through other people's eyes. Thus, this particular wave of global education marked a period when many U.S. educators emphasized the ways in which citizens were connected to the rest of the world.

Since this clarion call by Hanvey over 36 years ago for teachers to infuse a global perspective, the world, its people, and its tools have changed dramatically. No longer are the U.S. and its allies locked into a Cold War with the Soviet Union and its allies. Organizations, institutions, and citizens understand the profound impact of global markets, investment, natural disasters, diseases, conflicts, and issues on their everyday activities and opportunities. In a world marred by such man-made disasters as 9/11, the global financial crisis, and climate change, it is essential all citizens directly engage with geographically diverse populations to learn about events and movements that impact the quality of life on our planet. Researchers over the past 30 years have added a great deal of depth and needed conceptual clarity to advancing scholarship in global education (e.g., Alger, 1974; Anderson, 1991; Case, 1993; Gaudelli, 2003; Kirkwood-Tucker, 2009; Merryfield, 2002; Pike & Selby, 1988; Subedi, 2010; Tye, 1999; Willinsky, 1998). Due to the efforts of these scholars and others, the goals, content, and pedagogies associated with global learning have been greatly enhanced. Even though their work was often misperceived as being un-American and hostile to capitalism and Western values, the past 30-plus years have ushered in growing commitments by policy makers and educators to ensure citizens were being prepared for an increasingly global age (Merryfield & Wilson, 2005).

Advancements in new technologies like the Internet, satellite television, and low-cost transportation systems have redefined global interactions and learning opportunities. Today, new opportunities exist for global study tours and study abroad experiences. A record number of U.S. college students (283,332) traveled abroad for academic credit in 2011–12, up 150 percent more than a decade earlier (Institute of International Education, 2013). In addition to physical global travel, new digital tools have provided students and teachers with low-cost, synchronous (e.g., Skype) and asynchronous (e.g., YouTube) global communication opportunities (Maguth, 2012). Websites like iearn.org, TakingITGlobal, Google Earth, and epals that are predicated on helping teachers and students learn about the world, its people, and issues are increasingly used in the education community. Outside of new face-to-face and virtual global learning opportunities, today's 24/7 media have become instantaneous and global in scope. Events in the Middle East are not reported in days or hours (as noted by Hanvey in 1976) but within seconds. These events, and others, are instantaneously shared, with commentary, by users around the world through social networking websites like Twitter.

The need for students to learn about global interconnectedness in schools has garnered a great deal of support from members of different political leanings. On the one hand, progressives and humanitarians have advocated a form of global education that fosters a citizenry ready and willing to collaborate across geographic and cultural boundaries to confront some of our world's most serious issues. Through this lens, a globally literate citizenry must be sensitive to the heightened role of culture on human behavior and be equipped to build bridges of understanding and respect to foster meaningful and trusting global partnerships (Merryfield, 2002; Noddings, 2005). On the other hand, neoliberals, who have dominated contemporary discourse on globalization, have advocated a form of global education that promotes global capitalism overseas, which ensures strong, open markets for U.S. exports (Ball, 2012; Gaudelli & Donaldson, 2012). This focus has been on spreading free trade zones and world trade agreements to export as many goods globally as possible in order to maximize profits. Through this lens, nations must be committed to fostering a globally literate citizenry that's strong enough to out-compete foreigners for jobs and entrepreneurial opportunities (Friedman, 2005; Friedman & Mandelbaum, 2012). While their justifications for the curricular integration of global education differ, progressives and neoliberals tend to support teachers and students learning about ways in which people, businesses, and organizations are connected to one another in complex global systems.

This book presents a series of research studies and innovative instructional practices that help to initiate a conversation on ways to build healthy global partnerships and literacies—not in an attempt to push a narrow, neoliberal free-market agenda, but to better prepare citizens to undertake the "office" of citizen responsibly in an age confounded by global opportunities, challenges, and issues. A battle is being waged in classrooms and capitals around the world over the goals and objectives of the future of global education. What types of global citizens will schools promote? What types of policies, programs, and instructional practices at the primary, secondary, and tertiary levels best promote effective global citizenship? Will global education curricula advance an unwavering loyalty to the profit motive and corporate interests over the strengthening of human rights and the environmental health of our planet? How many more wars, famines, and other man-made acts of disasters must occur before we empower students with the tools and competencies to facilitate real and meaningful global change?

This book is an attempt to promote global education research and practice that are founded on advancing inclusivity, building rich and meaningful cross-cultural relationships through empathy and understanding, and leveraging the technological resources and assets of the 21st century to collaboratively build a more equitable, socially just, and sustainable planet. In advancing this goal, this book focuses on ways in which students learn *with* the world and its people (in school and out of school) conceptually, and on those educative programs, policies, and practices that foster global learning and action to help build a better future for all citizens of our planet.

As a collection, the chapters in this book present a variety of findings, strategies, and tools aimed at moving the field of global education forward. This volume offers a great deal of breadth on the topic of global education. The authors included in this volume come from many different countries (Australia, China, England, Japan, Singapore, and the U.S.). The scholarship included herein spans four continents in a multitude of educational contexts (elementary, secondary, and university). Likewise, some chapters focus on in-service teacher development while others focus on preservice teacher education. Several of these chapters are conceptual pieces that are intended to engage the reader in the theoretical underpinnings and new directions of global education, while others are based on newly collected empirical data. The intended audience of this volume includes teachers, teacher educators, global education scholars, primary and secondary school leaders, university leaders, and policy makers. While each of these chapters has a different focus, all of the chapters are linked by a focus on learning with the world and its people. The chapter authors offer greatly needed insights from experienced global educators who are also linked by their collective commitment to successfully prepare the next generation of informed and active global citizens.

ORGANIZATION OF THIS VOLUME

This book is divided into two parts. Part I presents theoretical and conceptual arguments that hold great promise in advancing the field of global education, with an emphasis on global citizenship, intercultural competence, and development. Part II presents scholarship on effective programmatic efforts and instructional practices in global education. We have divided Part III into three sections: Section I centers on research on the promise and perils of experiential education in global education, Section II focuses on university initiatives to advance global learning and the intended and unintended consequences of those initiatives, and Section III promotes innovative conceptual approaches in teaching and learning of global education. In the following space, we briefly summarize the chapters in this volume.

Part 1: Global Education in Theory

Chapter 2, "A Pedagogy of Development Education: Lessons for a More Critical Global Education" suggests that by looking at concepts and pedagogies within development education, global educators can adopt a more radical and challenging approach to global education. Douglas Bourn proposes a new pedagogical framework for global education that places specific emphasis on an understanding of power dynamics and inequality in the world, the influence of colonialism, the importance of reflection and dialogue, and, above all, a belief in social justice.

Chapter 3, "Global Aspects of Citizenship Education: Challenges and Perspectives" notes how the growing popularity and interest in global citizenship, a concept born millennia ago, have been widely discussed by politicians and scholars for the last several decades. However, schools are still largely outside of these debates. In this chapter, Anatoli Rapoport reports on the factors that contribute to many teachers' discomfort with the concept of global citizenship. His chapter includes a discussion on obstacles that prevent the expansion of global citizenship education in schools and the role of teacher education programs in advancing education for global citizenship.

Chapter 4, "Global Education in Theory: The Centrality of Intercultural Competence," investigates a key aspect of global education—intercultural competence—in the context of higher education. Caprice Lantz and Ian Davies from the United Kingdom begin their chapter with brief remarks about the history and background of global education and its connection to intercultural communication. In particular, they note that while the seeming necessity of educating about and for a globalized world is commonplace, the status levels of global education and intercultural competence in schools are still relatively low. While acknowledging significant challenges to the advancement of global learning, the authors conclude the chapter by discussing institutional and pedagogical initiatives that hold promise in raising the stature and reach of the field.

Part II: Global Education Programs and Practices

Section 1: Experiential Education

Chapter 5, "On the Modern Silk Road: A Case Study of the Limits and Promise of International In-Service Teacher Professional Development," considers the challenges and affordances of in-service teacher professional development through international experiential learning (global study tours). Timothy Patterson presents a case study of a study tour in which American teachers traveled along the historic Silk Road in China. Drawing from participant experiences, his own reflections of the tour, and relevant literature on international experiences and computer-mediated communication, the author debunks the notion that international experiences are inherently transformative for teachers. Here he challenges the dominant discourse on this topic and calls for structural changes to international teacher professional development. The author suggests this is one area where the potential to develop truly global educators may be blunted if international experiential learning opportunities are not properly planned and executed.

Chapter 6, "Teacher Conceptualizations of Global Citizenship: Global Immersion Experiences and Implications for the Empathy/Threat Dialectic," reports findings of a multistate study in which teachers were surveyed about their perspectives on global education and preparing students to be global citizens. Debora Hinderlitter Ortloff and Olga Shonia purposefully sampled 108 teachers falling into three categories: teachers with no significant experience outside of the U.S., teachers with significant international experience outside of the U.S., and teachers who migrated to the U.S. from other countries. Their findings indicated significant differences in the way teachers in the three categories conceptualized global citizenship. Teachers without experience outside of the U.S. recognize the preparation of global citizens as an important part of the schooling process, but are primarily motivated to teach for global citizenship out of a perspective of fear. These teachers situate the need for global citizenship in order to compete or keep up with other industrialized countries. In contrast, the teachers in the other two categories had much more nuanced and grounded ideas of global citizenship, invoking notions of empathy, cooperation, and social justice.

Chapter 7, "Globalization and Teacher Education: Teaching about Globalization through Community-Based Inquiry," notes how globalization remains an underexplored yet significant topic for teacher education scholars. Guichun Zong describes how globalization in teacher education is often framed as an uncritical acceptance of the taken-for-granted context. In this chapter, she explores approaches to integrating the concept of globalization into teacher education curricula. Using "Atlanta in the World" as a case study, the author presents how local communities can be used as resources by teacher educators to help university students demystify globalization and develop rich historical understandings of global and local connections. In so doing, she adds to existing scholarship on effective strategies to improve teacher education students' understanding of globalization. Teacher educators who focus on teaching globalization may find this chapter particularly helpful.

Section 2: University Initiatives

Chapter 8, "Globalization of Elementary Teacher Preparation in the United States: A National Snapshot," presents findings from a nationwide study on the extent to which global education university coursework and cross-cultural/co-curricular activities have been incorporated into American elementary teacher preparation programs before and after the year 2000 and the effects of this incorporation on the global perspectives of current elementary school teachers. Cyndi Mottola Poole and William Russell III's research findings indicate that while universities and teacher education programs have promoted global education, and global education courses have increased in elementary teacher preparation in recent years, there has been no significant increase in the global perspectives of the teachers graduating from those programs. The authors conclude with recommendations to counter this finding as universities and teacher education programs move forward with their global education initiatives.

Chapter 9, "Discussions within Online Learning Formats: Are Meaningful Encounters with Difference Possible?" builds on research using the Global Perspective Inventory (GPI) (Glass & Braskamp, 2012), which concludes that meaningful "encounters with difference" contribute significantly to students' development of a global perspective. Sarah A. Mathews and Hilary Landorf question, in an era when many colleges and universities are facing pressures to develop fully online programs and massive open online courses (MOOCs), whether it is possible to facilitate meaningful encounters with difference in online forums. The authors outline obstacles for fostering meaningful asynchronous discussions in online environments and highlight potential successful strategies to advance global learning that emerged from their research on distance education.

Section 3: Conceptual Approaches to Teaching and Learning
Chapter 10, "Learning from 21st-Century International Schools: Global Education That Is Action-Oriented, Globally Connected, and Inclusive," presents insights and recommendations for instructional strategies and school organization from a team of experienced global learning practitioners at international schools. Adrienne Michetti, Rebekah Madrid, and Kimberly Cofino discuss the commitment and significant steps taken by many international schools to promote global education. In this chapter, the authors draw on their collective experiences working in international schools in Europe, the Middle East, and Asia to offer specific examples of how international school–style curriculum, service, activities, leadership, and systems can contribute to changing a school culture to be more action-oriented, globally connected, and inclusive. Their framework may be particularly helpful to school leaders in national schools that wish to promote a school culture focused on global education.

Chapter 11, "A Values-Based Pedagogical Stance: Teaching Teachers for Global Education in Australia," presents scholarship from the Global Education Research and Teaching (GERT) team from the University of Newcastle in Australia. This collaborative is centered on advancing global education perspectives in preservice teacher education programs. Ruth Reynolds, Debbie Bradbery, Joanna Brown, Debra Donnelly, Kate Ferguson-Patrick, Suzanne Macqueen, and Anne Ross propose teaching should focus on "learning about" a global world, but also "learning for" a global world and "learning with" a global world. Each of these foci implies a particular pedagogy and set of values to be clarified and explored. The authors draw from teacher educators' (n=7) reflective diaries and student survey data (n=930) over a three-year period to explore the group's journey to better understand the field. As a result of their research, the authors present a values-based pedagogical stance that has emerged as a central tenet of their global education approach. Adopting this stance may help teacher educators, scholars, and preservice and in-service teachers promote a form of global education that is distinct from neoliberal approaches.

In closing, it is our hope that this book will be a valuable resource for scholars, practitioners, and all constituents related to global education. We hope to inspire more research to advance this line of inquiry. Most of all, we hope this book will push the conversation on global education from learning *about* the world's people to a conversation *with* the world's people.

REFERENCES

Alger, C. (1974). *Your city and the world/The world and your city*. Columbus, OH: Mershon Center.

Anderson, L. F. (1991). A rationale for global education. In K.A. Tye (Ed.), *Global education: From thought to action* (pp. 13–34). Alexandria, VA: Association for Supervision and Curriculum Development.

Ball, S. (2012). *Global education inc.: New policy networks and the neoliberal imaginary*. New York: Routledge.

Case, R. (1993). Key elements of a global perspective. *Social Education 57*, 318–325.

Friedman, T (2005). *The world is flat: A brief history of the twenty-first century*. New York: Farrar, Straus & Giroux.

Friedman, T., & Mandelbaum, M. (2012). *That used to be us: How America fell behind in the world it invented and how we can come back*. New York: Farrar, Straus & Giroux.

Gaudelli, W. (2003). *World class: Teaching and learning in global times*. Mahwah, NJ: Erlbaum.

Gaudelli, W., & Davidson, D. (2012, November). Creating spaces beyond schools for global citizenship education. Paper presented at B. Maguth (Chair), The influence of technology and globalization on the lives of students. Symposium conducted at Annual Meeting of the College and University Faculty Assembly of the National Council for the Social Studies, Seattle, WA.

Glass, R., & Braskamp, L. A. (2012, October 26). *Foreign students and tolerance: I. Inside higher education*. Retrieved at http://blogs.luc.edu/mediaclips/files/2012/10/Inside-Higher-Ed_Foreign-Students-and-Tolerance_10.26.12.pdf

Hanvey, R. (1976). *An attainable global perspective*. American Forum for Global Education. Retrieved from www.globaled.org/an_att_glob_persp_04_11_29.pdf

Institute of International Education. (2013). *Open doors 2013 report on international educational exchange*. Washington, DC: National Press Club. Retrieved from www.iie.org/~/media/Files/Corporate/Open-Doors/Open-Doors-Briefing-November-2013.ashx

Kirkwood-Tucker, T. (2009). *Visions in global education: The globalization of curriculum and pedagogy in teacher education and schools: Perspectives from Canada, Russia, and the United States*. New York: Peter Lang.

Maguth, B. (2012). *New directions in social education research: The influence of technology and globalization on the lives of students*. Charlotte, NC: Information Age Press.

Merryfield, M. (2002). The difference a global educator can make. *Educational Leadership 60*(2), 18–21.

Merryfield, M., & Wilson, A. (2005). *Social studies and the world: Teaching global perspectives*. Silver Spring, MD: National Council for the Social Studies.

Noddings, N. (2005). Global citizenship: Promise and problems. In N. Noddings (Ed.), *Educating citizens for global awareness* (pp. 1–21). New York: Teachers College Press.

Pike, G., & Selby, D. (1988). *Global teacher, global learner*. London: Hodder and Stoughton.

Subedi, B. (2010). *Critical global perspectives: Rethinking knowledge about global societies*. Charlotte, NC: Information Age Press.

Tye, K. A. (1999). *Global education: A worldwide movement*. Orange, CA: Interdependence Press.

Willinsky, L. (1998). *Learning to divide the world: Education at empire's end*. Minneapolis: University of Minnesota Press.

Part I
Global Education in Theory

2 A Pedagogy of Development Education
Lessons for a More Critical Global Education

Douglas Bourn

HISTORICAL TRADITIONS

Global education, as Gaudelli (2003) suggests, has suffered from a multiplicity of definitions, but there is a common goal of "preparing students to inherit an interconnected world that is complex and diverse" (p. 8). Within the global education tradition, some academics emphasize curriculum themes (Woyach & Remy, 1989) while others such as Merryfield (2009) emphasize the role of the educator, to be more world-minded and critically reflective. Tye (1999) stressed the importance of four distinct themes: promoting an awareness of the wider world; having a global outlook; the development of intercultural competences; and a critical approach to global issues. Pike (2000) has suggested a holistic approach that includes an equal emphasis on the affective and the cognitive domains. Gaudelli (2003) makes reference to seeing global education as a "pedagogical style that promotes critical engagement of complex, diverse information towards socially meaningful action" (p. 10).

Many of these themes can be seen in development education. While learning and understanding about development issues such as global poverty were included in curricular approaches to global education, development education has its own distinctive history and evolution where specific pedagogical approaches can be identified. It is suggested in this chapter that these pedagogical approaches in development education have relevance in advancing the field of global education.

DEVELOPMENT EDUCATION AND GLOBAL EDUCATION

The practice of development education in the 1960s and 1970s was influenced by changing relationships between countries in Europe and their former colonies. International aid and development programs emerged, which led to recognition by governments of the desirability of providing funding to encourage public support for development (Harrison, 2008). Thus funding primarily went to non-governmental organizations (NGOs) to produce resources for schools and young people in countries such as the UK and the Netherlands.

The link between an international outlook and the growth of development assistance programs influenced not only policy makers but also non-governmental organizations. One feature of this link was that more critical views on aid and development emerged, as a consequence of educationalists from the Global North spending time in the Global South. The work of Paulo Freire (1972) and his pedagogical approach, which questioned the "banking method of education" and promoted instead more participatory methods of learning, also helped to reinforce the ideas of educationalists who were looking for more radical approaches to the role of education in changing societies (Cronkhite, 2000).

By the 1990s in countries such as the UK, Canada, Germany, the Netherlands, and Japan there were movements of educationalists, mainly working in NGOs with some support from teachers and academics, promoting an approach primarily influenced by critical perspectives on development. This brought together the pedagogy of Freire and progressive classroom practices, influenced particularly by global educationalists such as Pike, Selby, and Tye (Kirby, 1994; Walkington, 2000).

At the beginning of the 21st century there was a shift on the part of educationalists toward the term *global* and away from *development*. There were a number of reasons for this movement. Development education had always been a difficult term to articulate and conceptualize. Individuals often confused personal human development with global economic development. Secondly for many organizations there was increasing unease about working within the dominant paradigm of development, which many felt inhibited a more critical approach. Biccum (2010), for example, has written about the "shift in vocabulary" and the need to have a strategy of ambivalence towards discourses on development. Reviews of the practice of development education in England, for example, identified that there was a need for concepts and themes that were unambiguous and gave a clear indication as to the nature and focus of learning. This led to, for example, the publication of *Developing a Global Dimension for the School Curriculum* (DfES 2005), *Education for Global Citizenship: A Guide for Schools* (Oxfam, 2006), and *Global Youth Work* (Sallah & Cooper, 2008). Within Europe, particularly in Germany and Austria, global educators such as Scheunpflug and Seitz stated that the world is much more complex than a Global North versus a Global South (Hartmeyer, 2008), with globalization being suggested as the dominant influence. In the UK, the umbrella body for development education, the Development Education Association, changed its name to Think Global and started to focus on global learning rather than development education because they felt it promoted a more concrete and concise articulation of their mission.

While development education and global education diverged in the 1980s and 1990s as a result of the different external influences noted earlier, they grew closer together in the first and second decades of the 21st century. Themes such as interconnectedness, having a global outlook, and understanding the perspectives of the "other" are today common themes within both development and global education. Globalization, as Kirkwood-Tucker (2009) noted, is ever-present and cannot be ignored. Less overt, however, in global education discourses today are direct references to power, inequality, the legacy of colonialism, belief in social justice, and personal reflection and transformation. Merryfield (2009) is perhaps one of a few global educators that has offered a more historical and critical perspective of the field. She suggests that global education today needs to bring to the "center of the curriculum the voices of people past and present who were silenced because they had little or no power to be heard" (p. 224). Aspects of these ideas can be seen in the work of Andreotti (2006, 2014), who takes a particular postcolonial perspective. It is suggested that alongside Andreotti's influence, the work of Scheunpflug and a range of practitioner-based organizations can provide models and frameworks that take forward the ideas posed by Merryfield.

CURRENT CONCEPTUAL INTERPRETATIONS OF TERMS

The starting point to identifying a potential conceptual and pedagogic framework of relevance and value to global education has to include a review of the different interpretations of learning about global themes. Various terms can be identified, such as *global learning, global citizenship education, global perspectives, global dimension, education for sustainable development,* and *international education*. The role and usage of these terms vary from country to country. In some cases, terms or concepts emerged in response to broader policy initiatives, such as those on global skills (Bourn, 2008) or global initiatives on sustainable development (Chalkley, Mahigh, & Higgitt, 2008). But in some instances the terminology was constructed by practitioners and researchers in order to move the debates forward, as, for example, in the increasing use of phrases such as being a global citizen or equipping the learner with skills to live and work in a global society.

The term *global education* still has a number of different interpretations in education from all around the world. However, where it has been used as encouraging a more values-based approach, the concept has been linked to themes such as human rights, social justice, sustainability, and creating a better world. An example in Europe has been the Council of Europe's definition, which states,

> Global Education is education that opens people's eyes and minds to the realities of the world and awakens them to bring about a world of greater justice, equity and human rights for all.
> (Maastricht Global Education Declaration,
> quoted in De Silva, 2012, p. 66)

A second unifying theme in Europe has been the desire of policy makers and funders to make a direct link to greater understanding of development themes. However, this has been taken forward by non-governmental organizations to encourage engagement in changing the world. An example of this approach is the European Consensus Document on Development Education, which states,

> The aim of development education and awareness raising is to enable every person. . . to be aware of and understand global development concerns and the local and personal relevance of those concerns, and to enact their rights and responsibilities as inhabitants of an interdependent and changing world by effecting change for a just and sustainable world.
> (Multi-Stakeholder Forum, 2005, p. 5)

Beyond Europe, the term *development education* has come to have rather different meanings. With regard to African contexts, Hoppers (2009) sees "development as a pedagogical field and human development as a goal" (p. 602), with transformative action needed to achieve these goals. Her perspective is based on knowledge development, especially indigenous knowledge systems and the anchoring and articulation of the African perspective within disciplines and the curriculum. Her approach is more than challenging dominant Western ideologies within education but about recognizing the "multiplicity of worlds and forms of life" (Odora Hoppers, 2009). This diversity of knowledge means that development education should be more inclusive, responsive, and dialogic to expose learners to different experiences and approaches.

Kumar (2008) raises similar themes with regard to development education in India. He looks at notions of human development with concepts of dialogical learning and critical humanism, bringing together the influence of Freire and Gandhi. Kumar states that development education must be concerned with

> how learning, knowledge and education can be used to assist individuals and groups to overcome educational disadvantage, combat social exclusion and discrimination, and challenge economic and political inequalities—with a view to securing their own emancipation and promoting progressive social change.
> (2008, p. 41)

Kumar goes on to suggest that development education is a kind of "emancipatory and dialogical learning" based on "critical humanist pedagogy." Dialogic education, he suggests, is where learners together pose problems, enquire, and seek solutions. These discourses and interpretations of development education are relevant not so much because of the continued use of the term, but because of the issues they pose in relation to the links between learning, human development, and social change.

A term that has gained currency in both North America and Europe to bring these themes together, while also recognizing the agenda of globalization, is *global citizenship education*. This term emerged in response to the influence of globalization and the desire of organizations to encourage learners to take action to secure a more just and sustainable world. As Andreotti (2014) has stated, however, the different interpretations of global citizenship education need to be situated within "assumptions about globalization, citizenship and education that prompt questions about boundaries, flows, power relations, belonging, rights, responsibilities, otherness, interdependence" (p. 1). She also makes a distinction between "soft" and "hard" interpretations of global citizenship education. To Andreotti (2006), the goal of soft global citizenship, influenced by cosmopolitan notions, is to "empower individuals to act (or become active citizens) according to what has been defined for them as a good life or ideal world" (p. 48). On the other hand, she sees a harder and more critical global citizenship, influenced by postcolonialist and cultural literacy theory, as about empowering "individuals to reflect critically on the legacies and processes of their cultures, to imagine different futures and to take responsibility for decisions and actions (Andreotti, 2006, p. 48).

Finally, in any discussion on terminology there needs to be an inclusion of the term *global learning*, which in Europe at least is rapidly becoming the dominant term for expressing both the pedagogical themes behind development education and the broader elements underpinning global education, to ensure that learning, and not campaigning, advocacy, or awareness raising, is part of the practice. The leading proponent of this approach internationally has been Scheunpflug (2011). Global learning, she suggests, should not be a new subject in schools but a guiding principle defined by thematic issues, such as development, environment, peace and interculturalism, and spatial dimensions, and by competencies that need to be acquired to live in a global society. These competencies include the ability to

> understand and critically reflect global interdependencies, own values and attitudes, develop own positions and perspectives, see options, capability to make choices, to participate in communication and decisions within a global context.
>
> (Scheunpflug, 2011, pp. 33–34)

Hunt (2012), in her research on global learning in primary schools in England, found that the starting points for teachers' engagement in learning about development issues came through themes such as fairness, rights, empathy, and intercultural understanding. This research was based on a survey with over 200 teachers and group interviews with older children in primary schools. This evidence reinforced the view that using the term *development education* is often confusing among practitioners; when they hear the term *development* or *development education* teachers initially think of personal growth and professional development.

Regardless of the debates around terminology, what is evident from the research mentioned earlier is that learning about themes such as social justice, inequality, and global poverty cannot be reduced to additional bodies of knowledge. They pose challenges to the learner about their sense of place, influences on their own learning journey, and the skills required to engage effectively in a global society. It is proposed here that a new pedagogical framework should be considered, one that builds on the experiences and practices from development education but using an approach that is located within the discourses around global education, global learning, and global citizenship education.

PEDAGOGICAL FRAMEWORK

Alexander (2004) refers to pedagogy as involving "what one needs to know and the skills one needs to command, in order to make and justify the many different kinds of decisions of which teaching is constituted" (p. 11). While he notes that this pedagogy needs to take into account culture and self and identity, there is a danger that this interpretation could lead to a lack of recognition of the influence of power and a critical understanding of the world. This is where the work of Freire (1972) and the writings of critical pedagogical writers such as Giroux (2005) can provide a valuable framework (Au, 2009).

I have suggested elsewhere (Bourn, 2014) that development education as a concept still has value if it is seen as a pedagogical approach, as a process of learning that implies deepening understanding, space for reflection, and potential movement of viewpoint. This process of learning may come about from exposure to different approaches, personal experiences, further learning, and study. Development education could therefore be proposed as an approach to learning that:

- Is framed within an understanding of development and global themes.
- Is located within a values base of social justice.
- Promotes critical and reflective thinking.
- Encourages the learner to make connections between their own lives and others throughout the world.
- Provides opportunities for the learner to have positive and active engagements in society that can contribute to the learner's own perspectives of what a better world would look like.

How this knowledge is perceived, constructed, and promoted is what makes it a pedagogy of development education. Learners will have different starting points, and will be influenced by a range of different external factors; for the learning to have a lasting impact, links need to be made to the learners' own sense of place and identity in the world.

A PEDAGOGY OF DEVELOPMENT EDUCATION AND LESSONS FOR A MORE CRITICAL GLOBAL EDUCATION FRAMEWORK

Four main elements are proposed as the basis for this pedagogy, bringing together the main elements of current practice with a range of theoretical approaches. This pedagogical framework could equally be posed as a framework for a more critical approach to global education in general.

The four elements are as follows:

- A sense of global outlook.
- Recognition of power and inequality in the world.
- Belief in social justice and equity.
- Commitment to reflection, dialogue, and transformation (Bourn, 2014).

A SENSE OF GLOBAL OUTLOOK

Learning about and understanding development and global issues in themselves could be said to encourage a global outlook. But this is not necessarily always the case. Learning about poverty and development, while deemed necessary by some teachers and learners as part of understanding the wider world, could be seen as being about distant places and peoples, with no direct relevance or connection to the learner. In proposing the concept of a global outlook as a key element of this pedagogy, it is hoped that learners will be drawn into debates about their own sense of identity and place in the world, and how as individuals they relate to inequality and poverty. This means encouraging and supporting learning that questions and critically reflects upon a concern for the poor, international solidarity, and a sense of global responsibility.

For the learner, an understanding of global themes and issues presents questions about one's relationship to the wider world. Evidence from research into how both young people and adults perceive international development themes and issues suggests that a dominant view is that of seeing the poor of the world as either helpless victims or beneficiaries of aid—in other words, in a negative context (Hunt, 2012; VSO, 2002).

A moral concern for the poor may well be the starting point for many teachers and young people learning about development. While this moral positioning could be criticized as patronizing and benevolent, it is suggested here that the educational approach should not be to condemn or directly criticize but rather to show that a moral concern for the poor in itself will not necessarily lead to change, and could result in a reinforcement of existing dependency relations. Within the pedagogic framework of developing a global outlook is the recognition of the consequences of one's own actions and those of others.

POWER, INEQUALITY, AND DIVISIONS IN THE WORLD

A concern for the poor is often linked to a broader social and political viewpoint that is inherently critical of dominant economic forces around the world and their consequences in reproducing inequalities. A theme within development education is the underlying assumption that we live in an unequal world where economic, political, and social power rests in the Global North to the detriment of the Global South (Andreotti, 2012; McCloskey, 2014; Regan, 2006).

An understanding of what is meant by power needs to be part of the process of learning, but power is all too often seen in purely economic terms. Power needs systems and bodies of knowledge to support it (McNay, 1994). Looking at power and inequality in relation to divisions in the world between the North and the South requires understanding the historical forces—social, cultural, and economic—that have shaped and informed the power relations and inequalities that exist in the world.

There is, however, a danger in seeing power purely in colonial terms. Globalization has transformed many of the social, cultural, and economic relationships that exist around the world. China, India, and Brazil are becoming global economic players today, whereas a decade ago the dominant lens through which they were seen economically and politically was as part of the Global South. Globalization is not just about economics; it has as much to do with social and cultural forces. This means that in the context of learning about development and global issues, there is a need to include recognition of the changing nature of social, economic, and cultural forces, which are likely to have a direct impact on the learner. Any learning about power and inequality in the world needs to make reference to themes such as globalization, identity, and a sense of historical perspective, to enable an understanding of the changing nature of social relationships around the world.

BELIEF IN SOCIAL JUSTICE AND A MORE EQUAL WORLD

An underlying theme of development education practice has been a value base of concern for a more just and equitable world (Hartmeyer, 2008; Hicks & Holden, 2007; Oxfam, 2006). This phrase, or variations of it, can be seen in most definitions of development education. Yet, concepts of social justice by their very nature can be ideologically and culturally laden—in whose interests of social justice, for example, and in terms of equity, and on what basis? A belief in social justice will come from a wide range of personal, social, and cultural influences. From a pedagogical perspective, this means recognizing that for many people their concern about global poverty is likely to start from a moral position, influenced perhaps by factors such as personal experience, religion, peer group and family, and the media. At the other end of the spectrum, you may also find an individual who has been campaigning against global poverty but has not seen the relationship of the values implicit in this action, in terms of social justice and desire for greater equality, to other aspects of their own lives or those of other people.

For many educators who are supportive of these approaches, there is a connection between their interest in the pedagogy and their own personal value system. This, however, can lead to a perception that only those educators who subscribe to a social justice perspective can be true development educators. To avoid these dangers of elitist notions, the process of engaging with what social justice means needs to be part of the learning and not taken as given.

COMMITMENT TO REFLECTION, DIALOGUE, AND PERSONAL AND SOCIAL TRANSFORMATION

Learning about global and development issues can be unsettling to the learner, leading to questioning one's own assumptions about oneself and one's relationship to the wider world. It suggests notions of critical thinking, reflection, dialogue, and engagement that can lead to personal transformation, which in turn may lead to concerns for social change. This means ensuring that discussions on social change are based not on some form of activist model, but on depth of understanding through increased knowledge, and engagement with debates on processes of learning, notably transformative learning (Mezirow, 2000) and global citizenship (Andreotti et al., 2010; Oxley & Morris, 2013).

Another theme of global and development education has been to encourage questioning of existing views about the world (Andreotti, 2012; Kirkwood-Tucker, 2009; Regan, 2006; Tormey, 2014). This approach to learning has much in common with the discourses around critical thinking. At one level, critical thinking could be reduced to looking at different sorts of information, weighing up evidence, and building an argument in order to solve problems. Within this pedagogical framework, critical thinking might include the following:

- Imagining a range of global perspectives—looking at topics and issues through different lenses.
- Looking critically at images of other countries as presented in the media and by organizations such as NGOs.

- Challenging assumptions about how poor people live.
- Looking at the causes of inequalities.
- Exploring power relations—including questions such as who has power, who is voiceless, and who benefits?
- Exploring our own prejudices about poorer countries.

Thinking critically and engaging with different viewpoints and assumptions often leads to the learner reflecting on his or her own viewpoints, and engaging in dialogue to listen to, question, and respect different views.

Dialogue, reflection, and questioning one's own assumptions are themes common to many discussions on learning (Illeris, 2006), but what this proposed pedagogy adds here is the importance of transformation. While at a general level, all forms of education may be seen as transformative if they involve a shift of consciousness that dramatically and permanently alters our way of being in the world, it is the nature of this transformation that is particularly relevant to the debates on learning about global and development issues. It is here perhaps that we can learn from the work of Mezirow (2000), who refers to transformative learning as

> the process by which we transform our taken-for-granted frames of reference (meaning perspectives, habits of mind, mind-sets), to make them more inclusive, discriminating, open, emotionally capable of change, and reflective so that they may generate beliefs and opinions that will prove more true or justified to guide action.
>
> (pp. 7–8)

PEDAGOGY OF DEVELOPMENT EDUCATION IN PRACTICE

This pedagogy will not by itself help motivate school teachers to bring a global element into their teaching. The themes identified are possible elements that could form part of a professional development program for teachers, but they need to be adapted and refined for classroom practice. In order to be of use to teachers, this pedagogy needs to be translated into approaches that are relevant and user friendly to teachers. One way of doing this is to pose the following questions, informed by this pedagogy, as a way of taking forward a global learning approach:

- To what extent in the process of learning about development are connections made to developing a global outlook, having a concern for the poor, and being disposed to be supportive of a sense of social justice and solidarity?
- Within the debates on development, to what extent is there recognition of historical antecedents of colonialism, the consequential divisions

between North and South, and the implications for how countries societies, economies, and cultures develop?
- A charitable mentality is often a natural starting point and response to learning about development. However, to what extent does the learning progress incorporate an understanding of social justice and equity?
- Learning about themes such as poverty and inequality poses challenges to the learners about their own viewpoints, sense of place in the world, and how they should respond. To what extent does learning about development encourage critical thinking, reflection, and dialogue, and pose challenges in terms of personal and social transformation (Bourn, 2014)?

Some aspects of these four areas are more appropriate than others to introduce with different age groups, and the starting point for each of these questions will be different if the teacher is working with 8-year-olds rather than 14-year-olds. The emphasis will vary considerably between subjects, based on pupils' age and maturity. In taking forward this pedagogy into school environments, teachers need to consider the relevant starting points for learning, the appropriate teaching styles, and the opportunities within different subjects.

Learning about development can be simply at the level of knowledge about distant places or data about poverty, or stories of change and transformation within specific communities. This approach implies that learning about development is value-free and that data is incontestable. It also suggests a narrative of one type of story. If global learning is to be built around a pedagogy as suggested here, teaching practice must reflect the different starting points of the learner and be located within a process of learning that opens up minds to see a broader global vision, to deepen knowledge and understanding, to encourage critical thinking and reflection, and to encourage dialogue around a values base of social justice and challenge to inequality.

CONCLUSION

This chapter has suggested that global education could and perhaps should take a more radical direction, making stronger connections to themes of power, inequality, social justice, and critical reflection. The development education tradition, particularly in Europe, provides some practical examples that show these potential connections. But even within this practice in Europe, a clearer pedagogical focus is needed that recognizes the processes of learning, and potential change and transformation in the learner.

Many teachers and schools around the world will be delivering good global education, opening up learners' minds to the world of today and the relevance of global issues. But all too often this approach to learning can easily be reduced to a series of well-intentioned activities and one-off activities that may do more harm than good. The pedagogical framework outlined here starts from recognizing that educators will engage in learning about global and development themes from a wide range of viewpoints, perspectives, and experiences.

Global learning needs to be relevant to the curriculum and to the student. It needs above all to be seen not as the application of a specific series of topics or themes but as an approach to learning that necessitates reflection and critical thinking on the part of the educator. It is not about reproducing bodies of knowledge about development but rather engaging in a process of learning that recognizes different approaches and ways of understanding the world, and that engages in the issues through different lenses.

The discussions outlined here are particularly relevant to broader discourses and debates in global education for three reasons. First, they show the historical evolution of the various concepts, and the links between their implementation and a range of political and educational influences. Second, they remind those engaged in global education that any discussion of global themes should have at its heart an understanding of power and inequality in the world, including the causes of poverty. And finally, learning about the wider world poses questions to the learners about themselves and their relationship to that world, their perceptions about their sense of place in the world, and the role they could potentially play in securing a more just and egalitarian world.

REFERENCES

Alexander, R. (2004). Still no pedagogy? Principle, pragmatism and compliance in primary education. *Cambridge Journal of Education, 34*(1), 7–33.

Andreotti, V. (2006). Soft versus critical global citizenship. *Policy and Practice, 3*, 40–51.

Andreotti, V. (2012). *Actionable postcolonial theory in education.* New York: Palgrave MacMillan.

Andreotti, V. (2014). Introduction: The political economy of global citizenship education. In V. Andreotti (Ed.), *The political economy of global citizenship education* (pp. 1–4). Abingdon, UK: Routledge.

Andreotti, V., Jefferess. D., Pashby, K., Rowe, C., Tarc, P., & Taylor, L. (2010). Difference and conflict in global citizenship in higher education in Canada. *International Journal of Development Education and Global Learning, 2*(3), 5–24.

Au, W. (2009). Fighting with the text: Contextualising and re-contextualising Freire's critical pedagogy. In M. Apple, W. Au, & L. A. Gandin (Eds.), *The Routledge international handbook of critical education* (pp. 22–231). New York: Routledge.

Biccum, A. (2010). *Global citizenship and the legacy of empire.* Abingdon, UK: Routledge

Bourn, D. (2008). *Global skills.* London: Learning Skills and Improvement Service.

Bourn, D. (2014). *The theory and practice of global learning.* DERC Research Paper no. 11. London: IOE.

Chalkley, B., Mahigh, M., & Higgitt, D. (2008). *Education for sustainable development: Papers in honour of the United Nations decade of education for sustainable development (2005–2014)*. Abingdon, UK: Routledge.
Cronkhite, L. (2000). Development education: Making connections north and south. In T. Goldstein & D. Selby (Eds.), *Weaving connections: Education for peace, social and environmental justice* (pp. 146–167). Toronto: Sumach Press.
Department of Education Association (DEA). (2003). *Citizenship education: The global dimension*. London: DEA.
Department for Education and Skills (DFES). (2005). *Developing a global dimension for the school curriculum*. London: DFES.
De Silva, M. C. (2012). *Global education guidelines*. Lisbon: Council of Europe.
Freire, P. (1972). *Pedagogy of the oppressed*. Harmondsworth: Penguin.
Gaudelli, W. (2003). *World class teaching and learning in global times*. New York: Routledge.
Giroux, H. (2005). *Border crossing*. New York: Routledge.
Harrison, D. (2008). *Oxfam and the rise of development education in England from 1959 to 1979*. Unpublished dissertation. Institute of Education, London.
Hartmeyer, H. (2008). *Experiencing the world global learning in Austria: Developing, reaching out, crossing borders*. Munster: Waxmann.
Hicks, D., & Holden, C. (2007). *Teaching the global dimension: Key principles and effective practice*. London: Routledge.
Hunt, F. (2012). *Global learning in primary schools: Practices and impacts*. DERC Research Paper no. 9. London: IOE.
Illeris, K. (2006). *How we learn*. London: Routledge.
Kirby, B. (1994). *Education for change: Grassroots development education in Europe*. London: DEA.
Kirkwood-Tucker, T. F. (2009). *Visions in global education: The globalization of curriculum and pedagogy in teacher education and schools*. New York: Peter Lang.
Kumar, A. (2008). Development education and dialogic learning in the 21st century. *International Journal of Development Education and Global Learning*, 1(1), 37–48.
McNay, L. (1994). *Foucault, a critical introduction*. Cambridge: Polity Press.
Merryfield, M. (2009). Moving the center of global education: From imperial worldviews that divide the world to double consciousness, contrapuntal pedagogy, hybridity, and cross-cultural competence. In T. F. Kirkwood-Tucker (Ed.), *Visions in global education* (pp. 215–239). New York: Peter Lang.
McCloskey, S. (2014). *Development education in policy and practice*. Basingstoke, UK: Palgrave Macmillan.
Mezirow, J. (2000). Learning to think like an adult: Core concepts of transformation theory. In J. Mezirow & Associates (Eds.), *Learning as transformation: Critical perspectives in a theory in progress* (pp. 3–24). San Francisco: Jossey Bass.
Multi-Stakeholder Forum. (2005). *The European consensus on development: The contribution of development education and awareness raising*. Brussels: DEEEP.
Odora Hoppers, C. (2009). Education, culture and society in a globalizing world: Implications for comparative and international education. *COMPARE*, 39(5), 601–614.
Oxfam. (2006). *Education for Global Citizenship: A Guide for Schools*. London: Oxfam. Retrieved from www.oxfam.org.uk/~/media/Files/Education/Global%20 Citizenship/education_for_global_citizenship_a_guide_for_schools.ashx
Oxley, L., & Morris, P. (2013). Global citizenship: A typology for distinguishing its multiple conceptions. *British Journal of Educational Studies*, 61(3), 1–25.
Pike, G. (2000). A tapestry in the making: The strands of global education. In T. Goldstein & D. Selby (Eds.), *Weaving connections: Education for peace, social and environmental justice* (pp. 218–241). Toronto: Sumach Press.

Regan, C. (Ed.) (2006). *Development in an unequal world*. Dublin: UNISA.
Sallah, M., & Cooper, S. (2008) *Global youth work: Taking it personally*. Leicester: National Youth Agency.
Scheunpflug, A. (2011). Global education and cross-cultural learning: A challenge for a research-based approach to international teacher education. *International Journal of Development Education and Global Learning, 3*(3), 29–44.
Tormey, R. (2014). Critical thinking and development education: How do we develop meta-cognitive capacities? In S. McCloskey (Ed.), *Development education in policy and practice* (pp. 65–80). Basingstoke, UK: Palgrave Macmillan.
Tye, K. (1999). *Global education: A worldwide movement*. Orange, CA: Interdependence Press.
VSO. (2002). *The live aid legacy*. London: VSO.
Walkington, H. (2000). The educational methodology of Paulo Freire: To what extent is it reflected in development education in the UK classroom? *Development Education Journal, 7*(1), 15–17.
Woyach, R. B., & Remy, R. C. (1989). *Approaches to world studies: A handbook for curriculum planners*. Boston: Allyn & Bacon.

3 Global Aspects of Citizenship Education
Challenges and Perspectives

Anatoli Rapoport

It has become almost commonplace in all recent debates to refer to globalization as one of the most influential factors in the reconceptualization of political, ideological, and social phenomena. Citizenship, as an ultimate form of political, economic, cultural, and moral membership, is one of such phenomena. The concept of world, or global, citizenship that was born millennia ago has been widely discussed by politicians and scholars for the last several decades. Many aspects of global citizenship, including global citizenship education (GCE), are the subject of numerous presentations at conferences and symposia. However, schools are still largely outside of these debates. Studies conducted among preservice and in-service teachers (Gallavan, 2008; Gaudelli, 2009; Leduc, 2013; Myers, 2006; Rapoport, 2010; Robbins, Francis, & Elliot, 2003; Yamashita, 2006) demonstrate, on the one hand, a growing interest among education practitioners in various aspects of global education but, on the other hand, very limited knowledge about or motivation to introduce and integrate the ideas of global citizenship in their instruction. Why are teachers still uncomfortable teaching global citizenship? It seems this is a multi-dimensional problem that can be resolved only if we address it on both institutional and personal levels. In this chapter I will outline what I believe are the most general obstacles in the way of the expansion of GCE in schools and the role of teacher education programs in advancing education for global citizenship: (a) conceptual vagueness of global citizenship, (b) propensity to teach national or regional citizenship, (c) curricular insecurity, and (d) lack of administrative support. To support my arguments, I will use some data from the study I conducted among Indiana teachers in 2009 and 2010 (Rapoport, 2010). In the course of the study, six high school teachers, who were interested and actively involved in global education, were interviewed about their attitudes toward global citizenship and its place in social studies curricula.

CONCEPTUAL VAGUENESS AND AMBIGUITY

Despite the fact that people have been talking about the idea of global or world citizenship since the Stoics and Socrates, it became a subject of intense theoretical debates only fairly recently (Armstrong, 2006; Banks, 2004; Heater, 1999; Noddings, 2005; Wood, 2008). Although in very general terms global citizenship means belonging to a global community, every next step in the deconstruction of this term raises questions. What is globalization? What is citizenship? Does a global community really exist? How inclusive should global citizenship be? Is global citizenship regulated? Who or what determines its boundaries? How devastating will the impact of global citizenship be on national or local citizenship if we accept it? These and many other questions challenge our routine understanding of citizenship, a construct that since the very inception of nations several centuries ago has been regarded mostly as a nation-state–related concept (Davies, Evans, & Reid, 2005; Delanty, 2002). As such, citizenship has been presented, taught, and negotiated among groups and individuals. The difficulty of conceptualizing global citizenship becomes even more apparent if we consider that even the key components of this construct, global and citizenship, are both contestant concepts that spark vigorous debates.

Dower (2003) outlined four challenges that call the prospects of global citizenship into question. First, is there a global ethic? If we do not accept that a global ethic exists, because an ethic is a function of a culture, we should not accept global citizenship. Second, are there global institutions that are needed to make us global citizens? There is no global government or any other robust global institution that would outline what constitutes the global citizen element in the global context. Third, is the claim of global citizenship relevant? We can make all ethical decisions about global rights and responsibilities without invoking the idea of global citizenship, which makes this concept redundant and unnecessary. And finally, the idea of global citizenship is misleading: our world is structurally and institutionally sound, although not without faults. We need a better functioning order at the state or regional levels instead of creating a new world order. Wood (2008) calls global citizenship an impossibility because citizenship functions as a part of a formal political structure that still does not exist on a global level and also because citizenship is "a technology of governance enacted by the state" (p. 25) rather than an emancipatory and empowering institution. Building a case against global education in general, Standish (2012) argues that "advocates for 'global citizenship' seek to nurture children who are not tied to one culture or the nation state" (p. 3).

The emerging global civil society faces several accusations itself: that it is terminologically ambiguous, that its supporters uncritically apply nation-state phenomena to global processes, and that it undermines democracy by weakening the democratic institutions of nation-states (Corry, 2006). Armstrong (2006) argues that the supposedly "global" elements of global citizenship are much less universal and transcendent. Miller (in Carter, 2001, p. 5) calls the idea of global citizenship utopian because "the conditions for global citizenship do not exist and the term is therefore at best metaphorical."

The skepticism about global citizenship is buttressed by two major assumptions: citizenship is an inherently state-related construct and the absence of a world government makes global citizenship impossible. Although these two assumptions are being constantly debated and contested in academic literature, the discussion very rarely if ever descends to practical discourses among educators or education stakeholders. As a result, the majority of teachers either have never heard about the idea of citizenship that transcends national boundaries (Gallavan, 2008; Myers, 2006, Rapoport, 2010), or ignore it as white noise unrelated to real curricula or problems of school. As one of the teachers whom I interviewed admitted, he had never heard about global citizenship before I invited him to participate in the study.

PROPENSITY TO TEACH NATIONAL CITIZENSHIP IN PUBLIC SCHOOLS

One of the major goals of public education is creating citizens. Thus, citizenship education is in the core of public schooling. Since the end of the 18th and the beginning of the 19th centuries, when nationalism played a particularly important role in unifying new nations and emerging nation-states, nationality and citizenship have been virtually synonymous terms (Davies, Evans, & Reid, 2005; Heater, 1999). As a result, the socially constructed symbiosis of citizenship and national identity has influenced state-supported citizenship education in the most profound way. Reid, Gill, and Sears (2010) outlined basic features in the relationship between citizenship, schooling, and the state that have been common across nations. Among those features are formal representations of the idea of citizenship in the curriculum, including subjects and materials that instill very particular knowledge, skills, and dispositions in students; and school culture that includes ceremonies, class organization, and pedagogy. In this way, school curricula, particularly in public schools, reflect, produce, and reinforce the dominant version of citizenship in a given society. Needless to say, the dominant version of citizenship is national citizenship, which determines membership in the nation and the relationship between government and the individual. The history of citizenship in the United States has been closely intertwined with the history of education and the development of public schooling. From the beginning, schools were expected to prepare future loyal citizens who would identify themselves with the nation (Graham, 2005; Reimers, 2006; Reuben, 2005). The new nation, as all new nations, needed legitimation that could be easily achieved, at least for its own citizens, through indoctrination in nationalism and patriotism. The public school system was a perfect means for achieving this goal.

The development of national citizenship and national identity has been the essence of school curricula in the U.S., particularly in such areas as history, social studies, or literacy, for centuries. Samuel Chester Parker, dean of the University of Chicago at the beginning of the 20th century, reported that, prior to 1880s, patriotism was the purpose of teaching history in schools (Bohan, 2005). Historians of education and curricular reform demonstrated that public schools were a robust component of nationalization. Nationalism and allegiance to the nation-state were a product of mandatory public schooling and its corresponding core curriculum (Bohan, 2005; Cremin, 1988; Tyack, 1974). As a result, the everlasting, never-ending process of nation-building has been cited as justification for concentrating on national citizenship at the expense of developing within the students a broader and more comprehensive picture of the world. A nation-state–centered public school curriculum is not idiosyncratic to the U.S. It is a common feature of public education in all countries (Macedo, 2011; Pinar, 2011; Rapoport, 2012; Tsolidis, 2011).

Although global contexts have always been present to a varying degrees in public school curricula and even considering growing interest in such subjects as world history or world geography (Cavanagh, 2007), the traditionalistic, nation-centered citizenship approach dominates curricula (Myers, 2006; Reimers, 2006). It is also true that numerous attempts have been made to introduce international and global themes to students for the last several decades, and many of those attempts have been successful. However, the general direction of citizenship education, the conceptualization of citizenship in its legalistic form as a strictly nation-state–related construct, has not changed much. There is not much evidence that teacher education programs are successful in challenging preservice teachers' beliefs about citizenship, despite a growing number of college courses in global and multicultural education (Gallavan, 2008; Robbins et al., 2003). New teachers normally return to classrooms with an unchallenged legalistic concept of citizenship securely tied to their previously constructed ideas of state and nation. And the circle starts all over again. No wonder that, for teachers, citizenship is by definition a state-related concept (Parker, Ninimiya, & Cogan, 1999). When I asked participants of my study to explain how they understand the terms citizenship or citizen, the idea of direct relationship to a state or nation was present, although to a different extent, in all of their answers: "Citizens are people who belong to the same culture and live in the same territory."

LACK OF DISCIPLINARY HERITAGE

Very few people question whether citizenship education should be a part of the public school curriculum. Even the contemporary "social studies wars" are more about the place of history education and methods of teaching citizenship than debates about the importance of citizenship education itself (Evans, 2004; Leming, Ellington, & Porter-Magee, 2003). As a part of a broad socialization process, citizenship education is a multicomponent system that involves a number of agencies—the government, community, media, parents, peers, and school—which all play a role in socializing a child, in turning a child into a responsible and informed citizen. Public schools, unlike other agencies, were created specifically for the purpose of educating citizens. Therefore, it follows that the public school system is best equipped to provide the conditions, space, and guidance for developing the knowledge, skills, and dispositions needed to educate globally minded citizens. Public education can play the leading role in this process, as school is designed to reflect on and to react to emerging challenges, particularly cultural, social, or ideological. School remains the core element of the citizenship education network. But the school curriculum, which is a set of ideas, texts, practices, and pedagogies, usually focuses on the disciplines. Global citizenship education, as an inherently multi- and interdisciplinary area, lacks what Gaudelli (2009) called "disciplinary heritage" (p. 78). A global citizenship paradigm, as well as a non-legalistic concept of citizenship, has not secured its place in school curricula in the U.S.

Such an "unfixed" status of citizenship education (Reid, Gill, & Sears, 2010) presents a serious challenge. When educators discuss programmatic challenges related to the introduction of ideas of global citizenship in the curriculum, they usually focus on two approaches. One approach is to design stand-alone courses that teach a plethora of global and international topics. Stand-alone courses and programs, such as *International Relations, World/Global/International Studies*, or *International Perspectives*, have become an important part of many schools' curricula. Undoubtedly, these courses provide frameworks for teaching global citizenship components. However, such courses are vulnerable: they depend on teachers' mobility, students' interests, ideological and cultural environments, and most often funding opportunities. Furthermore, budget cuts and excessive focus on testing make such elective courses almost nonexistent in low-income communities (Thornton, 2005).

Another approach to teaching global citizenship is to incorporate elements of global citizenship models into existing courses, social studies courses in particular (Collins, 2008; Noddings, 2005; Smith & Faiman, 2005; Thornton, 2005). This approach has both positive and negative consequences. The possible negative effect of curriculum integration is that the discipline-based approach narrows a school's capacities to present any model of citizenship in its entirety. Ostensibly, global citizenship education is usually conceptualized within the frameworks of international education, global education (Davies et al., 2005), multicultural education (Banks, 2004; Dunn, 2002), peace education (Smith & Fairman, 2005), human rights education (Gaudelli & Fernekes, 2004; Osler & Starkey, 2010), or economics education. None of these approaches, with the possible exception of economics education, has yet secured a position in school curricula. Thus, global citizenship education, if taught as one of the topics within these frameworks, would become even more secondary. Paradoxically, the positive effect of curriculum integration is also related to the fact that teachers have an opportunity to discuss elements of global citizenship in various disciplinary contexts, thus using the content and framework of every course to raise issues related to global citizenship. The success of this approach depends upon a number of factors. Time is the most precious asset in the instructional process: teachers rarely have enough time to cover required materials, let alone to incorporate something new. Curricular documents are usually vague about topics of globalization and global citizenship–related issues, and the absence of such curricular pressure either from programmatic documents or from the community discourages teachers from taking additional proactive steps to teach about global citizenship. The lack of epistemic and disciplinary heritage (Gaudelli, 2009) is an additional obstacle to curriculum integration and negatively affects global citizenship education. However, the biggest challenge to the curriculum integration approach may be the lack of the teacher's own interest, motivation, and pedagogical knowledge. The teacher may not be interested or know how to integrate global citizenship perspectives into classroom instruction. The teacher's role is critical. Schools need professionals who understand the importance of global and international perspectives in citizenship education, who are interested in these topics, motivated to step outside the box, and not afraid to challenge their own views.

LACK OF ADMINISTRATIVE SUPPORT OR CURRICULAR PRESSURE

Administrative or curricular pressure as an incentive to introduce GCE in schools seems controversial and potentially discouraging. One of the most comprehensive studies of teachers' perceptions of and roles in GCE, *Global Citizenship Education: The Needs of Teachers and Learners* (Davies, Harber, & Yamashita, 2005), clearly demonstrates that the national curriculum was seen by teachers in England as an obstacle to the creativity and flexibility that are necessary in GCE. "The pressure of educational system, such as curriculum expectations, standards and requirements like tests and exams" (p. 29) are mentioned among the factors that inhibit Canadian teachers' abilities to educate for global citizenship (Evans, Ingram, MacDonald, & Weber, 2009). The teachers whom I interviewed admitted that even if and when they wanted to teach global citizenship–related topics, they simply did not have time to do it because they had to cover other topics to prepare students for standardized tests. Rigid formal curricula stifle teachers' ability to teach global citizenship. There is other empirical evidence that citizenship education in general suffers from overreaching standardization and accountability policies (McEchorn, 2010; VanFossen & McGrew, 2008). Obviously, in practitioners' opinions, the already rigid curriculum prevents teachers from including GCE in their instruction. However, if we look at what exactly teachers specifically complain about, we will notice some nuances. Teachers interviewed for the *Global Citizenship Education* report (Davies, Harber, & Yamashita, 2005) saw the national curriculum as a potential barrier to a global citizenship program because it was too Eurocentric, because the bulk of the resources went to core areas, and because testing further shifted the focus to core activities. Teachers here demonstrated a legitimate expectation from a curriculum to guide what content to teach. For example, Ontario teachers who were determined to make global education a priority, as reported by Schwisfurth (2006), found curriculum guidelines very helpful; they were able to creatively adjust curriculum requirements to justify their approaches to global education. Considering the problems that GCE encounters in schools mentioned earlier (conceptual vagueness, the dominant role of national citizenship, and curricular insecurity), it is not surprising that many teachers who want to teach and believe they know how to teach global citizenship need some sort of institutionalization, formal programmatic justification of their interest and intent. Particularly because the concept of global citizenship is still ideologically and politically contested and not uniformly accepted, teachers need a curricular incentive to teach global citizenship–related ideas.

Research shows that such concepts as globalization and global or world citizenship are still rarely mentioned in states' content standards. Or, if these concepts are mentioned, standards disproportionally emphasize only one side of globalization—namely, its economic impact—rather than a holistic nature of global processes (Beltramo & Duncheon, 2013). The development and implementation of state content standards possess their own dynamics that explain, in part, why standards lag behind contemporary developments. This is particularly the case in the social sciences, where the rapidly changing world dictates its own pace, incompatible with other areas of education. For example, in 2009 the social studies standards of only two states, Maryland and Mississippi, contained the term *global citizen* (Rapoport, 2009). Standards play a twofold role: they are a channel of political influence of the society on education and, at the same time, they are the major document that guides curricular policy. By ignoring such powerful concepts as globalization or global citizenship, standards developers and state boards of education send a mixed message to educators. The descriptors used in the standards, such as "informed, responsible, and participating citizens at the. . . international level," "responsible citizens and active participants in. . . global society," "productive, informed citizens in a global society," or "capable citizens in a culturally diverse and interdependent world," are even more obscure and shift the focus. Blurred messages like these in a prescriptive curricular document eventually turn into neglect of a very important concept in the classroom.

Teachers lack academic freedom, as well as curricular justification and support, if they decide to include elements of global citizenship education in their curricula. Under the pressure of omnipresent accountability that, as many practitioners know, usually means that what is not tested is not taught, topics related to global citizenship are buried under more "necessary" materials. As a result, many teachers lack the confidence needed to translate their generally positive attitude toward global citizenship education into classroom practices (Merryfield, 1998, 2000; Robbins et al., 2003; Schweisfurth, 2006) and tend to rationalize the unfamiliar concept of global citizenship through more familiar concepts and discourses (Schweisfurth, 2006). Therefore, a curricular pressure in the form of the institutionalization of the language and terminology related to globalization and global citizenship may in reality become a valuable asset that will eventually incentivize teachers and administrators to be more responsive to the new global realities. However, curricular pressure will never turn into a curricular incentive without bona fide administrative support. Administrative support plays a critical role in any school innovation. In the case of GCE, the support of district or building administrators is particularly valuable because, in many communities, skeptical attitudes regarding global matters prevail.

Administrative support for teaching topics related to GCE is also very important because, as a number of researchers noted, many teachers refuse even to use the language of global citizenship for fear of being accused of a lack of patriotism (Loewen, 1996; Myers, 2006; White & Openshaw, 2002). Although the traditional or rather traditionalistic meaning of patriotism has been challenged more and more often (Apple, 2002; Branson, 2002; Merry, 2009; Nussbaum, 1994), and the idea of patriotism as a more inclusive construct, particularly in regard to multicultural and intercultural discourses, is becoming more acceptable, it is too optimistic to assume that the majority of education practitioners embrace the idea of "critical" (Merry, 2009) or "constructive patriotism" (Staub, 1997). "A useful definition of patriotism," noted Akhmad and Szpara (2005) "should not hinge on the legal status in a polity but embrace citizens' allegiance to universal human values, democratic ideals, and the human rights and dignity of all people in the world" (p. 10). It is noteworthy that teachers themselves rarely admit to the fear of being accused of being unpatriotic (Merryfield, 2007; Myers, 2006). For example, the participants in my 2009 study were not very concerned about being accused of teaching anything unpatriotic when they taught international or global issues in the sense that the content or pedagogies they used would not in any way undermine or violate what is routinely understood as patriotic sentiment. However, they saw a much bigger challenge for anyone who would attempt to teach global citizenship in a way that would upset what could be called a local mind-set. And that challenge seemed to them more serious than false accusations of a lack of patriotism. They never mentioned that parents, their colleagues, or their superiors had questioned their patriotism. Nevertheless, after one of the participants began to receive parents' complaints about "excessive" Islam-related materials in his World History course, he decided immediately to change the topic. He explained his decision not as fear but as unwillingness to challenge local conservative values. We can easily assume that what my participant referred to as "local conservative values" is called true patriotism by the people who hold those values. Definitely, the relationship between patriotism or patriotic education on the one hand and global citizenship education on the other requires more attention and empirical research.

Conceptual vagueness and terminological ambiguity of global citizenship, propensity to develop and teach national citizenship, and lack of curricular security and administrative support are major obstacles that GCE faces in schools. When we say "global citizenship education," what we usually mean is creating an atmosphere in the classroom or school conducive to raising questions about global issues; discussing local, regional, or national problems by placing them in a global context; being able to ask difficult questions that do not always have definite answers; and not being afraid to discuss controversial issues. In a word, the teacher becomes the most important link in the educational chain that connects our young generation with the growing societal understanding of the inevitability of global changes. Society, business, and even the legislature, although to a lesser extent, are ready for a paradigmatic shift that will eventually result in embracing global citizenship on the same level as we now experience national or local citizenships. Are education practitioners, both classroom teachers and school administrators, prepared to translate the societal need for a new, more globally oriented citizenship paradigm into meaningful changes in curricula and instruction in classroom discourse? Do teacher education programs or professional development programs equip practitioners with the necessary tools that will facilitate the education of globally minded citizens? To answer this question, we first have to identify content and tools that will define and direct global citizenship education discourse.

MOVING FORWARD

There is a consensus among theorists that the defining topics in global citizenship education narrative are those that problematize such areas as universal ethics, universal human rights, social justice, globalization, mono- vs. multicultural dichotomy, and all types of inequalities (Banks, 2004, 2008; Carter, 2001; Dower, 2003; Gaudelli & Fernekes, 2004; Heater, 2004; Osler & Starkey, 2010; Oxfam, 2006; Suárez-Orozco & Qin-Hilliard, 2004). As for techniques and strategies in GCE, there is a growing body of literature, mostly exploratory empirical studies, that analyzes both best practices and general experiences of teachers and administrators in all aspects of global education (Davies et al., 2005; Evans et al., 2009; Leduc, 2013, Merryfield, 2007; Oxfam, 2006; Rapoport, 2013). However, despite all evidence of the rising interest in GCE among educators, we will never be able to achieve success, even relative success, similar to, for example, that of multicultural education if the ideas of GCE are ignored in teacher preparation programs. Preservice teachers are normally exposed to the themes and discourses of GCE: many teacher education programs list courses on multicultural and international education among basic requirements, and the ideas of social justice, morality, and human rights are included in a number of preparatory courses. At methods courses, particularly social science methods courses, future teachers acquire knowledge of techniques and strategies, such as various types of discussions and debates. They learn how to work with primary sources, how to teach controversial issues, and how to use comparative techniques, case studies, and other techniques and strategies that have been identified as most useful in GCE. What is currently lacking is a combination of place and time that would serve as a nexus, a space where future teachers can connect their newly obtained knowledge and skills and translate them into global competencies. This nexus, in the form of a course, seminar, or system of workshops, would help preservice teachers look at the problems and perspectives of global citizenship holistically.

It should be kept in mind that understanding and embracing the concept of global citizenship requires the development of a certain mental paradigm that is quite different from the national citizenship paradigm we currently use. This shift is so complex and multifaceted that it requires a significant change in a child's outlook. We all were born with the idea of citizenship as a function of a state because all the means of socialization, such as family, school, media, church, or government institutions, have taught us so. It is simply difficult to comprehend that citizenship can be anything but a nation-centered phenomenon. In fact, in some languages, the term *citizenship education* is translated as citizenship upbringing, which demonstrates a clear link between citizenship education and socialization. Although socialization through its agents, such as family, school, or other institutions, constructs and reconstructs identities both locally and globally (Kiwako Okuma-Nyström, 2009; Zajda, 2009), citizenship still remains a predominantly locality-centered and nation-centered phenomenon. Socialization has been nation-centered probably since the emergence of nations and later nation-states. Discussing the unavoidable tensions in a democracy between individual liberty, diversity, and social conformity, Engle and Ochoa (1988) argued that any socialization is a form of coercion. To counterbalance socialization, they set forth the idea of countersocialization, which they defined as "a learning process designed to foster the independent thought and social criticism that is crucial to political freedom" (p. 31). In this regard, the view of citizenship education as countersocialization presents an intriguing theoretical issue: if we all are already global citizens by the virtue of birth, by our existential status (Dower, 2003), then the task of global citizenship education is to challenge traditional nation-oriented citizenship models and to resocialize children by making them aware of their global citizenship status.

Like countersocialization, resocialization does not lead to a rejection of previous practices and established values; rather, it offers a balance to the socialization experience that is void of reflective thought (Kaviani, 2006) and expands the boundaries of individual rights, freedoms, and responsibilities.

Changes occur because the time has come and there are people who understand that the time for changes has come. Very few doubt that the time for meaningful changes in education for global citizenship has come; many would even say these changes are long overdue. We need teachers who understand that the time has come. We need teachers who will not be afraid to face obstacles. We need teachers who will not be afraid to change themselves. "Changing the poor work schools do at present in preparing students for global civility," Fernando Reimers wrote in 2006, "will be a challenging task because it will require much more than including new objectives in the curriculum and instruction. It will require developing capacity among teachers . . . to change their minds about the need to change" (p. 291). But such teachers cannot appear by themselves. Teacher educators, particularly in the areas related to civics and citizenship education, should look critically at their programs to incorporate global citizenship–focused curricula.

REFERENCES

Ahmad, I., & Szpara, M. Y. (2005). Education for democratic citizenship and peace: Proposal for a cosmopolitan model. *Educational Studies, 38*(1), 8–23.

Apple, M. (2002). Patriotism, pedagogy, and freedom: On the educational meaning of September 11th. *Teachers College Record, 104*(8), 1760–1772.

Armstrong, C. (2006). Global civil society and the question of global citizenship. *Voluntas, 17*(4), 349–357.

Banks, J. (2004). Teaching for social justice, diversity, and citizenship in a global world. *Educational Forum, 68*(2), 289–298.

Banks, J. (2008). Diversity, group identity, and citizenship education in a global age. *Educational Researcher, 37*(3), 129–139.

Beltramo, J. L., & Duncheon, J. (2013). Globalization standards: A comparison of U.S. and non-U.S. social studies curricula. *Journal of Social Studies Research, 37*(2), 97–109.

Branson, M. (2002). *Patriotism and civic literacy*. Paper presented at the We the People State and District Coordinators Conference, Washington, DC, June 30. (ERIC Document Reproductive Service No. ED477598)

Bohan, Ch. (2005). Digging trenches: Nationalism and the first national report on the elementary history curriculum. *Theory and Practice in Social Education, 33*(2), 266–291.

Carter, A. (2001). *The political theory of global citizenship*. London: Routledge.

Cavanagh, S. (2007). World history and geography gain traction in class. *Education Week, 26*(28), 10.

Collins, M. (2008). *Global citizenship for young children*. London: Paul Chapman.

Corry, O. (2006). Global civil society and its discontents. *Voluntas, 17*(4), 303–324.

Cremin, L. (1988). *American education: The metropolitan experience, 1876–1980*. New York: HarperCollins.

Delanty, G. (2002). *Citizenship in a global age: Society, culture, politics.* Philadelphia: Open University Press.
Davies, I., Evans, M., & Reid, A. (2005). Globalizing citizenship education? A critique of "global education" and "citizenship education." *British Journal of Educational Studies, 53*(1), 66–89.
Davies, L., Harber, C., & Yamashita, H. (2005). *Global citizenship education: The needs of teachers and learners.* Birmingham, UK: Center for International Education and Research (CIER), University of Birmingham.
Dower, N. (2003). *An introduction to global citizenship.* Edinburgh: Edinburgh University Press.
Dunn, R. E. (2002). Growing good citizens with a world-centered curriculum. *Educational Leadership, 60*(2), 10–13.
Engle S. H., & Ochoa, A. S. (1988). *Education for democratic citizenship.* New York: Teachers College Press.
Evans, M., Ingram, L. A., MacDonald A. A., & Weber, N. (2009). Mapping the "global dimension" of citizenship education in Canada: The complex interplay of theory, practice, and context. *Citizenship, Teaching and Learning, 5*(2), 16–34.
Evans, R. (2004). *The social studies wars: What should we teach the children?* New York: Teachers College Press.
Gallavan, N. (2008). Examining teacher candidates' views on teaching world citizenship. *Social Studies, 99*(6), 249–254. doi: 10.3200/TSSS.99.6.249-254.
Gaudelli, W. (2009). Heuristics of global citizenship discourses towards curriculum enhancement. *Journal of Curriculum Theorizing, 25*(1), 68–85.
Gaudelli, W., & Fernekes, W. (2004). Teaching about global human rights for global citizenship. *Social Studies, 95*(1), 16–26.
Graham, P. (2005). *Schooling America: How the public schools meet the nation's changing needs.* New York: Oxford University Press.
Heater, D. (1999). *What is citizenship?* Cambridge: Polity Press.
Heater, D. (2004). *Citizenship: The civil ideal in world history, politics and education.* Manchester, UK: Manchester University Press.
Kaviani, K. (2006). Influences on social studies teachers' issue-selection for classroom discussion: Social positioning and media. *Social Studies Research and Practice, 1*(2), 201–222.
Kiwako Okuma-Nyström, M. (2009). Globalization, identities, and diversified school education. In J. Zajda, H. Daun, & L. Saha (Eds.), *Nation-building, identity and citizenship education: Cross-cultural perspectives* (pp. 25–42). London: Springer.
Leduc, R. (2013). Global citizenship instruction through active participation: What is being learned about global citizenship? *Educational Forum, 77*(4), 394–406.
Leming, J., Ellington, L., & Porter-Magee, K. (2003). *Where did social studies go wrong?* Washington, DC: Thomas B. Fordham Foundation.
Loewen, J. (1996). *Lies my teacher told me: Everything your American History textbook got wrong.* New York: Touchstone.
Macedo, E. (2011). Curriculum policies in Brazil: The citizenship discourse. In L. Yates & M. Grumet (Eds.), *World yearbook of education 2011. Curriculum in today's world: Configuring knowledge, identities, work and policies* (pp. 44–57). London: Routledge.
McEachorn, G. (2010). Study of allocated social studies time in elementary classrooms in Virginia: 1987–2009. *Journal of Social Studies Research, 34*(2), 208–228.
Merry, M. (2009). Patriotism, history, and the legitimate aim of American education. *Educational Philosophy and Theory, 41*(4), 378–398.
Merryfield, M. M. (1998). Pedagogy for global perspectives in education: Studies for teachers' thinking and practice. *Theory and Research in Social Education, 26*(3), 342–379.

Merryfield, M. M. (2000). Why aren't teachers being prepared to teach for diversity, equity, and global interconnectedness? A study of lived experiences in the making of multicultural and global educators. *Teaching and Teacher Education, 16*, 429–443.
Merryfield, M. M. (2007). The web and teachers' decision-making in global education. *Theory and Research in Social Education, 35*(2), 256–276.
Myers, J. (2006). Rethinking the social studies curriculum in the context of globalization: Education for global citizenship in the U.S. *Theory and Research in Social Education, 34*(3), 370–394.
Noddings, N. (2005). Global citizenship: Promises and problems. In N. Noddings (Ed.), *Educating citizens for global awareness* (pp. 1–21). New York: Teachers College, Columbia University.
Nussbaum, M. (1994). Patriotism and cosmopolitanism. *Boston Review, 19*(5), 3–16.
Osler, A., & Starkey, H. (2010). *Teachers and human rights education*. Stoke-on-Trent: Trentham Books.
Oxfam. (2006). *Cool planet for teachers: Global citizenship*. Retrieved from www.oxfam.org.uk/coolplanet/teachers/globciti/curric/index.htm
Parker, W. C., Ninimiya, A., & Cogan, J. (1999). Educating world citizens: Toward multinational curriculum development. *American Educational Research Journal, 36*, 117–45.
Pinar, W. (2011). Nationalism, anti-Americanism, Canadian identity. In L. Yates & M. Grumet, (Eds.), *World yearbook of education 2011. Curriculum in today's world: Configuring knowledge, identities, work and policies* (pp. 31–43). London: Routledge.
Rapoport, A. (2009). A forgotten concept: Global citizenship education and state social studies standards. *Journal of Social Studies Research, 33*(1), 75–93.
Rapoport, A. (2010). We cannot teach what we don't know: Indiana teachers talk about global citizenship education. *Education, Citizenship and Social Justice, 5*(3), 1–11.
Rapoport, A. (2012). Educating new citizens: The role of patriotic education in the post-Soviet countries. *Educational Practice and Theory, 34*(2), 81–105.
Rapoport, A. (2013). Global citizenship themes in the social studies classroom: Teaching devices and teachers' attitudes. *Educational Forum, 77*(4), 407–421.
Reid, A., Gill, J., & Sears, A. (2010). The forming of citizens in a globalizing world. In A. Reid, J. Gill, J., & A. Sears (Eds.), *Globalization, the nation-state and the citizen: Dilemmas and directions for civics and citizenship education* (pp. 3–16). New York: Routledge.
Reimers, F. (2006). Citizenship, identity and education: Examining the public purposes of schools in an age of globalization. *Prospects, 36*(3), 275–294.
Reuben, J. (2005). Patriotic purposes: Public schools and the education of citizens. In S. Fuhrman & M. Lazerson (Eds.), *The public schools* (pp. 1–24). Oxford: Oxford University Press.
Robbins, M., Francis, L. J., & Elliott, E. (2003). Attitudes toward education for global citizenship among trainee teachers. *Research in Education, 69*(1), 93–98.
Schweisfurth, M. (2006). Education for global citizenship: Teacher agency and curricular structure in Ontario schools. *Educational Review, 58*(1), 41–50.
Smith, S. N., & Fairman, D. (2005). The integration of conflict resolution into the high school curriculum: The example of workable peace. In N. Noddings (Ed.), *Educating citizens for global awareness* (pp. 40–56). New York: Teachers College Press.
Standish, A. (2012). *The false promise of global learning: Why education needs boundaries*. New York: Continuum International.
Staub, E. (1997). Blind versus constructive patriotism: Moving from embeddedness in the group to critical loyalty and action. In D. Bar-Tal & E. Staub (Eds.),

Patriotism in the lives of individuals and nations (pp. 213–228). Chicago: Nelson-Hall.

Suárez-Orozco, M., & Qin-Hilliard, D. (2004). Globalization: Culture and education in the new millennium. In M. Suárez-Orozco & D. Qin-Hilliard, (Eds.), *Globalization: Culture and education in the new millennium* (pp. 1–37). Berkeley: University of California Press.

Thornton, S. J. (2005). Incorporating internationalism into the social studies curriculum. In N. Noddings (Ed.), *Educating citizens for global awareness* (pp. 81–92). New York: Teachers College Press.

Tsolidis, G. (2011). Dressing the national imaginary: Making space for the veiled student in curriculum policy. In L. Yates & M. Grumet (Eds.), *World yearbook of education 2011. Curriculum in today's world: Configuring knowledge, identities, work and policies* (pp. 17–30). London: Routledge.

Tyack, D. (1974). *The one best system: A history of American urban education.* Cambridge, MA: Harvard University Press.

VanFossen, P. J., & McGrew, C. (2008). Is the sky really falling?: An update on the status of social studies in the K-5 curriculum in Indiana. *International Journal of Social Education, 23*(1), 139–179.

White, C., & Openshaw, R. (2002). Translating the national to the global in citizenship education. In D. Scott & H. Lawson (Eds.), *Citizenship education and the curriculum* (pp. 151–166). Westport, CT: Ablex.

Wood, P. (2008). The impossibility of global citizenship. *Brock Education, 17,* 22–37.

Yamashita, H. (2006). Global citizenship education and war: The needs of teachers and learners. *Educational Review, 58*(1), 27–39.

Zajda, J. (2009). Nation-building, identity, and citizenship education: Introduction. In J. Zajda, H. Daun, & L. Saha (Eds.), *Nation-building, identity and citizenship education: Cross-cultural perspectives* (pp. 1–11). London: Springer.

4 Global Education in Theory
The Centrality of Intercultural Competence

Caprice Lantz and Ian Davies

It is possible to trace the development of global education to at least the early years of the 20th century when in a quest for peace and understanding several organizations were established, including the League of Nations Union, the Council for Education in World Citizenship, and the Parliamentary Group for World Government (Fujikane, 2003; Heater, 1980; Richardson, 1996). Similar motivations to overcome lack of knowledge and to reduce tension could be seen in the Cold War era with work by, for example, Lee Anderson (1979), James Becker (1979), and Robert Hanvey (1975). Since the 1960s, with explicit connections being made to educate in relation to the forces of globalization, there has been a significant growth in global education initiatives (Tye, 1999). Many have called for a need to understand an interdependent world and warned about the dangers of ignoring those political, economic, and cultural realities (Merryfield, 1991).

When the seeming necessity of educating about and for a globalized world is commonplace, the status levels of global education and intercultural competence are low. In this chapter we argue there are significant challenges to global education and the promotion of intercultural competence. In light of our argument about these challenges we develop three sets of recommendations regarding what we view as a positive characterization of global education and intercultural education; we suggest institutional and pedagogical initiatives that may help in the realization of that vision; and finally we suggest areas for further research. While some of the references focus specifically upon the United Kingdom and European Union, in line with our own context, we continue to strive for a genuinely global approach to key issues in the field.

CHALLENGES FOR GLOBAL EDUCATORS AND INTERCULTURAL COMPETENCE (ICC)

We refer ahead to five of the many challenges faced by global educators who wish to promote ICC: the contested characterizations of the field; the continuing strength of the nation-state; the conflict between internationalization (which often highlights the primacy of commercial relations between nation-states) and intercultural education; an unrealistic expectation for ICC to automatically develop among students; and the accusations about low levels of academic work associated with global education and ICC. In referring to these challenges we do not pretend to provide a comprehensive outline of all that needs to be considered, but we have referred to some of the issues that relate to the fundamental ideas, political contexts, and institutional and pedagogical practices that make difficult the achievement of progress toward the realization of forms of global education that recognize the centrality of ICC. In a later stage of this chapter, we link these challenges to our recommendations (without pretending that scholarship, research, and education can deal with all the problematic areas referred to ahead).

Contested Characterizations

Global education is connected with globalization, but that does not mean that it is straightforward to provide precise meanings that enjoy widespread agreement. Very many issues are relevant in any discussion about globalization, including identity, law, social and environmental matters, and political citizenship (Heater, 2002). For others (e.g., Scholte, 2000) production, governance, community, and knowledge are the key elements. Cogan (1998) highlights the global economy, technology and communication, and population and the environment. Particular aspects are emphasized by emphasizing rights (e.g., Ignatieff, 2001), feminist perspectives (e.g., Arnot & Dillabough, 2009), hybridity (e.g., Appiah, 2006; Merryfield, 2001), and localities and regions (e.g., Hyslop, 1999), with some highlighting the need to avoid a narrow Westernized approach (e.g., Isin & Wood, 1999). There are differences regarding levels of acceptance and about whether positive or negative outcomes occur as a result of globalization (e.g., Held, McGrew, Goldblatt, and Perraton [1999] refer to hyperglobalists, skeptics, and transformationalists; see also Giddens, 1999).

Attempts have been made to summarize what is done in the name of global education. Davies and Pike (2009) have discussed some of those efforts by Richardson (1979), Davies, Evans, and Reid (2005), and others. There have been attempts made to identify the content of global education (global connections and interdependence, global systems, global issues and problems, cross-cultural understanding, human beliefs and values, and awareness of choices for the future [Pike, 2008]) alongside a range of approaches that span from simply describing what seems to be occurring to arguing for a transformative approach in an empowering pedagogy (Pike, 2008; Toh, 1993). Within these very broad positions are more detailed issues about the emphasis on cognitive as opposed to affective matters. We suggest that all of these approaches are relevant to global education and that a clearer, simpler approach is necessary in order to avoid fragmentation and confusion. It is in light of this contested characterization that we provide later in this chapter an exploration of one particular aspect of global education, the development of intercultural competence in students.

The contestation that applies generally to global education also applies specifically to intercultural education. Developing from the field of multicultural education, which focused upon promoting cultural tolerance, intercultural education focuses instead upon viewing cultural difference as enriching with the potential to further understanding through interactions between individuals (Portera, 2008). Intercultural competence (ICC), a fundamental outcome of intercultural education, is generally thought to be "the ability to communicate effectively and appropriately in intercultural situations" (Deardorff, 2006, p. 247). Although this is seemingly simple, ICC is actually an ambiguous concept, with at least 20 different terms used to refer to it (e.g., global competitive intelligence, international competence [Fantini & Tirmizi, 2006]) and well over 300 theoretical constructs associated with it [Spitzberg & Changnon, 2010]). Part of this confusion stems from the fact that research in this area emanates from a variety of disciplines. While early roots can be found in cross-cultural psychology studies conducted during the 1800s, the field expanded after World War II when researchers focused more attention on efforts to understand war and the psychology of other cultures (Segall, Lonner, & Berry, 1998). It was at this time that people began to work and study abroad more and researchers in other fields (e.g., languages, communication, management, anthropology) began to offer their own interpretations of it (Spencer-Oatey & Franklin, 2009).

While debates continue regarding the origin, meaning, and disciplinary home of intercultural competence, recently Spencer-Oatey and Franklin released a multidisciplinary analysis of ICC through which they found some overlap among approaches, and a survey of leading intercultural experts (Deardorff, 2006) similarly found common ground leading to the foregoing definition. These analyses suggest that ICC is made up of a set of competencies related to attitude (e.g., openness, respecting difference), behavior (e.g., active listening, behavioral accommodation), and cognitions (e.g., cultural self-awareness, awareness of values of other cultures) relative to communicating with people across cultures.

While the aforementioned research suggests rather specific components that make up ICC, it is a complex concept that requires a much broader understanding relevant to educating university students. ICC is not simply about training students to attain a set of attitudes, behaviors, and cognitions. It is about helping them to move from simple to complex modes of thinking about culture, similar to cognitive development as outlined by Piaget (1932) and ethical development as outlined by Perry (1970). Intercultural development (e.g., Bennett, 1986) involves advancing cognitive complexity, which relates directly to fostering critical thinking skills, arguably an important outcome for university students (Pithers & Soden, 2000).

We do not wish to suggest that debate about the meaning of global education and ICC is necessarily a bad thing. But there may be a narrow dividing line between necessary and meaningful debate and confusion. We suspect that there could be a clearer identification of common ground within the strands that make up global education and ICC.

Continuing Strength of the Nation-State

Heater (1997) has shown the range of ideas about global citizenship from the vague (member of the human race) to the specific (promotion of world government), but in concrete terms international law is limited. Transnational political organizations (e.g., the Organization of African Unity, the Association of Southeast Asian Nations, and the most developed—and, currently, crisis-ridden and challenged—the European Union) are, relative to the nation-state, rather weak. This does not mean that all nation-states are always strong and continuing. Nation-states come and go (Davies, 2012). But there is little global governance, and education systems are organized by, and largely for, the nation (Green, 1997), even (and perhaps especially) when the nation is actually just one privileged part of the population (Aldrich, 1996). For some, any opposition to the nation-state is seized upon as evidence not of constructive critique and inclusiveness in the form of multiple citizenships but as an act of betrayal:

> How strange to teach a student born in this country to be proud of his parents' or grandparents' land of birth but not of his or her own. Or to teach a student whose family fled to this country from a tyrannical regime or from dire poverty to identify with that nation rather than the one that gave the family refuge.
>
> (Ravitch, 2006, p. 579)

The continuing strength of the nation-state does not, of course, exclude proper attention to intercultural competence. The nation-state is not necessarily defined mono-culturally and exclusively from global perspectives. But global education, in the perspective of personal as well as geographical and conceptual frameworks, requires at least some particular and probably explicit attention to the need to overcome narrow state perspectives.

Internationalization as a Form of Commercial Activity between Nations and Global Citizenship

Our third challenge for global educators may be seen in Pike's (2012) argument that the attention often given to internationalism runs counter to what is wanted by most proponents of global education. While recent studies (e.g., Egron-Polak & Hudson, 2010) point to the ubiquitous rhetorical commitment to international linkages, Pike suggests that this may be evidence only of opposition to global education:

A neoliberal approach to education—standardisation, quantifiable outcomes, accountability—presented considerable challenges to the fundamental tenets of global education that view learning as a journey with an undetermined destination and adopt the beliefs and values of the student as the starting point for that journey. The predominant neoliberal focus on the acquisition of a fixed body of knowledge, inevitably prioritised by educational goals that insist on measurable outcomes, was largely at odds with the nascent global education movement that was struggling to define its epistemological parameters and which, in any case, wished to give more weight to skills development and the exploration of values.

(Pike, 2012, p. 136)

Although universities now prioritize internationalization activities, such as the promotion of ICC in students, the way in which institutions internationalize varies and is often dependent upon the motivations of university leaders. While motivations can be economic, academic, social/cultural, or political (Knight, 2004), researchers (e.g., Bone, 2008; Middlehurst & Woodfield, 2007; Toyoshima, 2007) suggest that they are most often economic. This marketization orientation (Caruana & Spurling, 2007), connected to the points made by Pike (2012) and referred to earlier, often leads universities to recruit large numbers of higher-fee–paying international students under the guise of creating fertile sites for intercultural learning. While culturally diverse campuses in part created by these students do provide atmospheres through which intercultural learning can take place, the economic orientation of policy makers undermines social and cultural goals (De Vita & Case, 2003), such as promoting the intercultural development of students, with universities using terms like *valuing diversity* and *achieving cross-cultural capability* in strategy statements without converting them into definitive plans (Koutsantoni, 2006; Middlehurst & Woodfield, 2007). Indeed the focus is much more likely to be on international collaborations, producing internationally recognized research, creating overseas campuses, and other activities that enhance international profiles. Thus, the pursuit of developing interculturally competent students is often overshadowed by aspects of internationalization that favor profit motives and a neoliberal agenda.

The predominantly economic approach to internationalization may have impacted strongly on the characterization and effect of initiatives that have been assumed to be one of the main ways in which ICC may be developed: study abroad programs. A review of European action programs (e.g., Socrates) by the European Commission in 1998 concluded that most initiatives related to study abroad are aimed at improving the job prospects of high-status students. These findings have been supported by others, such as Teichler and Maiworm (1997), Osler and Starkey (1999), and Grainger

(2003), with the latter suggesting that while students' motivations for studying abroad relate to an interest in travelling or living abroad, having a foreign experience, or enhancing foreign language skills, they primarily focused upon enhancing employment potential.

Student motivations aside, the proportion of students that actually study abroad is relatively low despite efforts to encourage it. For example, Bologna Ministers set a target for 20 percent of university students in the European Higher Education area (EHEA) to experience a program of study or training abroad by 2020. Although the numbers of students in the EHEA are climbing (European Commission, 2011), the proportion of university students who study abroad is still very low in many countries. ERASMUS statistics suggest that 13,668 UK students studied abroad in 2011/12 (British Council, 2013), which is a small proportion considering that close to 2 million UK undergraduates were enrolled during that period (Higher Education Statistics Agency, 2013). Further, what students learn from their experiences is sometimes questionable. Study abroad trips can often be superficial sightseeing excursions, providing students with little meaningful interaction with local culture. Many researchers (e.g., Lederman, 2007; Pedersen, 2010; Vande Berg, 2009) suggest that in the absence of a program carefully structured to support intercultural development during study abroad, students may return no more interculturally advanced than when they left—as experience has shown that students will often stay with their compatriots and fail to reflect upon their intercultural experiences (assuming they have any meaningful ones) in ways that translate into intercultural development.

Unrealistic Expectation for ICC to Spontaneously Develop among Students

Growing domestic diversity (Vertovec, 2007) and increases in international student numbers (UK Higher Education International Unit, 2007) have helped to create many culturally heterogeneous campuses on which students have more opportunities to engage with those from different cultures and to develop interculturally (Volet & Ang, 1998). However, similar to what has been discussed in relation to study abroad, students studying on home campuses may not be developing interculturally (e.g., Pedersen, 2010). Limited mixing across cultures is often observed particularly among home and international students, and difficulties often emerge when students from different cultures do interact (e.g., Sovic, 2008; Thom, 2000; Williams & Johnson, 2011).

Students' segregating themselves along cultural lines is hardly surprising when understood in the context of typical intergroup relations. Ethnocentrism—preference for one's own cultural group—has been researched and theorized about since at least 1906 (Sumner). Ethnocentric views are based upon a psychological process known as categorization. Drawing upon social identity theory (Tajfel & Turner, 1986), Brewer (2003) outlines the way in which humans categorize themselves and other individuals into ingroups (groups to which one belongs) and outgroups (groups to which one does not belong). This process helps individuals to economize thinking about other individuals so that ingroup members are relied upon to be similar to oneself, whereas outgroup members are viewed according to stereotypes (see Allport, 1954).

In more egalitarian societies, people like to believe that they harbor no group preferences and refrain from stereotyping. However, research consistently shows that individuals favor ingroup members and negatively stereotype outgroup members even if they are not aware of it. National group preference, for example, has been experimentally demonstrated in children as young as six (Tajfel, Nemeth, Johoda, & Campbell, 1970). Other studies have found that just hearing similar accents generates more positive feelings than dissimilar accents and individuals act more cooperatively toward those in their ingroups (Brewer, 2003).

Stereotypes are, of course, problematic because individuals are classified according to group characteristics that may or may not apply to them and that may create breakdowns in communication and result in ill feelings. Moreover, interacting with outgroup members is often associated with anxiety and uncertainty as individuals may be confused by their behavior, not know what to expect, or view them as unapproachable. Grounded in integrated threat theory (Stephan & Stephan, 2000), a recent study of UK home and international student interactions (e.g., Harrison & Peacock, 2009) illustrates the variety of difficulties that students have when interacting across cultures, some of which include: anxiety around the absences of similar cultural references, the effort required for mindful communication, fear of causing offense, and peer disapproval; negative stereotyping, including a lack of differentiation between individuals; symbolic threats, including swamping by unfamiliar others, and breaches of shared norms.

Supplementing research into the psychological underpinnings of intergroup relations, understanding communication processes can further help to explain the difficulties that emerge when individuals from different cultures meet and interact. For instance, a variety of subjective cultural differences relating to beliefs, behaviors, and values often lead communication to break down. Providing an example related to taking turns in group discussions, Bennett wrote,

> The European American pattern involves eye contact to cue turns. The speaker ends with his or her eyes in contact with the conversational heir-apparent. If the speaker lowers her eyes at the end of an utterance, a confused babble of fits and starts may ensue. In contrast . . . some Asian cultures routinely require averted eyes and a period of silence between speakers. In groups including more eye-intensive cultures unacculturated Asians may never get a turn . . . on the other end of the continuum, some forms of . . . Middle Eastern and Mediterranean cultures tend to

prefer more of a "relay-race" pattern of turn taking. Whoever wants the turn next just begins talking, and eventually the conversational baton may be passed on.

(1998, p. 20)

The foregoing example demonstrates how people can ethnocentrically perceive and interpret even nonverbal cultural differences leading to misunderstanding, avoidance, and potentially hostility. Understanding such communication and psychological processes as described earlier helps to explain both the physical divisions seen between student groups on university campuses and the difficulties erupting when interactions occur. What is perhaps surprising is the persistent view in the academic community that students will seamlessly interact and develop interculturally without targeted support and instruction.

Accusations of Low-Level Intellectual and Academic Work

Our penultimate challenge for global educators is that the combination of contested characterizations, the strength of the nation-state, and a particular understanding of the purpose of education leads almost inevitably to a perception that what is being offered in the name of global—as opposed to international—education is simply not worthwhile. At times suggestions are made that a global approach is simply not possible. Naysayers often ask to whom or what loyalty would be offered and whether a coherent identity could be developed in the absence of agreed characterizations and established political structures. There is a reluctance to risk the appearance of denying difference and diversity by exploring a global approach that may suggest uniformity as well as universality. But more precisely relevant to the point we are making here is that the sort of exploratory, values-related, and explicitly political thinking that is an essential feature of global education is not valued as highly as more technocratic approaches that categorize people. This argument is made usually in relation not only to the area of global education per se but also to the way in which global educators have chosen to speak about their work. Superficially framed political statements have been easily subjected to ridicule by a range of commentators (e.g., Scruton, 1985), and we argue here for a form of intercultural competence that is appropriately challenging in intellectual as well as other ways.

There are various reasons why universities seem not to achieve high status for ICC. As already described, it can be overshadowed by the drive to achieve economic gain. As well, however, some may consider students' intercultural development to be irrelevant to the achievement of the principal goal in universities—that is, the teaching of disciplinary knowledge for career placement. However, while universities may turn out graduates with thorough knowledge of psychology, engineering, and management, if they cannot work, live, and collaborate with people from a variety of cultures, how useful will their disciplinary knowledge be (Nolan, 2009)? As well, as argued earlier, fostering intercultural development is a means through which critical thinking skills (a relative cornerstone in higher education) may also develop. Moore and Ortiz (1999), as noted by King and Baxter Magolda (2005), found that students who demonstrated higher levels of intercultural competence were "critical thinkers who suspended judgment until the evidence was in and who included a diverse range of knowledge in what they considered as evidence" (p. 577).

While some universities do prioritize ICC to an extent, most seem to focus upon it more as an outcome in relation to employability, as highlighted earlier in relation to study abroad. While we would not wish to argue against professional preparation, we feel that a rather narrow and unhelpful approach is often developed that is evident not only in relation to study abroad but also on home campuses. Currently, there are some early adopters of global competence–type awards among UK higher education institutions (e.g., Surrey, Kent, Warwick), which require students on home campuses to undertake activities that could enhance intercultural development. Such programs are often described almost exclusively in employability terms and may do little to address ICC. In one program, for example, students are required to attend eight two-hour lectures on various global topics (e.g., the role of banks in the economic crisis), attend six workshops predominantly on career topics (e.g., interviewing skills, CV writing), and reflect upon their learning through a final assessment. Just 1 out of the 22 sessions offered deals with cross-cultural communication—and it is not one that is required. Another award program appears to focus exclusively on language learning. While we would not argue against the merits of studying a foreign language, it is not observed by scholars to automatically equate to cultural fluency (e.g., M. J. Bennett, 1997; Byram, 1997), is not found by research to be necessarily linked to ICC (e.g., Jackson, 2011; Park, 2006), and is not identified as one of the most important factors in mainstream models (Deardorff, 2006).

The employability view of ICC and the means through which universities might aim to develop it fail to take in its broader definition—that is, developing graduates who are able to interact across cultures as friends, community members, and global citizens to realize benefits that stretch beyond employment and monetary gain, as discussed by authors such as Haigh and Clifford (2010). While the two agendas can be successfully fused (Shiel, Williams, & Mann, 2005), such narrow conceptions can be problematic not only because they fail to comprehend and encourage a broader understanding of ICC but also because they may promote competencies that conflict with what ICC represents. For example, Sercu (2010) criticizes (Kim, 2002) model of global intelligence, which uses statements such as "'be aggressively curious about other cultures', 'shift their paradigms as necessary' and 'challenge the negative cultural influence on the status quo'" (p. 22). Such statements have little relationship to the humanistic goals espoused by mainstream models, such as valuing cultural diversity, being open to people from other cultures, withholding judgment, and the ability to empathize, which is considered by leading interculturalists to be the most important element (Deardorff, 2009).

RECOMMENDATIONS TO STRENGTHEN GLOBAL EDUCATION AND ICC

In light of the foregoing challenges we offer, it's only fitting that we present a series of recommendations. Our challenges are—broadly, and as stated earlier—about fundamental ideas, political contexts, and institutional and pedagogical practice. Our recommendations do not address political contexts, but we do consider ahead fundamental ideas by first suggesting that global education and ICC could be characterized by reference to four overlapping features. Second, we discuss some current practice at universities related to ICC development, the main concerns surrounding practice, and review methods that might be useful going forward. Finally, we suggest some areas of research that should be explored. It is probably too much to hope and naive to expect that these three recommendations (for a clear characterization of the field with perhaps greater consensus; for better practice; and for more research) will change political contexts, but not to hope for some interconnections between thinking, education, and political action would be unhelpfully pessimistic.

Recognizing Four Overlapping Features

Our first recommendation is that we should recognize four interconnected elements of global education and ICC with awareness that ICC is more than just training—it also involves cultivating understanding of particular communication and psychological insights relevant to a complex developmental process through which students may learn to think critically about cultural difference. In particular, ahead we note four specific areas in which global education and ICC overlap.

Learning about Ourselves and Others
We do not see globalization and internationalization as simple phenomena existing within a center-periphery model, but instead we recognize they involve complex flows of information and ideas, goods and individuals, cultures and practices within and between national and other borders. We consider *all* students and staff to be international insofar as they are affected by and must concern themselves with international and global contexts and issues. The fact that *some* will have travelled recently across national borders is important, but we must realize the relevance of global issues for *all*.

The content of teaching and research is likely to become more internationalized in the future.

Maintaining and Developing International Excellence
We suggest that educators have a responsibility to see their work as being of interest and value to those who live within and beyond their national borders. In this sense *international* is an expression of a standard as well as a geographical reference. Work undertaken in relation to local, national, and international issues may due to its quality be of interest and value to many within and beyond a single country. A focus on excellence helps us to avoid narrow perceptions of "us" and "them."

Recognizing the Value of Diversity
There are different ways of knowing. This does not lead us to a simplistic relativist position but rather helps us to appreciate varied approaches to the acquisition and characterization of knowledge in different cultural contexts. Research that takes place comparatively and teaching that is informed by recognition of the commonalities and differences in the needs of learners are a more sophisticated and valuable approach than that which assumes the superiority of one particular process.

Promoting the Skills and Dispositions of Intercultural Competence
We recognize that educators live and work in diverse communities, and as such it is clear that there will always be the need to strengthen the various ways in which diversity is celebrated and expressed so as to allow for positive achievement in an open environment.

Developing Specific Approaches to Global Education and ICC

Institutionally and pedagogically, we should develop very specific approaches to global education to help students develop ICC. We wish not to prioritize this unthinkingly beyond all other aspects of global education, but we see intercultural competence as absolutely essential and as such explore it in more detail ahead.

Intercultural contact offers one of the most useful if not essential means to develop ICC, providing as it does the opportunity for intensive learning opportunities through which individuals can experience culture firsthand and test their abilities. There are a variety of emerging practices in higher education institutions in the UK and elsewhere that encourage intercultural contact. Culturally oriented buddy schemes (e.g., Devereux, 2004; Pain, 2011), volunteer work in the local ethnic communities, language learning that incorporates intercultural learning (Sercu, 2002), culturally mixed group work within the curriculum (Arkoudis et al., 2010), and placing students in culturally mixed accommodation are just some of those that involve contact.

While these approaches are promising, as outlined earlier, individuals often prefer the company of ingroup members, find contact with outgroup members difficult, may not always advance their learning in positive ways, and/or may choose to limit their intercultural contact. As described by Janet Bennett (2012) in order for learning to occur, one must do more than simply have intercultural interactions; experiences must be made sense of through an iterative process of experience, reflection, conceptualization, and experimentation (Gregersen-Hermans & Pusch, 2012). While some individuals may be able to achieve this through intercultural contact relatively independently, such development may not come quickly or easily or at all for the many. A study in progress by Lantz, for example, suggests that students studying on a UK campus in a department with one of highest proportions of international students (35 percent) generally did not develop interculturally over the first seven months of university. Other studies, as mentioned previously, have shown similar outcomes. Another difficulty in relation to ICC is that it tends to be poorly defined and not well integrated into program outcomes, as described earlier—whether they involve formal or informal curriculum. While dedicating appropriate resources to support ICC development is an issue that universities must grapple with individually, if resources are available there are many research-informed approaches to working with individuals around ICC.

Fowler and Blohm (2004) provide a good review of a variety of educational methods, such as case studies, critical incidents, cultural assimilators, and role-playing. Paige (2004) surveys intercultural assessment tools, which can be useful for helping learners be self-reflective, assessing audiences to customize training, and measuring outcomes. Another useful resource developed by the Council of Europe (2012) is the publicly available *Autobiography of Intercultural Encounters*, which includes a set of tools designed to facilitate reflection upon intercultural experiences.

Research suggests the benefits of an evidence-based approach to establishing program goals, identifying relevant theoretical frameworks, and choosing educational methods and program assessments (Stephan & Stephan, 2013). Designing programs requires a clear understanding of ICC, how it develops, and how barriers to development might be overcome. Various models (e.g., King & Baxter Magolda, 2005) can be used to guide students in moving from lower levels of development in which knowledge is certain, cultural difference is not understood, and alternative cultural perspectives are considered wrong to higher levels of cognitive complexity in which judgment of differences is suspended, multiple cultural frameworks are integrated, and individuals can consciously adopt alternative perspectives and behaviors.

The foregoing methods and tools may be useful in the contact-related schemes described earlier but also have potential within the curriculum. One department at Leeds Metropolitan University has embedded global perspectives across their curriculum based upon Killick's (2006) curriculum review guidelines (Reddy, Lantz, & Hulme, 2013). While some of the changes involve a wider range of global perspectives, others are more closely aligned with ICC. For example, in one core module, students explore the ethnocentrism of their discipline as it tends to be underpinned by Westernized ideas and concepts and students' final project requires them to reflect upon their own cultural attitudes (Reddy et al., 2013).

While the foregoing methods could be useful in facilitating ICC, researchers suggest that approaches require customization. Stephan and Stephan (2013) note the importance of identifying the cultures involved in the program, which can help to determine appropriate learning goals, theoretical frameworks, and educational techniques. Supporting intercultural development among cultural groups with a history of cultural conflict, for example, may look quite different than among culturally diverse students with little experience of one another.

Beyond group level differences, Milton Bennett's Developmental Model of Intercultural Sensitivity (DMIS) (1986) suggests that individual readiness should also be considered. Bennett suggests that individuals operate at one of six developmental stages and that development is best achieved through stage-appropriate activities. For instance, a person at an early stage with little experience with culture and more ethnocentric views would benefit from experiencing less threatening objective cultural elements, such as learning about national heroes, holidays, or food, to develop familiarity with different cultures, while someone more advanced could benefit more from reflecting upon their own cultural orientation and how it influences their perceptions of and interactions with others (J. M. Bennett & Bennett, 2004).

Whatever the approach to supporting students' intercultural development, educators are well positioned to facilitate it within and outside the curriculum. However, they are likely to find themselves similarly challenged by the increasing diversity of students. While it is not possible to understand all of the cultures represented on today's campuses or world's regions, it is possible and may be necessary for educators to reflect upon and develop their own ICC in order to be able to effectively work with individuals across cultures and to facilitate such intercultural development in students. Travel or living abroad or in diverse neighborhoods, the ability to speak multiple languages, having friends or interacting regularly with those from other cultures may lead some educators (and students) to think of themselves as already interculturally competent. However, anyone regardless of experience with cultural difference can benefit from critical self-reflection. While the term *competence* implies that ICC can be somehow attained, it unlikely if not impossible that any one person will be adept in every intercultural situation. Pursuit of intercultural competence is a lifelong developmental process, involving continual reflection upon the self as much as, if not more than, upon others.

Developing Understanding through Research

Finally, our third recommendation is that we continue to develop our understanding about global education and ICC through substantive research. Some of that research would be philosophical in nature and would help us to clarify the meaning of key concepts. Although the preceding description of ICC helps to clarify its meaning, this meaning emanates predominantly from Western societies and could benefit from being considered alongside alternative approaches and conceptualizations. This would need to be undertaken realistically with awareness of those who would, mischievously, choose to represent enquiry as confusion and with the aim of contributing to collaboration and a reasonable degree of consensus with respect for common values. We would need to know more about the extent to which universities are dependent on and benefit from global collaboration and—without ignoring the reality of economic considerations—explore the extent to which global education and ICC provide value in a variety of ways for students, universities, and economies. There is a need to know, in the context of our existing professional and research-based knowledge, more about how tutors, students, and others characterize global education and ICC and what sort of educational approach would best suit their needs. We need to know more about what types of students (including socioeconomic status, subject specialism, gender, ethnicity) take part in global education and ICC programs and what can be done to equalize opportunities. And, crucially, we need to explore the impact of global education and ICC programs: precisely what sorts of knowledge, understandings, and dispositions do they foster?

CONCLUSION

Global education and intercultural competence are vitally important. Currently these areas are rhetorically accepted and in practice denied. This strange juxtaposition of legitimation and low status must be challenged. We suggest that these necessarily contested areas may be discussed with a greater degree of clarity and consensus that is at times in evidence. We want to encourage a shift away from internationalization, which is often driven by economic considerations, and emphasize more fully the academically rigorous and affectively demanding approaches that will help us understand ourselves and others. This intellectual activity must be underpinned by a vigorous pedagogical and research base.

REFERENCES

Aldrich, R. (1996). *Education for the nation.* London: Cassell.
Allport, G. W. (1954). The nature of prejudice. Cambridge, MA: Addison-Wesley.

Anderson, L. F. (1979). *Schooling for citizenship in a global age: An exploration of the meaning and significance of global education.* Bloomington, IN: Social Studies Development Center.
Appiah, K. A. (2006). *Cosmopolitanism: Ethics in a world of strangers.* New York: W. W. Norton.
Arkoudis, S., Yu, X., Baik, C., Borland, H., Chang, S., Loang, I., . . . Watty, K. (2010). *Finding common ground: Enhancing interaction between domestic and international students: Guide for academics.* Retrieved from www.cshe.unimelb.edu.au/research/projectsites/enhancing_interact.html
Arnot, M., & Dillabough, J. (Eds.). (2009). *Educating the gendered citizen: Social engagements with national and global agendas.* Abingdon: Routledge.
Becker, J. (1979). *Schooling for a global age.* New York: McGraw Hill.
Bennett, J. (2012). The developing art of intercultural facilitation. In K. Berardo & D. K. Deardorff (Eds.), *Building intercultural competence innovative activities and models* (pp. 13–21). Sterling, VA: Stylus.
Bennett, J. M., & Bennett, M. J. (2004). Developing intercultural sensitivity. In D. Landis, J. M. Bennett, & M. J. Bennett (Eds.), *Handbook of intercultural training* (3rd ed., pp. 147–165). London: SAGE.
Bennett, M. J. (1986). A developmental approach to training for intercultural sensitivity. *International Journal of Intercultural Relations, 10*(2), 179–196.
Bennett, M. J. (1997). *How not to be a fluent fool: Understanding the cultural dimension of language.* Retrieved from http://digitalcollections.sit.edu/cgi/viewcontent.cgi?filename=10&article=1001&context=worldlearning_publications&type=additional
Bennett, M. J. (1998). Intercultural communication: A current perspective. In M. J. Bennett (Ed.), *Basic concepts of intercultural communication: Selected readings* (pp. 1–34). Yarmouth, ME: Intercultural Press.
Bone, D. (2008). *Internationalisation of HE: A ten-year view.* Retrieved from www.timeshighereducation.co.uk/Journals/THE/THE/13_November_2008/attachments/Internationalisation-Bone.pdf
Brewer, M. B. (2003). *Intergroup relations.* Philadelphia: Open University Press.
British Council (2013). *ERASMUS—Facts and figures at a glance.* Retrieved March 31, 2014, from www.britishcouncil.org/eu_and_uk_erasmus_stats_11_12_at_a_glance.pdf
Byram, M. (1997). *Teaching and assessing intercultural communicative competence.* New York: Multilingual Matters.
Caruana, V., & Spurling, N. (2007). *The internationalisation of UK Higher Education: A review of selected material.* York: Higher Education Academy.
Cogan, J. J. (1998). Citizenship education for the 21st century: Setting the context. In J. J. Cogan & R. Derricott (Eds.), *Citizenship for the 21st century.* London: Kogan Page.
Council of Europe. (2012). *Autobiography of intercultural encounters.* Retrieved from www.coe.int/t/DG4/AUTOBIOGRAPHY/AutobiographyTool_en.asp
Davies, I., Evans, M., & Reid, A. (2005). Globalising citizenship education? A critique of "global education" and "citizenship education. *British Journal of Educational Studies, 53*(1), 66–89.
Davies, I., & Pike, G. (2009). Global citizenship education: Challenges and possibilities. In R. Lewin (Ed.), *The handbook of practice and research in study abroad: Higher education and the quest for global citizenship* (pp. 61–78). New York: Routledge.
Davies, N. (2012). *Vanished kingdoms: The history of half-forgotten Europe.* London: Allen Lane.
Deardorff, D. K. (2006). Identification and assessment of intercultural competence as a student outcome of internationalization. *Journal of Studies in International Education, 10*(3), 241–265.

Deardorff, D. K. (2009). Understanding the challenges of assessing global citizenship. In R. Lewin (Ed.), *The handbook of practice and research in study abroad* (pp. 346–364). London: Routledge.

Devereux, L. (2004). *When Harry met Sarita: Using a peer-mentoring program to develop intercultural wisdom in students.* Canberra: University of Canberra.

De Vita, G., & Case, P. (2003). Rethinking the internationalisation agenda in UK higher education. *Journal of Further and Higher Education, 27*(4), 383–398.

Egron-Polak, E., & Hudson, R. (2010). *Internationalization of higher education: Global trends, regional perspectives.* IAU 3rd Global Survey Report, International Association of Universities.

European Commission. (1998). *Education and active citizenship in the European Union.* Brussels: European Commission.

European Commission. (2011). *The Erasmus programme 2010–2011: A statistical overview.* Brussels: European Commission.

Fantini, A. E., & Tirmizi, A. (2006). *Exploring and assessing intercultural competence.* St. Louis: Federation of the Experiment in International Living.

Fowler, S. M., & Blohm, J. M. (2004). An analysis of methods for intercultural training. In D. Landis, J. Bennett, & M. Bennett (Eds.), *Handbook of intercultural training* (pp. 37–84). London: SAGE.

Fujikane, H. (2003). Approaches to global education in the United States, the United Kingdom and Japan. *International Review of Education, 49*(1–2), 133–152.

Giddens, A. (1999). *Social change in Britain.* The 10th ESRC Annual Lecture.

Grainger, N. (2003). *Perceptions of some key respondents of the ERASMUS/SOCRATES programmes and the European dimension in education.* Unpublished PhD thesis. University of York, UK.

Green, A. (1997). *Education, globalization and the nation state.* Basingstoke: Macmillan.

Gregersen-Hermans, J., & Pusch, M. D. (2012). How to design and assess an intercultural learning experience. In K. Berardo & D. K. Deardorff (Eds.), *Building cultural competence innovative activities and models* (pp. 23–41). Sterling, VA: Stylus.

Haigh, M., & Clifford, V. (2010). Widening the graduate attribute debate: A higher education for global citizenship. *Brookes eJournal of Learning and Teaching, 2*(5). Retrieved from http://bejlt.brookes.ac.uk/article/widening_the_graduate_attribute_debate_a_higher_education_for_global_citize/

Harrison, N., & Peacock, N. (2009). Cultural distance, mindfulness and passive xenophobia: Using integrated threat theory to explore home higher education students' perspectives on "internationalisation at home." *British Educational Research Journal, 36*(6), 877–902.

Hanvey, R. G. (1975). *An attainable global perspective.* New York: Center for War/Peace Studies.

Heater, D. (1980). *World studies: Education for international understanding in Britain.* London: Harrap.

Heater, D. (1997). The reality of multiple citizenship. In I. Davies & A. Sobisch (Eds.), *Developing European citizens* (pp. 57–76). Sheffield: Sheffield Hallam University Press.

Heater, D. (2002). *World citizenship: Cosmopolitan thinking and its opponents.* London: Continuum.

Held, D., McGrew, A., Goldblatt, D., & Perraton, J. (1999). *Global transformations: Politics, economics and culture.* Cambridge: Polity Press.

Higher Education Statistics Agency. (2013). *Free online statistics—students and qualifiers.* Retrieved from www.hesa.ac.uk/content/view/1897/239/

Hyslop, J. (Ed.). (1999). *African democracy in the era of globalization.* Johannesburg: Witwatersrand University Press.

Ignatieff, M. (2001). *Human rights as politics and idolatry*. Woodstock: Princeton University Press.
Isin, E. F., & Wood, P. K. (1999). *Citizenship and identity*. London: SAGE.
Jackson, J. (2011). Host language proficiency, intercultural sensitivity, and study abroad. *Frontiers: The Interdisciplinary Journal of Study Abroad, 21* (Fall), 167–188.
Killick, D. (2006). *Cross-cultural capability and global perspectives. Guidelines for curriculum review*. Leeds: Leeds Metropolitan University.
Kim, E. Y. (2002). *Global intelligence: Seven pillars for new global leaders, a cross cultural reference of business practices in new Korea*. Westport, CT: Quorum Books.
King, P., & Baxter Magolda, M. (2005). A developmental model of intercultural maturity. *Journal of College Student Development, 46*(6), 571–592.
Knight, J. (2004). Internationalization remodeled: Definition, approaches, and rationales. *Journal of Studies in International Education, 8*(5), 5–30.
Koutsantoni, D. (2006). *Internationalisation in the UK*. Paper presented at the Leadership Summit 2006, London.
Lederman, D. (2007). Quality vs. quantity in study abroad. *Inside Higher Ed*. Retrieved from www.insidehighered.com/news/2007/02/21/abroad
Merryfield, M. M. (1991). Preparing American secondary social studies teachers to teach with a global perspective: A status report. *Journal of Teacher Education, 42*(1), 11–20.
Merryfield, M. M. (2001). Moving the center of global education: From imperial world views that divide the world to double consciousness, contrapuntal pedagogy, hybridity and cross-cultural competence. In W. B. Stanley (Ed.), *Critical issues in social studies research* (pp. 179–208). Greenwich, CT: Information Age.
Middlehurst, R., & Woodfield, S. (2007). *Responding to the internationalisation agenda: Implications for institutional strategy*. York: Higher Education Academy.
Nolan, R. W. (2009). Turning our back on the world. In R. Lewin (Ed.), *The handbook of practice and research in study abroad* (pp. 266–281). London: Routledge.
Osler, A., & Starkey, H. (1999). Rights, identities and inclusion: European action programmes as political education. *Oxford Review of Education, 25*(1–2), 199–215.
Paige, M. R. (2004). Instrumentation in intercultural training. In D. Landis, J. M. Bennett, & M. J. Bennett (Eds.), *Handbook of intercultural training* (pp. 85–128). London: SAGE.
Pain, R. (2011). Boundaries, processes and participation: Integrating peer support through a buddy scheme. *Enhancing the Learner Experience in Higher Education, 3*(1), 59–73.
Park, M. (2006). *A relational study of intercultural sensitivity with linguistic competence in English-as-a-Foreign-Language (EFL) pre-service teachers in Korea*. Unpublished doctoral thesis. University of Mississippi.
Pedersen, P. J. (2010). Assessing intercultural effectiveness outcomes in a year-long study abroad program. *International Journal of Intercultural Relations, 34*(1), 70–80.
Perry, W. (1970). *Forms of intellectual and ethical development in the college years*. New York: Holt, Rinehart & Winston.
Piaget, J. (1932). *The moral judgement of the child*. London: Routledge & Kegan Paul.
Pike, G. (2008). Global education. In J. Arthur, I. Davies, & C. Hahn (Eds.), *The SAGE handbook of education for citizenship and democracy* (pp. 468–480). London: SAGE.
Pike, G. (2012). From internationalism to internationalisation: The illusion of a global community in higher education. *Journal of Social Science Education, 11*(3), 133–149.
Pithers, R. T., & Soden, R. (2000). Critical thinking in education: A review. *Educational Research, 42*(3), 237–249.

Portera, A. (2008). Intercultural education in Europe: Epistemological and semantic aspects. *Intercultural Education, 19*(6), 481–491.
Ravitch, D. (2006). Should we teach patriotism? *Phi Delta Kappan, 87*(8), 579–581.
Reddy, P., Lantz, C., & Hulme, J. (2013). *Employability in psychology.* York: Higher Education Academy.
Richardson, R. (1979). World studies in the 1970s: A review of progress and unresolved tensions. *World Studies Journal, 1*(1), 5–15.
Richardson, R. (1996). The terrestrial teacher. In M. Steiner (Ed.), *Developing the global teacher: Theory and practice in initial teacher education* (pp. 3–10). Stoke-on-Trent: Trentham Books.
Scholte, J. A. (2000). *Globalization. A critical introduction.* London: Palgrave.
Scruton, R. (1985). *World studies: Education or indoctrination?* London: Institute for European Defence and Strategic Studies.
Segall, M. H., Lonner, W. J., & Berry, J. W. (1998). Cross-cultural psychology as a scholarly discipline: On the flowering of culture in behavioral research. *American Psychologist, 53*(10), 1101–1110.
Sercu, L. (2002). Autonomous learning and the acquisition of intercultural communicative competence: Some implications for course development. *Language, Culture and Curriculum, 15*(1), 61–74.
Sercu, L. (2010). Assessing intercultural competence: More questions than answers. In A. Paran & L. Sercu (Eds.), *Testing the untestable in language education* (pp. 17–34). Bristol: Multilingual Matters.
Shiel, C., Williams, A., & Mann, S. (2005). *Global perspectives and sustainable development in the curriculum: Enhanced employability, more thoughtful society?* Paper presented at the conference Enhancing Graduate Employability: The Roles of Learning, Teaching, Research and Knowledge Transfer, Poole, UK.
Sovic, S. (2008). *Lost in transition? The international students' experience project.* London: Institute of Education.
Spencer-Oatey, H., & Franklin, P. (2009). *Intercultural interaction: A multidisciplinary approach to intercultural communication.* Basingstoke: Palgrave Macmillan.
Spitzberg, B. H., & Changnon, G. (2010). Conceptualizing intercultural competence. In D. K. Deardorff (Ed.), *The SAGE handbook of intercultural competence* (pp. 2–52). London: SAGE.
Stephan, W. G., & Stephan, C. W. (2000). An integrated threat theory of prejudice. In S. Sokamp (Ed.), *Reducing prejudice and discrimination* (pp. 23–46). Mahwah, NJ: Lawrence Erlbaum Associates.
Stephan, W. G., & Stephan, C. W. (2013). Designing intercultural education and training programs: An evidence-based approach. *International Journal of Intercultural Relations, 37*(3), 277–286.
Sumner, W. G. (1906). *Folkways.* New York: Ginn.
Tajfel, H., Nemeth, C., Johoda, G., & Campbell, J. (1970). The development of children's preference for their own country: A cross-national study. *International Journal of Psychology, 5*(4), 245–253.
Tajfel, H., & Turner, J. (1986). The social identity theory of intergroup behavior. In S. Worchel & W. Austin (Eds.), *Psychology of intergroup relations* (pp. 7–24). Chicago: Nelson-Hall.
Teichler, U., & Maiworm, F. (1997). *The ERASMUS experience: Major findings of the ERASMUS evaluation research project.* Luxembourg: Office for Official Publications of the European Communities.
Thom, V. (2000). Promoting intercultural learning and social inclusion for international students. In B. Hudson & M. J. Todd (Eds.), *Internationalising the curriculum in higher education: Reflecting on practice* (pp. 50–57). Sheffield: Sheffield Hallam University Press.

Toh, S.-H., (1993). Bringing the world into the classroom: Global literacy and a question of paradigms. *Global Education, 1*(1), 9–17.

Toyoshima, M. (2007). International strategies of universities in England. *London Review of Education, 5*(3), 265–280.

Tye, K. A. (1999). *Global education: A worldwide movement.* Orange, CA: Interdependence Press.

UK Higher Education International Unit. (2007). *Global opportunities for UK higher education.* London.

Vande Berg, M. (2009). Intervening in student learning abroad: A research-based inquiry. *Intercultural Education, 20*(S1), S15–S27.

Vertovec, S. (2007). Super-diversity and its implications. *Ethnic and Racial Studies, 30*(6), 1024–1054.

Volet, S. E., & Ang, G. (1998). Culturally mixed groups on international campuses: An opportunity for inter-cultural learning. *Higher Education Research & Development, 17*(1), 5–23.

Williams, C. T., & Johnson, L. R. (2011). Why can't we be friends?: Multicultural attitudes and friendships with international students. *International Journal of Intercultural Relations, 35*(1), 41–48.

Part II
Global Education Programs and Practices

Section 1: Experiential Education

5 On the Modern Silk Road
A Case Study of the Limits and Promise of International In-Service Teacher Professional Development

Timothy Patterson

Although calls for global travel on the part of American teachers have grown more frequent in recent years (Association of International Educators, 2011), international travel is not a particularly new phenomenon for educators. For example, since the founding of the United States, Americans have traveled for a variety of reasons: tourism, business, military service, religious duty, and, not least of all, education. With American influence growing throughout the world during the 20th century, so too did the number of American teachers traveling abroad (Zimmerman, 2006). Some traveled as instructors, such as those who went to the Philippines at the turn of the century, working with the indigenous population in U.S.-sponsored schools. Others traveled as both instructors and students, such as Peace Corps volunteers who ventured into the world with the dual mission of promoting a better understanding of Americans on the part of the world and developing a better understanding of the world on the part of Americans.

The earliest study tour to bring Americans abroad for the purpose of learning traveled in the 1880s out of Indiana University (Hoffa, 2000). Since this first organized experience, universities, non-governmental organizations, and awards such as the Fulbright Fellowship have continued to provide educational experiences abroad. For global educators, there are a variety of international professional development opportunities: Fulbright-Hays Summer Seminar, the National Consortium for the Teaching about Asia, and the Korea Society Summer Fellowship for American Educators are just a handful of offerings that send American teachers overseas to further develop their content knowledge and teaching of global topics. Several researchers have concluded that these types of international experiences positively impact participants' knowledge, skills, and values with regards to global education (Kirkwood, 2002; Merryfield, 2000; Willard-Holt, 2001).

This chapter considers the challenges and potential of developing global educators through international experiences. The benefits of such experiences, as well as the impact of computer-mediated communication (CMC) on the international experience, the spread of Western hegemony through globalization, and the challenges inherent within the study abroad format, are explored. Because study tours exist for foreign language acquisition, scientific inquiry, and many other purposes, I have limited my scope to the research into the professional development of experienced PK-12 classroom teachers. This chapter reports findings from a case study of one international teacher professional development program in which American teachers traveled along the historic Silk Road in China. In this case study, I compare the firsthand observations I made while on the tour with the scholarship on international teacher professional development. Through this format, I highlight the tensions between the expectations for international teacher professional development and the difficulties in meeting such ambitious goals in one planned international experience.

My findings suggest that, while there are many calls to rethink global education in light of international terrorism, economic crises, and climate change, calls for changes at the *programmatic level* of international teacher professional development have been rare. Rather, the assumption that international experiences are inherently transformative for in-service educators dominates the discourse on this topic, suggesting that this is one area where the potential to develop truly global educators may be blunted if not carefully planned and executed. In light of these findings, I also propose reforms to international teacher professional development at the programmatic level that may begin to work toward the promise held by transnational interactions for the purpose of advancing a rigorous and meaningful global education experience. For the purposes of this chapter, I define international teacher professional development as programs that provide in-service teachers with international experiences with the goal of cultivating various aspects of their professional practices and perspectives.

CONTEXT OF THE STUDY

Data in the form of observations and interviews for this case study was collected through one international teacher professional development program. Hosted by an organization that provides professional development about global history and culture for American teachers of all subjects and grade levels, this program aimed at reinforcing the professional development participants completed in the U.S. through a three-week international experience. I acted as a participant-observer on this study tour, engaging with the participants before, during, and after the experience. The facilitators of this program explained that the goal of this international experience was to help the participants further develop the perceptual and substantive dimensions of their global perspectives (Case, 1993). To enact this goal, the facilitators developed a study tour that examined the historic Silk Road in China.

The format of this study tour was largely representative of international teacher professional development programs that have primarily academic goals guiding their planning and implementation (Engle & Engle, 2002).

On the Modern Silk Road: A Case Study   65

As such, the activities of the study tour were organized around a series of lectures at historical sites in major Chinese cities. Most days were highly structured, with the participants being shuttled from site to site in a large bus. All meals were eaten together, and participants roomed in four- or five-star amenities in cosmopolitan neighborhoods of Chinese cities. As a result, contact with the host population was rare and mediated by the presence of guides, who served as translators. However, while traveling in Xinjiang Autonomous Region participants were able to gain some unguided time to explore host cities. These opportunities came when the local guides, who were all Muslim men, left the tour group for afternoon and evening prayers. During that time, some participants spent their time interacting with locals, while others retreated to the comfort and safety of their hotel rooms.

There are limitations to this study. The data presented here is a snapshot within a snapshot. That is, I offer, from my limited vantage point, the events and interactions of one international teacher professional development program. As such, this study inquires into the workings of a "bounded system" (Smith, 1979); it emphasizes a detailed contextual analysis of a limited number of events. The findings in this study will be site-specific and not generalizable or transferable to other cases, although much of what champions and critics have described as the promises and challenges of international teacher professional development was evident in what I witnessed while in China. These limitations are reflective of the limitations inherent in qualitative and case study research in general (Marshall & Rossman, 2011; Stake, 1995).

PROMISE OF INTERNATIONAL TEACHER EDUCATION

In this chapter, the Silk Road acts as both a metaphor for international teacher professional development and a literal site of travel for my study tour. In global history, the Silk Road refers to 4,000 miles of overland trade routes that, at various points in time, connected Asia to the Mediterranean region. The Silk Road is often presented as "a model of idealized exchange" (Chin, 2013, p. 194), exemplifying the free, hopeful, and cosmopolitan flow of ideas, information, or products from distant locations. In similar fashion, the discourse about the rewards of international teacher professional development frames the experience is analogous to a modern Silk Road, with participants engaging in rich cultural learning, developing global perspectives, and bringing material culture from around the world into their classrooms. It is with this discourse of teacher international professional development that I first explore the promises of international teacher professional development in global education.

The promises of international professional development, evident in the scholarly research and the larger public discourse on such experiences (Feinberg, 2002), likely appear commonsensical to most people who have spent any amount of time abroad. In his guide to educational travel *Beyond Tourism*, Kenneth Cushner offers the testimony of six teachers who taught abroad (2004). Some spoke passionately about their increased confidence, resulting from navigating large cities as non-indigenous language speakers. Others spoke about developing a sense of empathy, a useful skill in working in diverse classrooms, resulting from their status as outsiders in a foreign place. The teachers in this study explained that their knowledge of world cultures and history became more sophisticated as a result of their firsthand experiences abroad. Several reported that their time in international schools led them to reevaluate their cultural beliefs, hitherto unchallenged by their experiences in the U.S. Their reflections sounded familiar to me. In my own development as a teacher, I often drew on my international experiences in discussing global content, and felt my open-mindedness and flexibility when working with diverse groups of students came directly from negotiating difficult situations abroad.

The empirical data seems to suggest that the faith put in international experiences for developing global perspectives in in-service educators is well placed. Many of the positive outcomes expressed by the teachers in Cushner's book are represented in studies on international teacher professional development. For example, Merryfield (2000) found that "the experience of living as an expatriate is frequently *the* lived experience that middle-class white teacher educators cite as turning points towards multicultural and global education" (p. 439). Their international experiences made these teacher educators aware of the multiple realities that exist in both their communities and the world. Germain (1998) argued that the culture shock of international experiences worked as a form of "cultural therapy" for six veteran teachers, allowing them to be more aware of their own biases while teaching. Researchers have also argued that having worldly experiences prepares teachers to present global content, while also providing them with an imperative to do so. Kirkwood (2002) found that teachers who have engaged in international experiences are often motivated to teach about pressing global issues and U.S. foreign policy decisions. Kirkwood examined how 33 teachers from 21 schools taught about Japan in the U.S. after a one-year commitment in the Japan Today program. She contended that the cross-cultural impact of the Japan Today program was significant, and as a result the participants found meaningful ways to incorporate Japanese history and culture into their curricula.

Challenges to Teachers Learning Abroad

Of course, the studies reviewed in the previous section represent only a glimpse into the research on international teacher professional development. Much has been written, for example, on the development of intercultural competences through study tour experiences (e.g., Savicki, 2008). Taken together, the studies cited in the previous section (and others) make a compelling case for the inherent value of international teacher professional development. The mission statements of colleges of education and professional development programs that provide teachers with an international component to their education offer a similar perspective. The very act of crossing national borders is an education, and it cannot be replicated by any other encounter. However, electronic communications and the hegemony of American culture call for the rethinking of international teacher professional development experiences. The inherent distance that has seemingly made international travel educative has been challenged by computer-mediated communication (CMC) technologies that allow students across the world to interact in real time (Coleman & Chafer, 2010). By making the following critique, I am not arguing that such experiences are not educational, but that their abilities to produce powerful outcomes are more complex than is often suggested.

For example, there is evidence that online teacher training courses, when embedded with reflective activities, hold the potential for true cross-cultural learning and allow preservice educators to connect with people around the world in powerful ways (Merryfield, 2003). Time and distance are the key components that CMC technologies bring to the cross-cultural interaction that has allowed for deeper meaning and reflection on the parts of preservice educators that would not be available in ordinary face-to-face interaction. Similarly, preservice teachers have shown the capacity to develop a more robust notion of global education and an appreciation for communication and dialogue across cultures when participating in an international CMC, such as International Education and Resource Network (Zong, 2009). Neither of these experiences required the participants to leave their campuses (or homes, for that matter) to have the cross-cultural experience often promised by international programs for preservice and in-service educators.

While international CMC has allowed Americans to have international experiences while physically staying local, these same technologies have also challenged travelers' ability to have truly "foreign" experiences while abroad. In the past, travelers were all but cut off from their friends and family at home. Phone calls were expensive and often infrequent due to time zone differences. Written letters were even more infrequent, as one would need to wait days or weeks before hearing from a loved one. This meant that travelers were truly on their own in foreign countries, forced to interact with the host population, crossing language barriers, and adapting (or not) to unfamiliar ways of life. Some have observed that communication technologies like electronic mail and Skype, which provide inexpensive and instantaneous communications and, in the case of Skype, face-to-face contact in real time, allow travelers to stay connected with friends and family at home and avoid cultural immersion. For homesick travelers, such technologies encourage detachment from the host cultures, preventing cross-cultural experiences (Coleman & Chafer, 2010). This is particularly problematic because international preservice education and professional development programs tend to focus explicitly on academic goals for participants, while the development of cross-cultural skills is seen as a natural by-product of the international experience.

Unfortunately, the format of many international teacher professional development programs is likely to limit participants' contact with host cultures. Rather than immersing themselves in a foreign culture, participants are more likely to interact with other members of the tour, creating a parallel world to their lives at home (Engle & Engle, 2002). This cocoon serves to shield participants from being exposed to local practices, let alone reflecting on their experiences abroad. The foreign becomes a new background to act out familiar behaviors, rather than a site of cultural transformation. At its worst this type of experience runs the risk of reinforcing stereotypes; at its best it provides surface-level understandings of host cultures, commonly associated with tourist trips (Cushner, 2004).

In addition, American hegemony and globalization may blunt the potential impacts of international teacher professional development. Cultural differences clearly still exist, but due to the fast travel of information and economic and social homogenization, differences appear less visible to students who are unprepared to negotiate them while learning abroad (Engle & Engle, 2002). In response to these trends, participants have begun to travel to sites that have been traditionally avoided by study abroad programs, such as China, India, and Argentina (Institute of International Education, 2009). Organizing trips to these locales creates a whole new set of health, safety, and access concerns. As a result, administrators are pushed to either establish programs in familiar environments where participants are likely to encounter Western reference points, or develop programs in non-Western nations that seek to create an American cocoon that protects students from discomfort. While pursuing destinations that expose participants to culture shock may develop their skills as multicultural and global educators, these trips can still be problematic. These experiences, if designed with the goal of taking a knowing possessing of the host culture, may reinforce distinctions such as self and other, distancing the participants from their implicated positions as travelers (Talburt, 2009). Likewise, a lack of mutually beneficial experiences for both host and visiting peoples often characterizes tours that send participants to nontraditional destinations. The tendency is to create a strain on the local infrastructure, while exacerbating the differences between traveler and travelee by highlighting disparities in voyeuristic ways that emphasizes the "exotic" lifestyles of host cultures (Woolf, 2006).

Despite the aforementioned limits of and challenges to international teacher professional development programs the general structure of these programs has been slow to evolve. Several factors have contributed to the staying power of the typical international teacher professional development programs. For instance, market factors play a role in restricting the abilities of many study abroad programs to impact significant cross-cultural understanding. Universities and organizations that send Americans abroad are under pressure to gain interest from as many potential participants as possible. As a result, they often craft programs that are touted as both comfortable and fun. These programs, however, are not expected to fundamentally challenge a participant's worldview.

Looming large throughout these critiques is the fundamental difficulty facing both researchers and practitioners of international professional development in challenging "traditional and imperial categories of global Others" (Subreenthduth, 2010, p. 205). Organizations offering international teacher professional development rarely factor in how the multilayered identities of their participants (e.g., race, gender, class) will impact experiences abroad (Malewski & Phillion, 2009). Likewise, programs that lack critically reflective and collaborative components threaten to flatten and simplify global Others, rather than assist in the development of knowledge about the world that is founded on authentic cross-cultural understanding. Subreenthduth (2010) offers alternative travel narratives of two educators that represent examples of international teacher professional development that complicated, rather than obscured, the privilege the participants brought to both their travel and teaching. These narratives are marked by prolonged engagement before and after travel, and show evidence of significant effects on their identities and pedagogy. However, posed as alternative narratives, these examples represent what is possible, but not necessarily what is typical or automatic during international teacher professional development.

On the Modern Silk Road: International Teacher Professional Development in Practice

Thus far I have discussed what the scholarly research has indicated about international teacher professional development as a form of preparation for global educators. In the following space, I explore the realities of the promises and challenges to the study tour in practice, based upon my participation in one international teacher professional development program (which I will henceforth refer to as the "study tour") that traveled to China in the summer of 2012. This study tour traveled by bus and plane westward from Beijing, stopping in cities that had historical sites of relevance to the ancient Silk Road, such as Xi'an, Dunhuang, Turpan, Hotan, and Kashgar.

Prior to the study tour, participants completed at least one full year of professional development seminars in their home states. However, the seminars themselves were stand-alone professional development courses that varied in content. They were not designed under the assumption that all participants would continue on to the study abroad component of this organization's professional development. To remedy this, participants joined online discussions about the study tour through a Wikispaces page hosted by the guides running the tour. On this page the guides offered practical advice (e.g., what to pack, how to dress when visiting religious sites) and answered participants' questions about the tour. Here they also recommended academic readings, curricular frameworks, and travel guides to the participants that they believed would best prepare them to view the historical and cultural sites they would be visiting in China.

After a two-hour orientation in Chicago, where basic travel concerns such as the exchange of currency in China and dealing with jetlag were explained, the study tour of 18 American teachers flew to Beijing. In order to nurture the perceptual dimension of the participants' global perspectives, which includes attitudes such as open-mindedness, resistance to stereotyping, and an inclination to empathize (Case, 1993, p. 320), this study tour offered opportunities for planned and unplanned cross-cultural experiences. Planned cross-cultural experiences typically involved a visit to the home of a Chinese family, such as a tour of an active hutong in Beijing or dinner in the dining room of a Uyghur family in Turpan. The unplanned cross-cultural experiences existed as a by-product of the study tour. Rare although they were, participants did have several evenings to themselves, where they were free to explore Chinese cities without the protective buffer of the guides. The types of experiences participants had during free time varied greatly, although by the time the tour reached Xi'an many of the participants reported that interacting with the local population was the most educational aspect of the study tour. Some, such as Michael (all participant names are pseudonyms), a middle school social studies teacher, even contrasted these moments with the learning activities on the itinerary of the study tour:

> I understand the main thing is, yes, we're looking at how to teach the Silk Road, and it's ancient, but in the end, still, people that are alive now in the 21st century and making connections, seeing how culture is, I want to say similarities and differences, I think that was, this trip was really devoid of encouraging that kind of interaction. It's really sad.

Cross-cultural experiential learning can be particularly impactful for teachers when accompanied by culture shock and reflection (Merryfield, 2001). The presence of the guides, however, tended to mediate the impact of culture shock during planned cross-cultural experiences. For example, the guides often spoke to local people for the participants, preventing them from negotiating language and cultural gaps. The guides also discouraged the participants from venturing out into Chinese cities unaccompanied, preferring to chaperone such experiences. Thus interactions tended to be buffered by the guides, with the stated goal of eliminating the anxiety that comes from being an outsider in a new place (Cushner, 2004). Still, during some unplanned cross-cultural experiences participants faced difficult situations, resulting in what some described as culture shock. Some of this was manifested in simple annoyance over cultural differences between China and the U.S., such as personal space between strangers and spitting in public. Other frustrations appeared more severe. The poverty in cities like Urumqi and Hotan was shocking for some of the participants, while the most pronounced moments of culture shock appeared to come out of the participants' identities as non-Muslim Westerners in predominantly Muslim locales while moving through the Xinjiang Autonomous Region.

While many of the participants occasionally wrote in their notebooks while traveling from site to site, reflection and journaling were not required features of this trip. Indeed, the pace of the trip led several of the participants to complain they did not have sufficient time to truly mull over what they were experiencing. As a result, throughout the trip I noted moments when the participants engaged in conversation that would constitute reflective practice. For example, during one conversation we talked about the feeling of being an ethnic or racial minority in a population different from one's own. This conversation was sparked by a comment by a Chinese tour guide, who said that she was not comfortable at all in Xinjiang, because she was an ethnic minority in Uyghur territory. Several other participants shared their own experiences of being "othered," either in China or on previous trips.

The study tour aimed to nurture the substantive dimension of the participants' global perspectives, or the "range of global topics about which people should be informed" (Case, 1993, p. 319), through visits to historical and cultural sites and lectures from two American historians of Asian history as well as Chinese docents. The study tour made stops at sites commonly visited by American tourists traveling in China, such as the Great Wall, the Terra Cotta Warriors, and the Summer Palace. In traveling along the historic Silk Road, the study tour also stopped at sites off the beaten path of traditional tourist destinations, such as the Bezeklik Thousand Buddha Caves in Turpan and the Mogao Grottoes in Dunhuang, which were looted by Western archeologists. As a result, the legacy of Western imperialism was a theme returned to multiple times by both the Chinese and American guides. Their lectures tended to focus on the impact of these actions, noting that while many of the artifacts survive in Western museums, their exhibition outside of China represents a legacy of humiliation and defeat (Merewether, 2003).

As gauged by conversations during the tour and after returning to the U.S., participants' confrontation with Western imperialism in China did not significantly impact the substantive dimension of their global perspectives. For example, Anthony, a high school modern world history teacher, characterized Europe as the central focus of his class before leaving for China. When we returned I asked if he conceptualized his Eurocentric curriculum any differently: "My ability to convey knowledge and captivate the interest of students is a lot better having gone on this trip. And I have more resources and materials to look at, but I wouldn't necessarily change the way I talk about [Europe and the rest of the world]." Several participants assumed the talk about the looting of historical sites was a product of anti-Americanism rather than valuable historical information. The final stop on the study tour, Shanghai, also seemed to challenge the impact of lectures by the guides.

Shanghai is a reminder of European imperialism, due in particular to the names of several neighborhoods, French and British Concessions, which were formerly occupied by those powers. However, several participants remarked that Shanghai was the most comfortable city they had visited in China, due largely to the abundance of Western reference points and the cosmopolitan character of the city itself. While walking through the city at night, several of the participants and I talked about the benefits of the imperial conquests for the Chinese people. When I questioned this interpretation, using examples from sites that the tour visited that had been ravaged by European archeologists, they pushed back, citing the wealth and architectural achievements in Shanghai.

CRITIQUES AND RECOMMENDATIONS

The findings of this case study serve to both confirm and complicate the existing literature. As such, there are lessons here for both those who plan these tours and teachers who choose to participate. I offer critiques and corresponding recommendations of three broad aspects of study tours aimed at international teacher professional development: the lack of mandated preparation and follow-through, the study tour format, and the presence of CMC.

Preparation and Follow-Through

While the facilitators of this study tour naturally directed the bulk of their attentions toward crafting the activities that happened abroad, events before and after the study tour appeared to be the key aspects to maximizing the potential of study abroad experiences for educators. Conversations with several participants after returning to the U.S. underscored just how essential preparation and reflection are to extending the experiences into classroom action. Many complained that both the Wikispaces page and the two-hour orientation in Chicago, with their focus on practical travel tips, were sadly absent of substantive content about the host population and how the host population was likely to view them as American visitors. While in China, the participants complained of the intense pace of site visits and movement from city to city. With little free time, journal writing, meeting in discussion groups, and other opportunities for reflective practices were limited. Following the study tour, the participants were "lone wolves" in their schools (Gaudelli, 2006), facing resistance to reforming their curricula utilizing knowledge from the study tour.

The facilitators of the study tour cited fiscal challenges to providing substantial support before and after as the primary limitation of this study tour. The Wikispaces page was an attempt at expanding the participants' substantive knowledge of Chinese history and culture prior to the study tour, but participation was minimal and hardly interactive. Given that participants' perceptual understanding of the host culture is the tool they will use to interpret their experiences, it is only sensible that programs ought to be in place to gauge participants' content knowledge, expectations, and attitudes, as well as support their reflection upon returning home. Of course, this is not an original insight on my part. Preparation before and reflection during and after have long been noted as essential features in the research on international experiences for educators (Germain, 1998; Kambutu & Nganga, 2008; Merryfield, 2001; Willard-Holt, 2001; Wilson, 1982). However, based on my observations of this study tour it is worth reinforcing this point.

Format

If cross-cultural experiences are the goal of international teacher professional development, then the format of the study tour was highly problematic. Being a part of the study tour meant that participants almost exclusively interacted with other Americans, rather than the host population. As such, cross-cultural exchanges typically occurred while shopping for souvenirs or during free time *despite* the format of the study tour. Upon returning to the U.S., Caroline, a world cultures teacher, complained that she got a "Best Western experience. I don't know that it was intended, but I felt like we were kept from interaction with the people. And even when we expressed a desire for interaction, I felt like there was no flexibility." Chinese tour guides mediated nearly all of these exchanges, and as a result only rarely were the participants challenged to traverse any language barriers.

Likewise, the pace of the tour left little time for reflection or debriefing on the participants' experiences. The facilitators of the tour argued that this was a result of their desire to have the participants visit as many sites in China as possible during their brief time there. I would argue against adding content/sites to international experiences at the expense of reducing time set aside for debriefing participant experiences and learning. Given the limited time practicing teachers are likely to have to devote to international professional development, it appears the most effective use of resources would be put toward spending as much time as possible in several cities rather than moving quickly between many cities (e.g., quality over quantity). In addition, several homestays, rather than lodgings in Western-styled hotels, would further divorce the participants from their lives in the U.S. and, given time constraints, create prolonged cross-cultural encounters. Although these experiences are likely to be uncomfortable for participants, they would also be potentially educational in ways hardly replicable in traditional forms of teacher development, at best fostering intercultural sensitivity (Bennett, 1993).

Presence of CMC

Even in far-flung cities such as Hotan, the hotels had high-speed Internet access, making contact with home easy. Many participants could be found in the lobbies talking with loved ones face-to-face through Skype communiqués on their laptops or tablets before the day's activities. Given the availability of high-speed Internet access throughout most of the study tour and that a decisive majority of participants brought either a laptop or a tablet with them, I recommend that organizations providing study tours to advance international teacher professional development embrace the potentials of CMC, rather than ignoring their presence abroad. Although research into the synthesis of online collaboration and study abroad experiences is relatively thin, initial studies demonstrate promise for maximizing the benefits for teachers who travel abroad for professional development (e.g., Lou & Bosley, 2008).

At a minimum, participants ought to be engaged in online collaboration before and after the experience, potentially attending to my critique of the lack of preparation and follow-through. Borrowing from best practices in distance learning, participants would be asked to examine their own assumptions about the host cultures and expectations for the study tour through discussion boards, Skype teleconferences, and reflective journaling (Palloff & Pratt, 2007). Facilitators of the study tour could then tailor experiences abroad in response to the particular characteristics of the participants, rather than applying a one-size-fits-all approach to professional development activities. Finally, upon returning home participants could engage once again in these digitally communicative activities, all with the goal of unpacking and making meaning out of their experiences. In essence, international teacher professional development should be reconceptualized as occurring in a blended learning environment, a format that has already shown gains in developing cross-cultural awareness without having participants cross borders (Lajoie et al., 2006; West, 2010). One need not reinvent the wheel to update the study tour format; programs such as What's Up with Culture, created by Bruce La Brack at the University of the Pacific, already provide facilitators with the framework to develop virtual interactions with the goal of supporting international experiences (2003).

CONCLUSIONS

While the analysis in this chapter is largely critical of the international experience observed here, it must be acknowledged that every participant I spoke with after returning to the U.S. was emphatic in describing the learning they say they experienced while in China. Although they tended to concentrate on experiences that occurred during their free time, as opposed to activities organized and facilitated by the study tour, participants reported that their experiences have inspired them to develop lessons that address both the global content and broad-minded perceptual attitudes in their students. In response to viewing murals in the Mogao Caves, Rebecca was inspired to develop an appreciation for cultural diffusion in her world history students:

> Exploring the change in the art and how that shows the idea of coming in contact with other groups. Cultural diffusion, I want to explore that. And the caves and art made me want to do that more.

Some discussed witnessing global interconnections first hand, allowing them to see their home nation as within a larger system, rather than as the center of it. Others spoke about having their stereotypical understandings of China challenged by their observations of this nation's religious, ethnic, and linguistic diversity. One current that flowed through all of our conversations regarded the power of their brief moments of cultural exchange with the host population.

Of course, this chapter is not a call for such experiences to be abandoned in developing global educators. Like many curricula and schools that promise to impart to students 21st-century global skills, without critical evaluation of the structures and outcomes of such experiences there exists a risk for international teacher education to be defined by buzzwords devoid of content. CMC in particular acts as a double-edged sword for international teacher professional development. On the one hand, the potential of professional development through digital technologies challenges the logic of spending significant amounts of money and time away from home when cross-cultural experiences appear available through such technologies. It also provides an out for homesick travelers, linking them to their home lives and preventing cultural immersion. On the other hand, such communications can aid in both the preparation for and support afterwards of international study tour experiences in potentially powerful ways.

When study tours are planned and executed under the assumption that they will be automatically educational for teachers, such programs run the risk of creating a traditional tourist experience, rather than international professional development. If participants are treated as a homogenous entity, and previous dispositions are not considered in the planning of international teacher professional development, a generic experience is likely. As such, a premium must be placed on the preparatory aspects of any international professional development experience, as well as the format that programs take while participants are abroad. Similarly, it is easier today to stay connected to home than ever before. These factors increase the chances of missed opportunities for the expansion of participants' global perspectives and teaching. Sadly, the study tour described in this chapter has largely characterized the field of international teacher development for the last three decades (Engle & Engle, 2002; Malewski & Phillion, 2009). In an effort to further internationalize teacher education, facilitators of such experiences would be wise to embrace the changes brought to the international experience by international CMC technologies.

REFERENCES

Association of International Educators. (2011). *Education students for success in the global economy: A public opinion survey on the importance of international education*. Washington, DC: National Association of Foreign Student Affairs.
Bennett, J. M. (1993). Towards ethnorelativism: A developmental model of intercultural sensitivity. In R. M. Paige (Ed.), *Education for the intercultural experience* (pp. 21–71). Yarmouth, ME: Intercultural Press.
Case, R. (1993). Key elements of a global perspective. *Social Education, 57*, 318–325.
Chin, T. (2013). The invention of the Silk Road, 1877. *Critical Inquiry, 40*(1), 194–219.
Coleman, J. A., & Chafer, T. (2010). Study abroad and the Internet: Physical and virtual context in an era of expanding telecommunications. *Frontiers: The Interdisciplinary Journal of Study Abroad, 19*, 151–167.
Cushner, K. (2004). *Beyond tourism: A practical guide to meaningful educational travel*. Lanham, MD: Scarecrow Education.
Engle, J., & Engle, L. (2002). Neither international nor educative: Study abroad in the time of globalization. In W. Grunzweig & N. Rinehart (Eds.), *Rockin' in Red Square: Critical approaches to international education in the age of cyberculture* (pp. 25–39). New Brunswick, NJ: Transaction.
Feinberg, B. (2002). What students don't learn abroad. *Chronicle of Higher Education, 48*(34). Retrieved from http://chronicle.com/article/What-Students-Don-t-Learn/23686
Gaudelli, W. (2006). Professional development for global education: Possibilities and limitations. *Policy and Practice in Education, 11*(2), 24–54.
Germain, M. H. (1998). *Worldly teachers: Cultural learning and pedagogy*. Westport, CT: Greenwood Press.
Hoffa, W. W. (2000). *A history of US study abroad: Beginnings to 1965*. Carlisle, PA: Journal of Study Abroad.
Institute of International Education. (2009). *Americans study abroad in increasing numbers*. Retrieved October 27, 2010, from http://opendoors.iienetwork.org/?p=150651
Kambutu, J., & Nganga, L. (2008). In these uncertain times: Educators build cultural awareness through planned international experiences. *Teaching and Teacher Education, 24*(4), 939–951.
Kirkwood, T. F. (2002). Teaching about Japan: Global perspectives in teacher decision-making, context, and practice. *Theory and Research in Social Education, 30*(1), 88–115.
La Brack, B. (2003). What's up with culture? Retrieved November 4, 2013, from www2.pacific.edu/sis/culture
Lajoie, S. P., Garcia, B., Berdugo, G., Márquez, L., Espíndola, S., & Nakamura, C. (2006). The creation of virtual and face-to-face learning communities: An international collaboration experience. *Journal of Educational Computing Research, 35*(2), 163–180.
Lou, K., & Bosley, G. (2008). Dynamics of cultural contexts: Meta-level intervention in the study abroad experience. In V. Savicki (Ed.), *Developing intercultural competence and transformation: Theory, research and application in international education* (pp. 276–296). Sterling, VA: Stylus.
Malewski, E., & Phillion, J. (2009). International field experiences: The impact of class, gender, and race on the perceptions and experiences of preservice teachers. *Teaching and Teacher Education, 25*(1), 52–60.
Marshall, C., & Rossman, G. B. (2011). *Designing qualitative research* (5th ed.). Thousand Oaks, CA: SAGE.

Merewether, C. (2003). Looting and empire. *Grand Street, 72,* 82–94.
Merryfield, M. M. (2000). Why aren't teachers being preparing to teach for diversity, equity, and global interconnectedness? A study of lived experiences in the making of multicultural and global educators. *Teaching and Teacher Education, 16*(4), 429–443.
Merryfield, M. M. (2001). Moving the center of global education: From imperial worldviews that divide the world to double consciousness, contrapuntal pedagogy, hybridity, and cross-cultural competence. In W. B. Stanley (Ed.), *Critical issues in social studies research for the 21st century* (pp. 179–207). Greenwich, CT: Information Age.
Merryfield, M. M. (2003). Like a veil: Cross-cultural experiential learning online. *Contemporary Issues in Technology and Teacher Education, 3*(2), 146–171.
Palloff, R. M., & Pratt, K. (2007). *Building online learning communities: Effective strategies from the virtual classroom* (2nd ed.). San Francisco: Jossey-Bass.
Savicki, V. (Ed.). (2008). *Developing intercultural competence and transformation.* Sterling, VA: Stylus.
Smith, L. (1979). An evolving logic of participant observation, educational ethnography, and other case studies. In L. Shuman (Ed.), *Review of research in education* (pp. 316–377). Itasca, IL: F. E. Peacock.
Stake, R. E. (1995). *The art of case study research.* Thousand Oaks, CA: SAGE.
Subreenduth, S. (2010). Travel dialogues of/to the Other: Complicating identities and global pedagogy. In B. Subedi (Ed.), *Critical global perspectives: Rethinking knowledge about global societies* (pp. 199–222). Greenwich, CT: Information Age.
Talburt, S. (2009). International travel and implication. *Journal of Curriculum Theorizing, 25*(3), 104–118.
West, C. (2010). Borderless via technology. *International Educator, 19*(2), 24–33.
Willard-Holt, C. (2001). The impact of a short-term international experience for preservice teachers. *Teaching and Teacher Education, 17*(4), 505–517.
Wilson, A. H. (1982). Cross-cultural experiential learning for teachers. *Theory into Practice, 21*(3), 184–192.
Woolf, M. (2006). Come and see the poor people: The pursuit of exotica. *Frontiers: The Interdisciplinary Journal of Study Abroad, 12,* 135–146.
Zimmerman, J. (2006). *Innocents abroad: American teachers in the American century.* Cambridge, MA: Harvard University Press.
Zong, G. (2009). Developing preservice teachers' global understanding through computer-mediated communication technology. *Teaching and Teacher Education, 25*(5), 617–625.

6 Teacher Conceptualizations of Global Citizenship
Global Immersion Experiences and Implications for the Empathy/Threat Dialectic

Debora Hinderliter Ortloff and Olga N. Shonia

INTRODUCTION

Global education, although manifesting in a variety of curricular forms (Dolby & Rahmen, 2008), attempts to reconceptualize the notion of citizenship, reconciling it with a changing world in which national boundaries are no longer clearly delineated (Kagan & Stewart, 2004; Keating, 2010; Ortloff, 2011; Suarez-Orozco & Sattin, 2007). Further, by drawing theoretically from cosmopolitanism (Nussbaum, 1997), global education provides a conceptual basis for reconciling the sometimes conflicting purposes of education: the fostering of national allegiance as well the development of universal empathy for all of humankind (Marshall, 2009; Shah, 2008; Suárez-Orozco, 2005). Thus, at its heart global education aims at education for global citizenship.

In 2012 the U.S. Department of Education released a framework for internationalizing K-12 education (U.S. Department of Education, 2012) that prioritized global citizenship as a critical outcome of compulsory education in the United States. Although global education, defined here as all those curricula, instructional practices, materials, and intentions that seek to give students global knowledge and dispositions toward global-mindedness, is not a new concept, this is the first major policy statement issued by the U.S. Department of Education on the topic. Although the framework itself is an unfunded policy initiative, it remains significant that the education of globally competent citizens has moved from a rhetorical topic to the focus of a policy framework. Indeed, in recent years more attention has been paid to global citizenship as an important outcome of public education in the U.S. (Council of Chief State School Officers, 2006; Ravitch, 2002; Schattle, 2008).

Despite a growing acknowledgment that global education is a critical component of a 21st-century education, there is little consensus in the literature about how this should be undertaken (Cushner, 2012; Ortloff et al., 2012). A central aspect of advancing teaching and learning in an increasingly international context is the capacity of educators to teach for global citizenship. It is interesting to note that the U.S. Department of Education specifically uses the term *globally competent citizen* as opposed to *global citizen*. The pragmatic emphasis does imply less of a cosmopolitan notion than is supported by the literature on global citizenship. Nonetheless, the development of a strategy with the aim of educating students globally is noteworthy.

The purpose of this study is to identify how prior global immersion experiences can sharpen an educator's approach to teaching for global citizenship or incorporating global issues into the classroom. We use James and Cherry McGee Banks' CATS model (2004) of four levels of integration of multicultural content to analyze the data and to organize our findings. Banks' CATS model includes: the Contributions approach, the Additive approach, the Transformation approach, the Social Action approach (Banks & Banks, 2004). Banks' framework is useful because it focuses on curricular reform and teacher action, while recognizing that teacher values influence instructional decisions. Likewise, the CATS model conforms to Merryfield's (2000) assertion that the preparation of global educators is an extension of preparing multicultural educators. Overall this chapter contributes to creating a more precise understanding of teacher conceptualizations of global citizenship as a means for developing empathy or a means to mediating external threats, especially as it relates to teachers' global immersion experiences.

LITERATURE REVIEW

The research on global education is in and of itself diverse, drawing on a wide variety of literatures and traditions (Dolby & Rahman, 2008). Beginning in the 1960s, as an awareness of social problems, such as poverty, war, and discrimination, created both national and international social movements, the idea of introducing international components to the compulsory school curriculum became the focus of policy, practice, and research discussions (Dolby & Rahman, 2008, p. 699).

Currently, the global education movement in the U.S., although it still remains a fragmented area of study, is largely based upon the belief that as national borders become more fluid and processes of globalization become more dominant, U.S. students need to be prepared in different ways to function and succeed in society (U.S. Department of Education, 2012). While globalization (Suarez-Orozco & Qin-Hillard, 2004) is a process widely interpreted as a contemporary phenomenon, an overall examination of education for global citizenship within a historical context reveals a conflicting relationship between understanding global education holistically and understanding global education as a response to global threats (Frey & Whitehead, 2009). This tension, while evidenced in the historical context surrounding global education, continues today and in fact is clearly evident in the Department of Education (DoE) framework (2012). Within this framework, the DoE justifies the need for internationalization in order to remain economically competitive, to respond to global challenges, and to preserve national security. All of these reasons position the need for global understanding and citizenship as a response to perceived *threats* to U.S. interests. Our data, likewise, revealed that, for many teachers, international forces were perceived as a threat to U.S. interests. However, the perception of international forces as threats can be lessened through global immersion experiences. Specifically, an emphasis on cross-cultural competence, empathy for others, and appreciation of other cultures emerged as a means of mediating the threat. As such, we adopt a theoretical lens that situates *empathy* and *threat* as dialectics. This dialectic approach to global citizenship was a useful lens for analyzing the data and interpreting the ways in which international immersion experiences mediated teachers' perspectives toward this dialectic.

METHODOLOGY

Research Design

Our primary data collection instrument for this study was an open-ended survey. Survey questions asked participants about their beliefs, values, and experiences with global education as well as a series of demographic questions, including their teaching biography. The intent of this instrument was not to create subscales for quantitative analysis as in traditional survey analysis (Creswell, 2007), but rather to generate a large amount of qualitative data from a larger sample of teachers to reflect on issues of global citizenship than would be possible in face-to-face interviews (N=15). We also conducted face-to-face interviews with a separate sample of teachers to make sure the survey was, in fact, functioning reliably when compared to a face-to-face interview. We found that the themes coded in the face-to-face interviews and the survey were in agreement 93.4 percent of the time. We also followed standard processes in qualitative research in order to increase validity. In terms of validity, we used both member checking (Creswell, 2007) with teachers who had agreed to follow up when they took the survey (n=10) and discussing with them our analysis and findings. We also used peer debriefing in order to check our own biases and assumptions (Carspecken, 1996).

Participants and Recruitment

This chapter reports the findings from two studies conducted as part of an ongoing, multistate project in which teachers of all levels and subjects are surveyed about their perspective on global citizenship and preparing students to be global citizens (Creswell, 2007). We purposefully sampled 108 teachers into three categories: teachers with no significant experience outside of the U.S., teachers with significant international experience outside of the U.S., defined as more than four months outside the U.S., and non-native teachers who emigrated to the U.S. from other countries. We choose four months as the line for demarcation when selecting teacher participants with significant travel experience, as it represents an amount of time beyond what could be experienced in a short-term summer (or other season) exchange. Our intent was to ensure that participants had enough time in-country to have experiences beyond those of a casual visitor. Participants were recruited through teacher education programs, requesting in-service teachers to complete the survey. We e-mailed a variety of teacher education programs (conveniently sampled), asking the chairs of the programs to forward the message to in-service teachers in their program. Of the 108 teachers in the sample, there was equal representation across the three targeted areas and across elementary and secondary schools. Eighty-two percent of respondents were women and 79 percent were White, with 9 percent reporting Hispanic ethnicity and 6 percent Black or African American. The remaining percentage did not report a race or ethnicity.

Data Analysis

We used a two-pronged data analysis process. First, we conducted an emergent analysis, followed by a second-level analysis using Banks and Banks' (2004) CATS model (2004) of four levels of integration of multicultural content. Banks and Banks' CATS model includes: the Contributions approach, the Additive approach, the Transformation approach, and the Social Action approach (Banks & Banks, 2004). For the emergent analysis we used the constant comparative method to analyze the open-ended responses in the survey. We analyzed our survey data using techniques adapted from Miles and Huberman (1984).

In order to understand the emergent findings as they related to curricular and instructional reform, we then coded the data based on Banks and Banks' CATS model (2004) of four levels of integration of multicultural content, to further analyze the data. Banks theorized that curricular and instructional reforms like multicultural education begin at more superficial levels and move toward levels that involve more personal investment of time, knowledge, and resources. Likewise he recognized that multicultural education reform requires a value transformation in the teaching force toward viewing multicultural education as essential for all students, in order for the reform to be successful. We argue that applying this framework to teachers' conceptualizations of global citizenship helps to illustrate internationalization as a reform process that requires both intellectual and values transformations.

FINDINGS

Of the questions on our 16-item survey instrument, two items related directly to the respondents' ways in which they conceptualized living in a globalized world and being a global citizen, and how they linked that to their own classroom, curriculum, and professional dispositions. Furthermore, two questions addressed participants' beliefs regarding the need for more emphasis on global education and citizenship, and, consequently, what actions participants deemed necessary to increase emphasis on global education and citizenship, if at all.

Conceptualization of Global Citizenship

We asked participants to unpack the notion of living in a globalized world and being a global citizen, evaluating the extent to which they viewed themselves as a global citizen. Overwhelmingly, our respondents seemed to believe that "having an understanding and being aware of other cultures" is an important aspect of being globally minded. For example, almost half (53) of the 108 participants who answered all of our questions reported the sentiment that "a global citizen is concerned with broadening her view to include an interest and concern for understanding more about the world as a whole," and that being a global citizen includes "knowing how to interact with cultures that are different from their own."

Other high-frequency responses reported by our participants in their conceptualization of a global citizen included: sense of responsibility/care, community and interconnectedness (38 responses), critical thinking and cultural sensitivity (28), acceptance, tolerance, and respect (20), technology and business/economic competition (18), traveling and immersion experiences (15), communication and knowledge of a foreign language (13). These responses reveal important insights into the ways these teachers perceive living and teaching in a globalized society.

As seen earlier, for many participants a stronger sense of interconnectedness, care, and responsibility not only for their own communities but also for the world as a whole and one's place in it was a significant trait of a global citizen. One teacher shared the following observation:

> I believe a global citizen is someone who sets aside their personal beliefs and helps others and sees them through whatever they need to, so they can be successful, caring citizens no matter what part of the world they live in.

According to another teacher,

> Students need to learn to connect with people around them—their community. When they feel connected and know how to reach out, they are more prepared to be a global citizen.

Evidence also indicates that teachers place high value on development of cultural sensitivity and critical thinking skills as major attributes of a global citizen. Indeed, more than 25 percent of our participants supported the sentiment that increased cultural sensitivity and empathy for others, coupled with critical thinking skills that allow students to recognize social issues that affect the world today, are essential characteristics of an engaged global citizen. Here is a representative quote:

> A global citizen must have the ability and cultural sensitivity to work with other communities around the world. They are critical thinkers who can recognize global implications of local, county and world issues.

Another teacher added,

> Students need to learn how to connect with people around them—their community. When they feel connected and know how to reach out, they are more prepared to be global citizens. A global citizen is one who takes an interest in political, social, economic norms around the world. Global citizens know how to find opposing viewpoints, and apply them to the culture and events of an area. To do this, one needs to think critically, judge impartially, and propose solutions.

Our study participants' voices are also compelling in the premise that acceptance, tolerance, and respect bear important implications for the idea of global citizenship. Here are some important participant insights reported on the topic:

> I think the best way to prepare to be a good global citizen is to be sure you understand and learn to respect the space, heritage, and culture of yourself, your family, your communities, and your country. Then, you can and will extend that respect and tolerance and curiosity to other people on this planet and to their spaces, customs, and views.

Several other teachers had similar perceptions:

> A global citizen is one who acknowledges and accepts all human beings.
>
> A global citizen is a person who is open to new ideas and takes the time to learn about other people regardless of their race, ethnicity, gender, religious beliefs, etc. Having opportunities to learn more about other cultures and be willing to be open minded about other people's ideas and decisions.
>
> To me, a good global citizen is someone who is not only aware of cultures beyond their own, but also sees their role in helping those in other cultures live better lives. A good global citizen recognizes that we are all connected as human beings and inhabitants of this Earth, and our actions (or lack thereof) have far-reaching effects. A good global citizen is not only tolerant of other cultures but looks for the value that can be gleaned from cultural differences.

Several of our respondents considered recent developments in technology as well as economic competition when reflecting on the concept of global citizenship. Educators acknowledged the fact that technology had changed the way we communicate, and that it is instrumental in facilitating global connections. Additionally, the participants point out that economic and business connections have transformed, and a global citizen needs to be aware of implications of such changes. Participants described it the following way:

> Big business develops worldwide; innovation and creativity lead to competition and wealth: the United States used to be leading the way in these areas but now it is a global race with China and India leading in some areas. World-wide students are being prepared for jobs that may not even exist yet due to globalization and advances in technology.
>
> Children today are world citizens because of the easy access to communication with students far away. The ease with which our young generation uses technology. . . they have multiple ways to connect with and learn from people throughout the world. I consider myself a citizen of the world although being at the end of my career, I am less proficient with some of the technology.

Interestingly, some teachers, while recognizing the impact of technology, saw it as less of a means to an end, but rather as a useful tool, a stepping stone to developing truly engaged and meaningful connections as well critical thinking skills among their students—the 21st-century global citizens. Here are the quotes supporting this important nuance:

> A global citizen is one who takes an interest in political, social, economic norms around the world. Global citizens know how to find opposing viewpoints, and apply them. To do this, one needs a background in technology, but first, they need instruction on how to think critically, judge impartially, and propose solutions.
>
> Though people are more and more connected by technology, I do not think that proper ideas of other cultures are being presented to young people. Technology may perpetuate stereotypes if students are not more informed about the global society they live in.

Here we include quotes related to cultural immersion and international travel voiced by our participants.

I may be a global citizen since I lived in different countries and travel abroad to learn about different cultures around the world.

I think a global citizen is somebody who gets used to living in a different country.

> I see myself as a global citizen first and American second. I feel I have learned a great deal about myself and others around me from my experiences abroad.

Shonia and Stachowski (2014) provided evidence that preservice overseas immersion experiences during student teaching have lasting and meaningful impact on teachers' perspectives and practices, both professionally and personally. Their study revealed that student teaching overseas leads to enhanced cross-cultural communication skills, an eagerness to foster relationships with people from other cultures and countries, and a clearer understanding of the challenges faced by children and families with limited English proficiency.

As seen from the foregoing quotes, our study participants, several of whom have undergone such immersion experiences themselves, draw on these as important aspects of developing global-mindedness. Using Banks' "stages of cultural identity," Kolar (2012) challenged teachers to "empower students to approach the stage 6 ideal of 'globalism and global competency,'" which is characterized by "a sense of solidarity with 'all human beings in the world community'" (p. 27). Yet, for educators to be able to do this meaningfully, Kolar argues, they first must engage in culturally diverse experiences themselves and "consciously challenge their own assumptions about themselves and others" (p. 28). This sentiment resonated with our study participants: teachers who have had immersion experiences outside the U.S. reported that such experiences had a profound influence in shaping their professional and personal perspectives and dispositions, while contributing to their global competency. We will discuss this important implication further as we move to our next research question of how these dimensions of global citizenship apply to our participants' classrooms and professional practice.

Earlier we presented six major dimensions that stemmed from the in-service teachers' reflections on the concept of global citizenship. These six high-frequency themes perceived by our participants as important facets of being a global citizen include: having an understanding and being aware of other cultures; sense of responsibility/care, community, and interconnectedness; critical thinking and cultural sensitivity; acceptance, tolerance, and respect; technology and business/economic competition; traveling and immersion experiences; and communication. These dimensions and their nuances that the teachers included in the conceptualization of what it means to be a global citizen have important implications for how these educators view their own professional practice and its impact on and contribution to creating a community of global learners in their schools and professional environments. In the following section, we report findings related to teachers' praxis.

Cultivating Global Citizenship in the Classroom

Our respondents' reflections on their lived experiences point to important details as teachers identified dimensions of their vision for today's global citizen. Educators in our study emphasized finding one's place in the world community, contributing to it effectively, and understanding the rights as well as responsibilities of living and working in a globalized world. Teachers' conceptualization of global citizenship was personal, rooted in lived experiences. Some participants framed the concept of global citizenship around the notion of cooperation and community, while for others global focus was important because of economic competition and external threats, in which fear seemed to be the driving force behind the need to understand the "other." We expand on these ideas ahead.

After their reflection on what constitutes global citizenship, participants were asked to consider how their professional practice may have been impacted by their vision of a globally minded person. Here the respondents described their engagement with students, community, and the content they taught. Some responses were more nuanced than others, framing education praxis as an important tool serving to promote social justice and global awareness.

Ahead we look at our participants' professional practice and experience using Banks' CATS model that presents four levels of integration of multicultural content (Banks & Banks, 2004). We adopted this model for our analysis of the teachers' praxis of global citizenship because of the similarity of process that is in place when the mainstream curriculum is being critically consumed via a cultural, global lens, with the focus shifting from an ethnocentric to an ethnorelative frame of reference (Bennett, 1986). Four approaches of the culturally relevant integration of ethnic content into the curriculum described by Banks include: the Contributions approach, where cultural components, heroes and heroines, holidays, and other isolated elements related to ethnic groups are added to the curriculum without changing its structure. The Additive approach consists of the addition of content, concepts, themes, and perspectives to the curriculum, with its structure remaining unchanged; it is still viewing ethnic content from the mainstream, majoritarian perspective. In the Transformation approach, the structure, goals, and nature of the curriculum are changed to enable students to view concepts, issues, and problems from diverse ethnic perspectives. Finally, the Social Action approach in Banks' model includes all elements of the Transformation approach, as well as elements that enable students to identify important social issues, gather data related to them, clarify their values, make reflective decisions, and take actions to implement their decisions. Teachers who employ the Social Action approach seek to make students social critics and reflective agents of change (Banks & Banks, 2004).

When we analyzed the reported data of how teachers cultivate ideas of global citizenship in the classroom, we noticed a direct correlation between the level of their own international exposure and the level of their engagement with the concept of global citizenship. Teachers with international professional and personal immersion experiences tended to work on the Transformation and Social Action approaches level as they engaged students with experiential learning and service learning projects that promoted cultural sensitivity, respect (not just passive tolerance), and community building, while advancing critical thinking skills and reflection about the current global issues as well as possible solutions for those. The following quotes illustrate this distinction:

> Global clubs/organizations are formed in the school that discuss and investigate current events and the life of individuals around the world. This serves an academic purpose to develop an understanding that the world is connected economically, environmentally, etc. As a teacher that has travelled to South America, Africa, Eastern Europe, and Europe, I provide my students with real experiential knowledge connected to topics that we discuss in the classroom.
>
> Students participate in a social justice project. This research-based project has students identifying issues in their community that need to be solved (causes, consequences), researching agencies that are designed to combat the issue of choice, and proposing what students like them or community members can do about it.
>
> As a Japanese teacher, it is easy to discuss the admirable qualities of Japanese culture and what ways we, as Americans, could improve. I encourage my students to be open-minded to all cultures, pointing out that there is good and bad in each of them. Last year when the earthquake and tsunami struck Japan, I helped my students implement a plan of action that helped us raise almost $1000 to support the victims. They were happy that they did not have to sit around thinking "Too bad we can't help," but were instead able to do something wonderful to help people they may never meet.
>
> At the school level, I am the assistant advisor to student council. Our goal is to encourage students to become involved in the community. We are pushing this into the global community by planning an international service trip for next summer.

As the educators were asked to reflect on their teaching and its connection to building global citizenship, the value of engaging with the community and service learning became recurrent themes, particularly among the group of educators in this study who had significant international experience, illustrating the broad influence of overseas professional and personal immersion on their professional performance. This is an important finding as the literature on the topic indeed supports that well-designed, community-based service learning opportunities foster individuals' dispositions toward and sustained participation in civic life (Hart, Donnelly, Youniss, & Atkins, 2007; Larkin & Mahoney, 2006; Shonia & Stachowski, 2014). Such extended forms of learning address critical issues that allow students to bridge multiple life worlds (Skerrett, 2010)—from their local neighborhoods to transnational communities in which they engage, nurturing responsible global citizenry.

On the other hand, the teachers with no immersion experience tended to fall within the Contributions or Additive approach of the CATS model when describing some of their involvement with the aspect of global citizenship education. Their praxis included discussions of the importance of learning about a globalized world, and learning for life and work in a global society. Participants' actions that conformed to this approach included: inviting an occasional guest speakers in the classroom representing a different culture, sharing family traditions, talking to students about diversity, and a Global Awareness Day/Fair. Here we included several examples from this group:

> I have Spanish language teaching certification so I teach my students some Spanish and we sing to each other in Spanish on our birthdays. In language, I share with the kids how our language has borrowed words from other languages and our root words have their basis in other languages.
> Global Awareness Day/Fair; speakers to enrich and educate.
> I teach about "holidays around the world," not just Christmas.
> Talking about/discussing different traditions in our own families as well as the traditions of others, especially holiday time!
> In my classroom I incorporate "fun facts" about the places all over the world. We take these fun facts and investigate them more in depth.

As follows from the earlier discussion and the quotes, both the conceptualization of global citizenship and the implementation of it in practice differ from teacher to teacher. Our study supports that educators' global immersion experiences are a considerable factor that contributes to a more robust and nuanced vision of global citizenship. Furthermore, the data suggests a relationship between more global immersion experiences and a more engaged pedagogy with an emphasis on social action. In fact, when cross tabulating a teacher's international experience with their conceptualization of global citizenship according to Banks and Banks' (2004) levels, a very clear pattern emerges. Of those respondents whose conceptualizations were coded into the first two levels of Banks' model, 98 percent had no global immersion experience. On the other end of the spectrum, those respondents whose answers were coded into the highest two levels all had at least some global immersion experience and over 90 percent had lived abroad for at least four consecutive months.

One salient fact, however, warrants special notice: when asked about whether there was a need for more emphasis on global education and global citizenship, the participants in our study overwhelmingly—more than 89 percent—responded affirmatively. This finding reveals that in spite of differences in levels of global literacy and competency, educators by and large acknowledge the importance of global awareness and advancing global competency in today's classrooms.

This echoes the programmatic statement in the U.S. DoE's (2012) internationalization strategy, which outlines the necessity of an international focus in our classrooms and communities:

> In today's globalized world, an effective domestic education agenda must address global needs and trends and aim to develop a globally competent citizenry. It is no longer enough to focus solely on ensuring that students have essential reading, writing, mathematics, and science skills. Our hyper-connected world also requires the ability to think critically and creatively to solve complex problems, the skills and disposition to engage globally. It is essential that we are all able to communicate and work with neighbors, coworkers, and friends with different cultural traditions and perspectives. Such interpersonal skills and appreciation for diverse viewpoints will facilitate civil discourse and a cohesive society. (p. 3)

As our study indicates, this pragmatic approach does not seem to translate to teachers' conceptualizations of global citizenship, unless educators have participated in meaningful global immersion experiences. While our research is limited to teachers' perceptions, clear next steps would be to examine how the dispositions we illustrate play out in classroom practice. Given our findings, the DoE strategy will remain only words on paper without providing teachers global immersion experiences and helping them translate to a more global classroom for students.

Implications

The current study explored the concept of global citizenship and its implementation as it related to teacher's different global immersion experiences. The data revealed six major dimensions perceived by the educators as important facets of being a global citizen: having an understanding and being aware of other cultures; sense of responsibility/care, community, and interconnectedness; critical thinking and cultural sensitivity; acceptance, tolerance, and respect; technology and business/economic competition; traveling and immersion experiences; and communication. These dimensions have important implications for how educators view their own professional practice and its impact on creating a community of global learners in their classrooms. Further, our study supports that educators' global immersion experiences are a considerable factor contributing to both a more robust vision of global citizenship and a more engaged pedagogy with an emphasis on social action. Indeed it was these immersion experiences that helped educators move beyond the idea of global education as a threat response and toward associating global education with building empathetic, active global citizens.

If teacher preparation institutions are interested in better preparing teacher candidates, they need to assess their proficiency in the areas of global/international and comparative education. Given the findings reported in this study, teacher preparation programs need to offer comparative education course work as well as well-constructed and implemented prolonged field experiences designed to advance international immersion in host nation schools (e.g., intercultural student teaching programs). In turn, in-service educators with limited international experience need to be encouraged to participate in opportunities of further professional development via both comparative education course work and overseas immersion summer practicums (e.g., Overseas Practicum for Experienced Teachers).

Authors' Note: Readers interested in accessing our survey instrument may do so by e-mailing the corresponding author, Debora Ortloff: Debora. Ortloff@gmail.com

REFERENCES

Banks, J. A., & Banks, C.A.M. (Eds.). (2004). *Multicultural education: Issues and perspectives.* Boston, MA: Allyn & Bacon.

Bennett, M. J. (1986). A developmental approach to training for intercultural sensitivity. *International Journal of Intercultural Relations, 10*(2), 179–195.

Carspecken, P. F. (1996). *Critical ethnography in educational research: A theoretical and practical guide.* New York: Routledge.

Council of Chief State School Officers. (2006). *Global education policy statement.* Washington DC: Council of Chief State School Officers. Retrieved from www.ccsso.org/content/pdfs/Global%20Education%20FINAL%20lowrez.pdf

Creswell, J. W. (2007). *Educational research: Planning, conducting, and evaluating quantitative and qualitative research* (2nd ed.). Upper Saddle River, NJ: Merrill.

Cushner, K. (2012). Intercultural competence for teaching and learning. In B. D. Shaklee & S. Baily (Eds.), *Internationalizing teacher education in the United States* (pp. 41–58). Lanham, MD: Rowman & Littlefield.

Dolby, N., & Rahman, A. (2008). Research in international education. *Review of Educational Research, 78*(3), 676–726.

Frey, C. J., & Whitehead, D. M. (2009). International education policies and the boundaries of global citizenship in the United States. *Journal of Curriculum Studies, 41*(2), 269–290.

Hart, D., Donnelly, T., Youniss, J., & Atkins, R. (2007). High school community service as a predictor of adult voting and volunteering. *American Educational Research Journal, 44*(1), 197–219.

Kagan, S. L., & Stewart, V. (2004). Putting the world into world-class education: Introduction. *Phi Delta Kappan, 86*(3), 195–196.

Keating, A. (2010). Educating Europe's citizens: Moving from national to post-national models of educating for European citizenship. *Citizenship Studies, 13*(2), 135–151. doi: 10.1080/13621020902731140

Kolar, N. G. (2012). A comparison of K-12 multicultural and international education in the United States. In B. D. Shaklee & S. Baily (Eds.), *Internationalizing teacher education in the United States* (pp. 17–40). Lanham, MD: Rowman & Littlefield.

Larkin, R., & Mahoney, A. (2006). Empowering youth to change their world: Identifying key components of a community service program to promote positive development. *Journal of Social Psychology, 44*, 513–531.

Marshall, H. (2009). Educating the European citizen in the global age: Engaging with the postnational and identifying a research agenda. *Journal of Curriculum Studies, 41*(2), 247–267. doi: 10.1080/00220270802642002

Merryfield, M. M. (2000). Why aren't teachers being prepared to teach for diversity, equity, and global interconnectedness? A study of lived experiences in the making of multicultural and global educators. *Teaching and Teacher Education, 16*(4), 429–443.

Miles, M., & Huberman, M. (1984). *Qualitative data analysis: A source book for new methods.* Beverly Hills, CA: SAGE.

Nussbaum, M. (1997). *Cultivating humanity.* Cambridge, MA: Harvard University Press.

Ortloff, D. H. (2011). Moving the borders: Multiculturalism and global citizenship in the German social studies classroom. *Educational Research, 53*(2), 137–149.

Ortloff, D. H., Shah, P., Hamilton, E., & Lou, J. (2012). Internationalizing K-12 education: A case study of one Midwestern state. *Intercultural Education, 23*(2), 33–46.

Ravitch, D. (2002). September 11: Seven lessons for the schools. *Educational Leadership, 60*(2), 6–9.

Schattle, H. (2008). *The practices of global citizenship.* Lanham, MD: Rowman & Littlefield.

Shah, P. P. (2008). From monsoons to Katarina: The civic implications of cosmopolitanism. In E. Doyle Stevick & B.A.U. Levinson (Eds.), *Advancing democracy through education? U.S. influence abroad and domestic practices* (pp. 207–227). Charlotte, NC: Information Age Press.

Shonia, O., & Stachowski, L. (2014). Standing the test of time: Overseas student teaching's lasting impact on participants' perspectives and practices. In J. Phillion, S. Sharma, & J. Rahatzad (Eds.), *Internationalizing teacher education for social justice: Theory, research, and practice* (pp. 21–48). Charlotte, NC: Information Age Press.

Skerrett, A. (2010). Teaching critical literacy for social justice. *Action in Teacher Education, 31*(4), 54–65.

Suárez-Orozco, M., & Sattin, C. (2007). Wanted: Global citizens. *Educational Leadership, 64*(7), 58–62.

Suárez-Orozco, M. M. (2005). Rethinking education in the global era. *Phi Delta Kappan, 87*(3), 209–212.

Suarez-Orozco, M. M., & Qin-Hillard, D. B. (Eds.). (2004). *Globalization: Culture and education in the new millennium.* Berkeley: University of California Press.

U.S. Department of Education. (2012). *Succeeding globally through international education and engagement: U.S. Department of Education International Strategy 2012–16.* Washington, DC: Author.

7 Globalization and Teacher Education
Teaching about Globalization through Community-Based Inquiry

Guichun Zong

> The need to understand globalization and to be able to respond and adapt is perhaps the most crucial challenge facing humanity. While its processes are inevitable, the direction and the shape of globalization remain in our control. The future depends on developing a sense of urgency, accepting responsibility to address global problems, and acting as world citizens.
>
> (Adams & Carfagna, 2006, p. xii)

INTRODUCTION

Rapid global changes in recent years, such as the unprecedented financial crisis in the Eurozone, the revolutionary wave of demonstrations and nonviolent and violent protests in the Arab world, and growing volumes of cross-border flow of information, technology, capital goods, services, and people worldwide has reshaped discussion of the connections between the local and the global in the United States and around the world. Meanwhile, there have been major shifts in the global balance of technological skill, economic power, world population growth, and distribution of the labor force (Alpert, 2013; Charan, 2013). The new and enduring challenges and mounting tide of public concern about where the world is heading have brought global perspectives to the forefront of education discourse (Gaudelli & Heilman, 2009; Hicks & Holden, 2007; Stearns, 2009). In response to the pressing need to produce a citizenry that is culturally literate and globally competent, the field of global education has taken on a new urgency and importance. Many argue there are opportunities to assert global education's contributions to analyzing and understanding the unfolding interactions of culture, politics, economics, science, and technology shaping the 21st-century world (Ferriter, 2010; Gaudelli & Wylie, 2012; Gibson, 2010; Marino, 2011; Stearns, 2009; Ukpokodu, 2010). In order to prepare the teachers and citizens required in this new global age, there has been a push for greater scholarship on global education theory and improved practice in K-12 and higher education.

The global education field has also been challenged to reexamine its rationale, scope, focus, and approaches toward teaching about the world. Some call for a critical social justice perspective to address the challenges and realities of the new global era (Landorf, 2013; Subedi, 2010; Ukpokodu, 2010). Others suggest an expanded curricular scope to teach about the world that explicitly addresses issues like globalization. Global education scholars suggest that as the primary conceptual lens for explaining the functioning of the world system, globalization has important and long-reaching implications for learning about the world (Gibson, 2010; Hytten & Bettez, 2008). Making sense of this discourse is important for educators as they set out to enact policies, programs, and practices that are relevant to current world conditions (Merryfield & Wilson, 2005; Myers, 2010; Sleeter, 2003; Spring, 2008; Zong, 2009). They argue that while theoretical and empirical research on globalization has generated a vast and growing literature in social sciences during the last two decades, the research and scholarship in teacher education on globalization have unfortunately lagged behind.

The available scholarly literature about globalization is dominated by disciplines outside of education, such as sociological, economic, geographical, and anthropological fields. Within the education research community, discussions of globalization are often limited to the areas of comparative education, foundations of education, or curriculum studies. Notably missing are articles from a teacher education perspective. In the three prominent teacher education books published during the last decade, *Preparing Teachers for a Changing World* (Darling-Hammond & Bransford, 2005), *Handbook of Research on Teacher Education: Enduring Questions in Changing Contexts* (Cochran-Smith, Feiman-Nemser, McIntyre, & Demers, 2008), and *Studying Teacher Education: Report of the AERA Panel on Research and Teacher Education* (Cochran-Smith & Zeichner, 2005), there was no mention of global education or globalization as a topic of discussion. The word *globalization* was not mentioned in the index of any of these three books. Given the assessment- and accreditation-driven teacher education program and curriculum designs in the U.S., the accreditation standards rarely make globalization visible or required. Similarly, in a review of four leading peer-reviewed journals in multicultural education from 2000 to 2008, Gibson (2010) found that there is extremely limited engagement with globalization in teacher education, with only seven articles mentioning globalization. She also notes that when globalization is discussed, it is often as a taken-for-granted backdrop whose meaning and context are neither critiqued nor thoroughly discussed. Among these seven articles mentioning globalization, only three make explicit connections between globalization and classroom practice.

Because of such omissions, very little is known about the policy, research, or practices that connect the global domain to teacher education. There is little practical information available about how to teach globalization in the teacher education context. As a result of this lack of discussion and action in the teacher education community, most teachers in the U.S. are not prepared with knowledge and skills to teach the concept. They are unsure how the term of globalization differs from concepts such as internationalization, world studies, or even multicultural education or diversity education and whether it would fit into their curriculum or relate to their students' developmental levels (Sleeter, 2003).

At the scholarly intersection of globalization and teacher education, many questions remain: How can the concept of globalization be integrated in teacher education curricula? What are the core concepts and critical debates that should be examined? How should readings and resources for students be selected? How does one create activities and assignments that are meaningful and manageable in teacher education courses that often have to meet mandated accreditation standards and have embedded field experiences? This chapter describes how teacher educators can begin conceptualizing how to incorporate globalization into their curricula. In what follows, I provide an overview of definitions and characteristics of globalization. I then briefly review literature on different approaches to teaching globalization in higher education, including teacher education settings. The second half of the chapter presents my own curricular and pedagogical decisions in selecting instructional strategies and resources to integrate the concept of globalization in teacher education courses. Specifically, the chapter focuses on creating experiential learning opportunities through community-based inquiry as a means to engage undergraduate and graduate teacher education students in exploring the interconnection between global forces and local influences in the contemporary American South. At the end, I reflect on course dynamics and student responses, and discuss challenges and possibilities of this pedagogical approach to teaching about globalization in teacher education.

LITERATURE REVIEW

Defining Globalization: A Contested Topic

In the last two decades, globalization has become one of the most powerful concepts for explaining the major changes in the world and the process of development of a global society. Many have stated that globalization encompasses a range of processes affecting different spheres of life, including culture and politics in addition to economics. There has been no other concept in social, political, and economic theory as publicly and passionately debated as globalization. From popular media and campaign slogans to calls for educating children for global completion, globalization is a highly contested concept in both the public arena and academic disciplines, especially in terms of its effects. Deep disputes have emerged with respect to the historical and cultural origins of globalization, its economic, political, and social consequences, and implications for educational policies and practices. Observers and theorists of globalization have argued that the rapid increase in cross-border economic, social, technological, and cultural exchange is a new source for optimism in a world that has witnessed much economic and cultural exploitation and human suffering (Murray, 2006). Proponents of globalization argue that the movement of people, money, and information across national and cultural boundaries allows people instantaneous access to markets, cultural practices, and products as never before witnessed and this access clearly has the potential for enriching people's lives (Bhagwati, 2004; Friedman, 2006; Ohmae, 1995, 2005). Critics of globalization tend to draw attention to the links between past and present global economic policies and social realities, such as widespread hunger and poverty, the massive displacement of small farmers, sweatshop working conditions, the breakdown of community, the rise of ethnic and religious fundamentalism, increased social conflict, rising global inequality, and an array of severe ecological crises (Smick, 2009; Smith, 2014; Smythe, 2009; Stiglitz, 2003).

While attitudes differ drastically, scholars of globalization define it in quite similar fashions, emphasizing the increasing interconnectivity between people around the world. For example, Guillen (2001) defined globalization as a "process leading to greater interdependence and mutual awareness (reflexivity) among economic, political, and social units in the world, and among actors in general" (p. 236). Drori, Meyer, and Hwang (2006) define it as "intensification of global interdependencies and the consolidation of the globe as a social horizon" (p. 1). Ostry (1999, p. 1) describes globalization as "an ongoing process of deeper integration" among countries that has proceeded in stages since the end of World War II and traces the roots of globalization from the early postwar decades, with the focus on reducing border barriers to trade, to the 1970s and 1980s, when the liberalization of the movement of capital and the deregulation of financial markets began the process of global integration. She argues that globalization further developed during the 1990s with the revolution in the development of information and communication technologies (ICT), which made it cheaper and easier to develop and manage global production networks and led to the prominence of multinational enterprise as the "main funnel for the three engines of growth: trade, capital and technology" (p. 2). She suggests that the final integration due to the ICT revolution is the growth in electronic commerce, global telecommunications, and the new world of cyberspace, which could eliminate national borders to the extent that "the term 'domestic policy' could become an oxymoron" (p. 2).

Similarly, in their leading book on globalization, *Global Transformations*, Held, McGre, Goldblatt, and Perraton (1999) also emphasize the historical evolution of globalization and argue that "globalization is neither wholly novel, nor a primarily modern social phenomena. Its form has changed over time and across the key domains of human interaction, from the political to the ecological" (p. 415). They suggest that the processes of globalization do not unfold according to a predetermined path or an inherent logic, but rather a collection of forces that may or may not converge at any given time: "Historical patterns of globalization have been punctuated by great shift and reversals, while the temporal rhythms of globalization differ between domains" (p. 415). With this in mind, they provide a detailed and historically rich interpretation of a fourfold periodization of globalization: premodern globalization, early modern globalization, modern globalization, and contemporary globalization. While acknowledging that globalization cannot be neatly measured and described, many scholars found A. T. Kearney and *Foreign Policy*'s (2005) annual index of globalization—which includes four broad categories: economic integration, technological connectivity, personal contact, and political engagement—a useful approach to conceptualizing globalization. More recently, the Brookings Institution's Global Cities Initiative has developed ten criteria to guide metro areas in the U.S. for their readiness to respond to globalization: leadership with a worldview, legacy of global orientation, specializations with global reach, adaptability to global dynamics, culture of knowledge and innovation, opportunity and appeal to the world, international connectivity, ability to secure investment for strategic priorities, government as global enabler, and compelling global identity.

For the purpose of this research, this chapter adopts the following definition suggested by the Levin Institute (n.d.):

> Globalization is a process of interaction and integration among the people, companies, and governments of different nations, a process driven by international trade and investment and aided by information technology. This process has effects on the environment, on culture, on political systems, on economic development and prosperity, and on human physical well-being in societies around the world.
>
> (para. 3)

Underpinning this definition is the proposition that globalization is a historical, multidimensional process or a set of intertwined processes with various complexities and contradictions. How globalization as a process works out both institutionally and culturally depends to a large extent on local cultures and conditions.

Teaching Globalization: Multiple Approaches

In recent years, there have been increasing calls for explicit and sustained inclusion of globalization in K-12 schools as well as in colleges and universities. Scholarship on teaching globalization has expanded in concert with the tidal waves of public debate and popular protest about the meaning and effects of globalization. For instance, Sleeter (2003) examines various ways of thinking and teaching about globalization, and how the concept is represented in some state and national curriculum standards. She presents these competing narratives of globalization using six metaphors: "global village," "military domination," "networks of interdependence," "McWorld," "spaceship earth," and "neo-colonialism." She further notes that metaphors that are less critical—"global village," "military domination," and "networks of interdependence"—are given far more attention in school curricula than are those that challenge the effects of globalization. These three metaphors therefore

> converge into an overall narrative: The world is interdependent, although made up of independent and competing nations. Western ideas and systems represent the culmination of human cultural evolution; in global competition these ideas and systems will eventually prevail.
>
> (p. 5)

Sleeter (2003) calls for a critical approach to examine the impact of globalization on education:

> Increasingly, schools are losing a vision of education for public good and shifting toward education for private consumption and the needs of transnational corporations. This means that, increasingly, schooling is helping to serve global imperialism.
>
> (p. 9)

Hytten and Bettez (2008) argue that teaching about globalization should become an integral part of teacher education curricula. They describe and reflect upon how their teacher education work is grounded in Noddings' (2005) dimensions of global citizenship, in which citizens advocate for social and economic justice, protection of the Earth, cultural pluralism, and world peace. Global citizens are committed to eliminating poverty, creating sustainable lifestyles, making well-informed choices, and maintaining an ecology of interdependence (Noddings, 2005; Sleeter, 2003). Hytten and Bettez (2008) also suggest that global educators should go "beyond a value-neutral look at globalization" and use "one that centralizes issues of justice and caring" (p. 175). To foster this kind of citizenship among preservice teachers, they explicitly teach about globalization with a focus on its multiple dimensions, its connection to the local, and its danger to democracy. They argue that teaching globalization should challenge "our students' sense of themselves as good people in a basically fair and meritocratic world, not people who in many ways benefit from inequitable social relations, even if they are not individually responsible for them" (p. 176). This, they hope, will cultivate social justice commitments.

Stearns' (2003) and Myers' (2010) work focuses on making globalization a topic of inquiry in history and social studies education. Stearns argues that the traditional way of teaching world history, Western history, and American history should be changed in a way that explicitly includes the dimension of globalization. Globalization provides history teachers with an opportunity to link past to present in new ways and to test historical thinking. He suggests several vantage points through which globalization can be approached in historical thinking and teaching: sorting out the unevenness of globalization as a process, discussing timing and precedent, and assessing the diversity of reactions. Meanwhile, Myers (2010) specifically focuses on the approach to teaching globalization in K-12 social studies curricula. He contends that the topic of globalization has not yet entered the U.S. social studies curriculum with the sufficient complexity and depth that are warranted. As a way to increase conversations among social studies educators regarding how to teach globalization in social studies, Myers outlines three curriculum approaches—global history, global civics, and 21st-century skills, which have different understandings of the significance of globalization as a curriculum topic, with different implications for students' learning about the world today. He argues that each of the suggested three approaches is "informed by the globalization scholarship and makes distinct contributions that help to bring the social studies curriculum in line with contemporary scholarship and world realities" (p. 110).

Drawing upon their work with 12 teachers from a range of disciplines to develop and teach units on globalization, Veronica Boix Mansilla and Howard Gardner (2007) developed an interdisciplinary framework to help teachers develop strategies to teach about globalization. This framework highlights four areas that are central to the understanding of complexities and contingencies of globalization: (a) *economic integration*, emphasizing the opportunities and costs for economies, societies, cultures, and individuals associated with the flux of capital and production around the globe; (b) *environmental stewardship*, raising awareness of the state of global environment (including global health) and what we can and should do to ensure its long-term sustainability and well-being; (c) *cultural encounters*, examining the forces of homogenization, hybridity, and localization that shape how nations, cultures, and small groups exchange ideas, people, and cultural products; and (d) *governance and citizenship*, comprehending emerging tensions between national and supranational forms of government, as well as the extent to which individuals enjoy global rights and responsibilities as a function of their humanity (Mansilla & Gardner, 2007, p. 52). They further argue that the primary purpose of teaching globalization is to nurture student global consciousness.

I have found the interdisciplinary framework especially helpful in creating a balanced approach to guiding my own work with teacher education students in learning about globalization. My work is also informed and guided by emerging scholarship on the intersections between global education and multicultural education. The aim of this chapter is to reflect on my own curriculum decisions and instructional approaches to engage teacher education students in exploring the concepts, theories, processes, and impacts of globalization on various societies, particularly my efforts in creating experiential learning opportunities through community-based inquiry to engage prospective and practicing teachers in learning about the impact of globalization on economic structure and cultural landscapes in the American South.

TEACHING GLOBALIZATION THROUGH COMMUNITY-BASED INQUIRY

Teaching Context

I teach at a large, doctoral-granting public university in the southeastern part of the U.S. The university has a long history of commitment to global learning. In 2006–07, it underwent the regular Reaffirmation Review by the Southern Association of Colleges and Schools (SACS), at which time the university set forth a Quality Enhancement Plan (QEP) entitled "Global Learning for Engaged Citizenship." The university since then has engaged in and supported a broad range of global learning initiatives in teaching, research, and community engagement. As a teacher education faculty member committed to global education, I approach the topic of globalization in a range of ways in the teacher education program, from including it as a topic or unit in undergraduate and graduate educational foundation courses (e.g., Exploring Sociocultural Perspectives on Diversity, Teaching and Schools in a Changing Society) and social studies teaching, learning, and research courses to developing and teaching a special advanced graduate seminar on globalization and education and a doctoral-level core course for leadership in teaching and learning, titled Intercultural Communication and Global Learning.

The majority of my students are from this southern state, where the university is located. Some live and teach in urban settings, others in suburban neighborhoods, and a few are from rural mountain communities. The majority of students enter my classes with limited knowledge of globalization and are not sure if the curriculum standards require the topic to be taught (Sleeter, 2003), something they readily admit. Some students openly express their doubts about the relevance of the topic as they live in communities where a trip to a Walmart grocery store takes 30 minutes. In contrasting these students' doubts, reluctance, and lack of knowledge, scholars have suggested the American South is arguably experiencing the greatest transformation across all sectors of any part of the U.S. as a result of globalization (Cobb & Stueck, 2005). They argue that while the transformation of work, corporate growth, and foreign investment due to globalization can be seen all over the country, some of the most striking changes are occurring in and to the South. For example, according to a newly released study by the Washington-based Brookings Institution, metro Atlanta ranked 7th in jobs created by foreign direct investment (FDI) from 1991 to 2011 out of the 100th largest metropolitan areas in the U.S. It had 134,610 jobs in foreign-owned firms, for a total of 6.8 percent of private employment in the area, a substantial jump in 20 years (Bolton, 2014).

Globalization has created some of the furthest-reaching and most complex transformations facing the American South. They are also among the most difficult ones to understand. The full meaning of globalization remains elusive because of the scale of the opportunities and challenges it brings to political economy, culture, and the individual (Peacock, Watson, & Matthews, 2005).

To bridge the gap between my teacher education students' lack of knowledge and the transformative impact of globalization on southern culture and economy, I have tried various approaches to integrate community-based experiential learning opportunities into formal study of people and cultures around the world in my teacher education courses. Sometimes, I take the whole class on global learning field trips. Most recently, I have designed a systematic approach that integrates scholarly readings with community-based inquiries to explore the effects of globalization on the local landscapes of the American South (see Table 7.1 and the appendix for a copy of the assignment and related readings and resources).

Conceptual Framework

My philosophy of teaching and learning draws upon the theoretical principles of social constructivism, which views knowledge as primarily a cultural product, shaped by micro- and macro-cultural influences and evolves through increasing participation within different communities of practice. In contrast to the traditional, acquisition-oriented learning model that emphasizes transmitting knowledge and skills, social constructivism conceptualizes learning as a collective, participatory process of active knowledge construction emphasizing context, interaction, and situatedness (Duffy & Cunningham, 1996). I have used this theoretical perspective as a guide to construct learning activities and assignments to engage prospective and practicing teachers in exploring, examining, and critically analyzing various aspects of globalization and its impact on their communities. In deciding the course content on globalization, I use Mansilla and Gardner's (2007) conceptual map to organize readings and resources that illuminate the complexities and contingencies of the concept and provide students with critical insights into the social, cultural and political impacts of the globalizing economic integration and communication technologies. My goal is to provide teacher education students with capacities to assess the costs and benefits in their lives and those of people in other parts of the world. This comprehensive and balanced approach provides an important ethical as well as analytical dimension to the study of globalization in four domains: economic integration, environmental stewardship, cultural encounters, and governance and citizenship.

Selecting Readings and Resources

Careful selection and appropriate use of readings and resources are essential for any successful teaching and learning experience. However, given the interdisciplinary nature of globalization and lack of scholarship and discussion of the concept among the teacher education community, educators who would like to locate practical lessons on globalization often find it challenging to select relevant books, articles, and other resources to use in the classroom. This is also the case with me. In creating the syllabus for a doctoral-level core course, "Intercultural Communication and Global Learning," I found it fairly easy to find several texts on the cultural component of the course that are appropriate for advanced graduate students from both the field of communication and field of education. In contrast, it takes much more time and effort to assemble a list of readings and resources that are useful in facilitating teaching and learning about globalization in a teacher education context. Guided by Mansilla and Gardner's (2007) interdisciplinary framework, I select readings and other resources that reflect the economic, environmental, and cultural aspects of globalization.

Since Friedman (2000, 2006) has written extensively about globalization and provided suggestions for countries, companies, and individuals who are increasingly required to compete against and collaborate with a global workforce, I always include his two books on the reading list, either as required texts or as selected books for discussion and review: *The Lexus and the Olive Tree: Understanding Globalization*, and *The World Is Flat: A Brief History of the Twenty-First Century*. Teacher education students in my classes also find Friedman's cogent description of the promise and peril of an economic and geopolitical future shaped by the forces of globalization wrought by technologically driven global connectivity, international commerce, and cross-cultural competition more accessible, and his ideas to "Connect, Compete, Collaborate" with the world resonate well with young students of a digital age.

To examine the impact of globalization on the state of the global environment, I have regularly incorporated resources produced by the World Watch Institute, the *State of The World* series, and Lester Brown's (2009) book, *PLAN B 4.0: Mobilizing to Save Civilization*. The readings from these resources provide an opportunity for students to discuss globalization from an interdisciplinary perspective. The mathematics and science teacher leaders in my classes always comment on the powerful learning they experienced from reading and discussing books by Lester Brown. Recently, I have added more resources examining the impact of globalization on the American South. These include books such as *The American South in a Global World* (Peacock, Watson, & Matthews, 2005) and *Globalization and the American South* (Cobb & Stueck, 2005). To guide class discussion on the implications of globalization for educational policies and practices, I have chosen to use *The Flat World and Education: How America's Commitment to Equity Will Determine Our Future* (Darling-Hammond, 2010), and *The Global Achievement Gap: Why Even Our Best Schools Don't Teach the New Survival Skills Our Children Need—And What We Can Do about It* (Wagner, 2008). In addition to the books, I also use supplementary resources, such as news articles, and Internet-based audio and video resources to ground the globalization analysis by showing how global economic relations impact ordinary individuals and shape social relations in local communities.

Importance of Local Inquiry and Community-Based Inquiry

Scholars of globalization recognize that globalization "often makes itself felt most powerfully through the reorganization of spaces and the transformation of local experience" (Lipsitz, 1994, p. 6) and the important role of local inquiries in contextualizing the economic underpinnings of globalization in everyday activities of individuals (Barner & Okech, 2013; DeTemple, 2012; Takacs, 2008). They argue that the best way to understand the inherent complexity of concepts and to interrogate critically the processes and agendas that characterize globalization is to undertake grounded research that analyzes the manifestations of global-local interaction processes in particular places (Dicken, 2004; Overton, Murray, & Banks, 2012). By grounding the local and everyday experiences with globalization, global educators strive to raise student awareness about the drivers and outcomes of globalization and to "give them a framework for understanding their lives in relation to, rather than apart from, others in the world" (Takacs, 2008, p. 224). In its recently launched initiative, "At Home in the World: Educating for Global Connections and Local Commitments," the American Council on Education (ACE) also makes the following call for increasing college graduates' cultural and global competency through analyzing global and local connections:

> The need for cultural competency among 21st century graduates becomes ever more pressing as U.S. demographics shift, local and global communities become further intertwined, the job market becomes increasingly global, and the workforce continues to diversify. In order to become responsible, productive citizens, our students must possess an understanding of their own cultures and those of their neighbors at

home and afar. They will also need the skills to analyze interconnections between global and local systems and effectively participate in their diverse communities. (ACE, 2009, p. 4)

The community-based study of globalization project I have designed for my classes, titled "Atlanta (Your Community) in the World/ the World in Atlanta (Your Community)," responds to this call by having teacher education students explore the processes and local impact of globalization in the communities in which they live. First, students were asked to read Raymond Mohl's (2003) article "Globalization, Latinization, and the Nuevo New South," in which he traces the historic and political forces that caused many of the immigration patterns from Latin America to the southeastern part of the U.S. during the last 50 years. He discussed how the passing of the NAFTA legislation changed industry in the U.S., and many foreign-owned businesses came to Alabama, Georgia, and other southern states. He explains that during the 1990s industries in the southeastern part of the U.S. were looking for cheap, reliable, non-unionized labor to take advantage of the new economic opportunities, while at the same time the economy of Mexico was suffering. These and other factors, such as the immigration reform act of 1986, coalesced to create the perfect conditions for a new surge in immigration from Latin America to Dixie. Mohl uses a narrative approach to discuss the economic, social, and cultural changes in the Southeast that were the result of the globalization and Latinization.

After reading and discussing the Mohl's (2003) article, individual students are expected to select one aspect of the metro Atlanta community, such as economy, government, arts, recreation, values and beliefs, food, or shelter. Students are directed to explore the Global Atlanta website (www.globalatlanta.com), which highlights global events happening in the metro Atlanta area as well as the state of Georgia. I also often bring local newspapers published in different languages to help students choose events or communities. After students have finalized their choices of community for inquiry, they will identify a person or persons who have been associated with this aspect of the community for an interview. To prepare for the interview, students need to search for background information about the chosen community's history and develop a set of questions to use for conducting interviews. Students are also directed to physically visit the community of their choice to conduct observations. Using information collected from background research, observation, and interviews, they are required to create a presentation about their findings. Students may use any of the following formats to prepare for their presentations: a traditional poster board, a digital video clip that eventually can be posted on YouTube or a class website, or a PowerPoint presentation. At the end of the presentation, students are required to write a short essay to reflect their understanding of globalization and its impact on the community and to address the following two questions: How has this aspect of the chosen community changed over the last two decades? What evidence is there that this aspect of the community has (or has not) been affected by globalization?

IMPACT ON STUDENTS' LEARNING

The primary goal for the project about understanding globalization through community inquiry is that students will begin to recognize how they are engaged in globalization even when they often fail to recognize it as an issue of relevance in education. I also hope that this experiential learning opportunity will encourage students to transfer their learning and understanding of globalization beyond the classroom setting. Content analysis of students' completed projects, presentations, and reflective essays demonstrates deepened and rich understanding of globalization's impact on local economic structure, cultural landscapes, religious institutions, schools, and government agencies. While some students choose projects that explore the impact and activities of specific U.S. and foreign multinational corporations' operations in Georgia, such as the global impact of Coca-Cola, CNN, Home Depot, Kia Motors' Georgia headquarters, and Port of Savannah, many students tend to select projects that revolve around globalization's impact on various aspects of local communities, such as parks, sports fields, grocery stores, public libraries, and religious institutions. One student explored how a local public library has added multilingual services and multicultural events to engage the changing demographics due to the impact of global migration. Students use these inquiries to consider how the concept of globalization has evolved and how communities have transformed as a result.

Regarding the instructional value of using local community as a site for inquiry in teaching globalization, many commented that the project has provided an authentic context to understand this rather abstract concept. One student reflected upon her project and visit to a recently built Hindu temple (BAPS Shri Swaminarayan Mandir), located in Lilburn, Georgia:

> One can never really understand nor feel the depth of a religion just by studying its concepts and beliefs in a classroom. I realized this personally when I actually visited the BAPS Shri Swaminarayan Mandir, a Hindu temple, one Sunday afternoon. The temple is located fairly close to my parents' house in Lawrenceville. I learned so much about the Hindu religion and Indian people. I was very impressed with the architecture of the temple and the quietness of the people in the mandir that gave me the feeling of peace and oneness. I truly believe that field trips like this would elevate their awareness, understanding, and even appreciation for other cultures and religion. I believe this community-based project added depth to our learning of changes and cultures.

Teacher education students' reflective essays demonstrate improved understanding of the complexity associated with the process and impacts of globalization. One student discussed how her interview of a native Georgian employee in the Korean-owned company Kia Motors' Georgia headquarters had changed her previous conceptions of globalization: Americans losing jobs because of American company outsourcing practices and cheap labor in other parts of the world, and immigrants stealing jobs from Americans. After completing the community-based global learning project, she has realized that despite some destructive forces, globalization has also opened possibilities for transnational collaboration and social transformation. This improved understanding has helped to increase students' commitment to teaching about globalization to their future students. The following comments from one high school social studies teacher who was in my doctoral-level class represent many powerful reflections:

> After studying, discussing, exploring and analyzing globalization over the past few months, I have compiled a list of five implications. I believe that these five implications are important for educators to understand in a world that is being affected so greatly by globalization: Students need to be taught and shown what globalization means to them. We need to change the way in which we and our students view other cultures; negative effects of globalization need to recognized, analyzed, discussed, and taught; teachers need to be taught how to interact and teach the new cultures they will be experiencing in their globalized classroom; the curriculum being taught in our schools needs to be re-focused.

While I found great value in using community-based inquiry in engaging teacher education students in exploring the nature and impacts of globalization, developing and implementing this experiential learning curriculum have also proved to be challenging. The completed students' projects have exclusively focused on economic integration and cultural encounters brought about by globalization. Very rarely they would choose topics that are related to environmental stewardship or governance and citizenship, the other two key dimensions of Mansilla and Gardner's (2007) framework for teaching globalization. In discussing issues related to environment, teacher candidates tend to blame emerging markets, such as China, India, Brazil, and Venezuela, for causing the air, land, and river pollutions, rather than critically analyze the roles and responsibilities of multinational corporations from developed nations. They prefer selecting projects that are perceived as safe and less controversial. They see most topics related to globalization as "controversial" or "overwhelming"; therefore, they reluctantly learn about topics such as immigration policies in the American southern states and the safety issues for workers in Bangladesh garment factories, which provide most products in retail stores in the U.S.

CONCLUSION

Much has been debated and discussed regarding the importance of globalization and its impact on world economics, politics, culture, technology, the environment, and general educational policies and practices. However, the concept of globalization remains an underexplored topic for teacher education scholars. The limited engagement with globalization is often framed as an uncritical acceptance of the taken-for-granted context. Too often, globalization presented by the media for students is a remote litany of tariffs, treaties, outsourced jobs, flows of foreign investments, and angry protests at the WTO Ministerial Conferences. This chapter aims to explore different approaches to integrate the concept of globalization into teacher education curricula and add to existing scholarship on effective strategies to improve teacher education students' understanding of the concept and its role in social and cultural changes of the 21st-century American South.

Using Atlanta in the world as a case study, this chapter examines how local communities can be used as resources by teacher educators to help students demystify globalization and develop rich historical understanding of global and local connections (Maguth & Hilburn, 2011; Marino, 2012; Noddings, 2005). I argue that to keep global education relevant in the shifting context of the 21st century, global education scholars must address globalization as an area of curricular inquiry and a site of sociopolitical and educational contestation. History has demonstrated that globalization, despite its destructive forces, has also opened possibilities for transnational collaboration and social transformation. How might scholars of global education reconcile these dual forces of increasing inequality and increasing possibility to help future teachers contextualize and problematize the dominant narratives of globalization? Clearly, a deeper, more deliberate, explicit, and sustained analysis of globalization in a teacher education context is highly needed for further research.

Author's Note: The author would like to thank the book editors and anonymous reviewers for their critical feedback to the chapter manuscript.

Appendix

Guidelines for Understanding Globalization through Community Inquiry

This is an inquiry-based project designed to help candidates understand the global connections within local communities in the state of Georgia. It also helps to establish the relevance and context to study intercultural communication. You may check the website (www.globalatlanta.com) for project ideas.

Table 7.1 Activities for Understanding Globalization through Community Inquiry

Activities	Possible grade
Read Globalization and the American South *Read* the *USA Today* article "U.S. Ports Racing to Get Ready for Bigger Ships" from the following website: www.usatoday.com/money/economy/story/2011-09-30/ports-bigger-ships/50637090/1 *Listen to* the following NPR story on deepening the Savannah harbor: www.npr.org/2012/01/05/144737372/the-race-to-dig-deeper-ports-for-bigger-cargo-ships *Select* one aspect of community: economy, government, arts, recreation, values and beliefs, food, shelter, and so forth. *Identify* a person or persons who have been associated with this aspect of the community. *Develop* a set of questions to use for your interviews. *Conduct* the interview. *Visit* the place and take some pictures of this aspect of the community. *Construct* your narratives using your interview data: • How has this aspect of the community changed over the last two decades? • What evidence is there that this aspect of community has (or has not) been affected by globalization? *Tell* your story through (choose one) • PPT presentation • Digital video • Traditional poster *Reflect* the process: Discuss and deliberate the impact of globalization. • What is your overall view about globalization? • What were the most challenging parts of this task? • Reflect upon ways that educational policies and practices have been and will be affected by globalization.	

REFERENCES

Adams, J. M., & Carfagna, A. (2006). *Coming of age in a globalized world: The next generation.* Bloomfield, CT: Kumarian Press.

Alpert, D. (2013). *The age of oversupply: Overcoming the greatest challenge to the global economy.* New York: Portfolio/Penguin.

American Council on Education. (2009). *Educating for global connections and local commitments.* Retrieved from www.acenet.edu/Content/NavigationMenu/ProgramsServices/cii/current/gap/index.htm

Barner, J. R., & Okech, D. (2013). Teaching globalization to social work students: In and out of the classroom. *Social Work Education, 32*(8), 1061–1074.

Bhagwati, J. (2004). *In defense of globalization.* Oxford: Oxford University Press.

Bolton, P. (2014). Atlanta ranks 7th among metro areas in jobs at foreign-owned firms. Retrieved from www.globalatlanta.com/article/26982/atlanta-ranks-7th-among-metro-areas-in-jobs-at-foreign-owned-firms

Brown, L. (2009). *Plan B 4.0: Mobilizing to save civilization*. New York: W. W. Norton.

Charan, R. (2013). *Global tilt: Leading your business through the great economic power shift*. New York: Crown Business.

Cobb, J., & Stueck, W. (2005). *Globalization and the American south*. Athens: University of Georgia Press.

Cochran-Smith, M., Feiman-Nemser, S., McIntyre, J., & Demers, K. (2008). *Handbook of research on teacher education: Enduring questions in changing contexts*. New York: Routledge.

Cochran-Smith, M., & Zeichner, K. (2005). *Studying teacher education: The report of the AERA Panel on Research and Teacher Education*. Mahwah, NJ: LEA.

Darling-Hammond, L. (2010). *The flat world and education: How America's commitment to equity will determine our future*. New York: Teachers College Press.

Darling-Hammond, L., & Bransford, J. (Eds.). (2005). *Preparing teachers for a changing world: What teachers should learn and be able to do*. San Francisco, CA: John Wiley & Sons.

DeTemple, J. (2012). Home is my area code: Thinking about teaching, and learning globalization in introductory world religions classes. *Teaching Theology & Religion, 15*(1), 61–71.

Diken, P. (2004). Geographers and "globalization": (yet) another missed boat? *Transactions of the Institute of British Geographers, 29*(1), 5–26.

Drori, G. S., Meyer, J. W., & Hwang, H. (2006). *Globalization and organizations: World society and organizational change*. Oxford: Oxford University Press.

Duffy, T., & Cunningham, D. (1996). Constructivism: Implications for the design and delivery of instruction. In D. H. Jonassen (Ed.), *Handbook of research for educational communications and technology* (pp. 170–198). New York: Simon & Schuster.

Ferriter, W. M. (2010). How flat is your classroom? *Educational Leadership, 67*(7), 86–87.

Friedman, T. L. (2000). *The Lexus and the olive tree: Understanding globalization*. New York: Anchor Books.

Friedman, T. L. (2006). *The world is flat: A brief history of the twenty-first century*. New York: Farrar, Straus, Giroux.

Gaudelli, W., & Heilman, E. (2009). Reconceptualizing geography as democratic global citizenship education. *Teachers College Record, 111*(11), 2657–2677.

Gaudelli, W., & Wylie, S. (2012). Global education and issues-centered education. In S. Totten & J. Pedersen (Eds.), *Educating about social issues in the 20th and 21st centuries: A critical annotated bibliography* (pp. 293–320). Charlotte, NC: Information Age.

Gibson, M. L. (2010). Are we "reading the world"? A review of multicultural literature on globalization. *Multicultural Perspectives, 12*(3), 129–137.

Guillen, M. F. (2001). Is globalization civilizing, destructive or feeble? A critique of five key debates in the social science literature. *Annual Review of Sociology, 27*(1), 135–260.

Held, D., McGre, A. G., Goldblatt, D., & Perraton, J. (1999). *Global transformations: Politics, economics and culture*. Cambridge: Polity Press.

Hicks, D., & Holden, C. (Eds.). (2007). *Teaching the global dimension: Key principles & effective practice*. London: Routledge.

Hytten, K., & Bettez, S. C. (2008). Teaching globalization issues to education students: What's the point? *Equity & Excellence in Education, 41*(2), 168–181.

Kearney, A. T./*Foreign Policy*. (2005, May/June). Measuring globalization: The global top 20. *Foreign Policy, 118*, 52–59.
Landorf, H. (2013). Using the dialectic of social justice to enliven the dialogue between global education and multicultural education. *Journal of International Social Studies, 3*(2), 99–105.
Levin Institute (n.d.). *What is globalization?* Retrieved from www.globalization101.org/about-us
Lipsitz, G. (1994). *Dangerous crossroads: Popular music, postmodernism, and the politics of place*. New York: Verso.
Maguth, B., & Hilburn, H. (2011). The community as a learning laboratory: Using place-based education to foster a global perspective in the social studies. *Ohio Social Studies Review, 47*(1), 27–34.
Mansilla, V., & Gardner, H. (2007). From teaching globalization to nurturing global consciousness. In M. Suarez-Orozco (Ed.), *Learning in the global era: International perspectives on globalization and education* (pp. 47–66). Berkeley: University of California Press.
Marino, M. (2011). World history and teacher education: Challenges and possibilities. *Social Studies, 102*, 3–8.
Marino, M. (2012). Urban space as primary source: Local history and historical thinking in New York City. *Social Studies, 103*, 107–116.
Merryfield, M., & Wilson, A. (2005). *Social studies and the world: Teaching global perspectives*. Silver Spring, MD: National Council for the Social Studies.
Mohl, R. A. (2003). Globalization, Latinization, and the nuevo new south. *Journal of American Ethnic History, 22*(4), 31–66.
Murray, W. (2006). *Geographies of globalization*. New York: Routledge.
Myers, J. P. (2010). The curriculum of globalization: Considerations for international and global education. In B. Subedi (Ed.), *Critical global perspectives: Rethinking knowledge about global studies* (pp. 103–120). Charlotte, NC: Information Age.
Noddings, N. (2005). Placed-based education to preserve the Earth and its people. In N. Noddings (Ed.), *Educating citizens for global awareness* (pp. 57–68). New York: Teachers College Press.
Ohmae, K. (1995). *The end of the nation state*. New York: Free Press.
Ohmae, K. (2005). *The next global stage: Challenges and opportunities in our borderless world*. Upper Saddle River, NJ: Warton School.
Ostry, S. (1999, March). *Globalization and sovereignty*. James R. Mallory Annual Lecture in Canada Studies. Montreal: McGill Institute for the Studies of Canada.
Overton, J., Murray, M., & Banks, G. (2012). The race to the bottom of the glass? Wine, geography, and globalization. *Globalizations, 9*(2), 273–287.
Peacock, J., Watson, H., & Matthews, C. (2005). *The American South in a global world*. Chapel Hill: University of North Carolina Press.
Sleeter, C. (2003). Teaching globalization. *Multicultural Perspectives, 5*(2), 3–9.
Smick, D. M. (2009). *The world is curved: Hidden dangers to the global economy*. New York: Penguin Group.
Smith, N. (2014). The dark side of globalization: Why Seattle's 1999 protesters were right. *Atlantic*. Retrieved from www.theatlantic.com/business/archive/2014/01/the-dark-side-of-globalization-why-seattles-1999-protesters-were-right/282831
Smythe, K. (2009). The dangers of teaching about globalization. *Globalization, 8*(1), 1–10.
Spring, J. (2008). Research on globalization and education. *Review of Educational Research, 78*(2), 330–363.
Stearns, P. (2003). Treating globalization in history surveys. *History Teacher, 36*, 154.
Stearns, P. (2009). *Educating global citizens in colleges and universities: Challenges and opportunities*. New York: Routledge.

Stiglitz, J. (2003). *Globalization and its discontents*. New York: W.W. Norton.
Subedi, B. (Ed.). (2010). *Critical global perspectives: Rethinking knowledge about global societies*. Charlotte, NC: Information Age Press.
Takacs, S. (2008). Making globalization ordinary: Teaching globalization in the American studies classroom. *American Studies, 49*, 221–254.
Ukpokodu, O. (2010). Teacher preparation for global perspectives pedagogy. In B. Subedi (Ed.), *Critical global perspectives: Rethinking knowledge about global studies* (pp. 121–142). Charlotte, NC: Information Age.
Wagner, T. (2008). *The global achievement gap: Why even our best schools don't teach the new survival skills our children need—And what we can do about it*. New York: Basic Books.
Zong, G. (2009). Global perspectives in teacher education research and practice. In T.F. Kirkwood-Tucker (Ed.), *Visions in global education: The globalization of curriculum and pedagogy in teacher education and schools* (pp. 71–89). New York: Peter Lang.

Section 2: University Initiatives

8 Globalization of Elementary Teacher Preparation in the United States
A National Snapshot

Cyndi Mottola Poole and William B. Russell III

Calls for the increased globalization of the American education system seem to come from all directions. International education organizations, such as the United Nations Educational, Social, and Cultural Organization (UNESCO) and the Organisation for Economic Cooperation and Development (OECD), have emphasized the need for all countries to incorporate such global education concepts as sustainability education, education for human rights, and intercultural and interfaith education into their school curricula to ensure the future social and economic success of their students (OECD, 2010; UNESCO, 2006). Within the United States, both the Partnership for 21st Century Skills' *Framework for 21st Century Learning* (2009) and the Common Core State Standards Initiative (2012) embrace the expansion of global awareness, civic literacy, and successful participation in the global economy in our nation's school curricula. Additionally, the National Council for the Social Studies' *National Curriculum Standards* (2010) specifies that American social studies programs should emphasize cultural diversity and global interdependence.

While educational organizations have been firm in their support for global education, there are many potential barriers to the integration of global perspectives into American elementary social studies classes. One of these barriers is state-mandated curriculum standards, which, coupled with standardized tests, have been most effective at driving curricular and instructional decisions within the American education system (Au, 2007; Landorf, 2009; Vogler & Virtue, 2007). Unfortunately, global education does not seem to be a priority in the standards of any state (Rapoport, 2009). Similarly, the "expanding environments" curriculum popular in most elementary social studies standards requires teachers to focus on the local and national, with true global instruction not included until the sixth grade (Turner, Russell, & Waters, 2012). Additionally, the sole emphasis on bolstering student standardized test performance in the areas of math and literacy within most states serves to marginalize instructional time, resources, and space in non-tested subjects like social studies (Au, 2009; Heafner & Fitchett, 2012; Russell, 2009; Tye, 2009; VanFossen & McGrew, 2008).

The most likely avenue to increased global education in schools, then, is directly through the teacher (Gragert, 2012; Merryfield, 1997). There is evidence that, despite the pressure to surrender intellectual autonomy to the established curriculum standards, most American teachers still exert at least some control over the learning opportunities within their own classroom (Barton, 2012; Gaudelli, 2003; Thornton, 1991). Many scholars have argued that teachers who have developed their own global perspectives and who have a personal commitment to global education will be more likely to integrate these themes into their classrooms (Browett, 2003; Merryfield, 1994b, 1997; O'Connor & Zeichner, 2011; Ukpokodu, 2010; Wilson, 1993). Global perspectives must therefore be nurtured within teacher preparation programs. While many suggestions for globalizing teacher preparation programs exist in the literature, the majority include the expansion of global content course requirements and frequent participation in cross-cultural activities as crucial components (AACTE, 1989; Klassen, 1975; Merryfield, 1997; Roberts, 2007).

The purpose of this study, then, was to obtain a snapshot of the extent to which global education courses and cross-cultural cocurricular activities have been incorporated into American elementary teacher preparation programs before and after the year 2000 and the effects of this incorporation on the global perspectives of current elementary school teachers. The study was guided by the following research questions:

- Is there a significant difference between American elementary teachers' year of graduation from their teacher preparation program and the total number of global education courses taken?
- Is there a significant difference between American elementary teachers' year of graduation from their teacher preparation program and rate of participation in cross-cultural activities?
- Is there a significant difference between American elementary teachers' year of graduation (pre- or post-2000) from their teacher preparation program and their global perspectives?

Definition of Terms

The researchers acknowledge the lack of a universally accepted definition of many of the terms utilized in this study (Gaudelli, 2003). For the purposes of this research, the following operational definitions were used:

- Cross-cultural activities: The researchers defined cross-cultural activities as activities in which teachers voluntarily engage that allow them the opportunity to further develop their skills in cross-cultural communication and understanding. The specific cross-cultural activities examined in this study included the following: cultural events, following

international events or crises through the media, and interacting with students or coworkers from other countries or ethnic groups.
- Global content courses: The researchers defined global content courses as those courses identified in the literature (Braskamp & Engberg, 2011; Crose, 2011; Merryfield, 1994; Muirhead, 2009; Wilson, 1993) as having the potential to increase participants' global perspectives, including such classes as multicultural courses, foreign language courses, world history courses, international comparison courses, and multicultural service learning courses.
- Global education: "the study of problems and issues that cut across national boundaries, and the interconnectedness of the systems involved . . . [and] the cultivation of cross-cultural understanding, which includes development of the skill of perspective-taking" (Tye & Tye, 1992, p. 6).
- Global perspective: "the acquisition of knowledge, attitudes, and skills important to intercultural communication and the development of more complex processes, identities, and interpersonal development" (Engberg & Fox, 2011, p. 85).
- Elementary school teacher: The researchers defined an elementary school teacher as a certified teacher currently employed to teach classes in grades K–5.

FRAMEWORK

Global Education

The main goal of global education, according to NCSS (2005), is to "develop in youth the knowledge, skills, and attitudes needed to live effectively in a world possessing limited natural resources and characterized by ethnic diversity, cultural pluralism, and increasing interdependence" (p. 1). Anderson and Anderson (1977) defined global education as "education for responsible citizen involvement and effective participation in global society" (p. 36). While learning about other countries, languages, and cultures is certainly a part of global education, it is not the only purpose, as students must also gain an awareness of how separate countries interact in the world to create a new transnational society. Hanvey (1976) outlined five key characteristics educators must promote in students for a real global perspective. These are perspective consciousness, state of the planet awareness, cross-cultural awareness, knowledge of global dynamics, and awareness of human choices. Perspective consciousness is the understanding that all peoples have a unique way of perceiving the world, ingrained in us by our natal culture, which may be decidedly different than the way other people perceive the world. State of the planet awareness is awareness of the issues that exist in the world in which we live, including such concerns as population growth, environmental issues, international conflicts, and other global matters. Cross-cultural awareness is a consciousness of the similarities and differences among the different groups of people who share this planet, including some realization of how one's particular culture is viewed by others. Knowledge of global dynamics is an understanding of how the world works as an interconnected system, and how one's actions can cause unintended effects around the world. Awareness of human choices is the realization that we have choices as individuals, societies, and a species that can potentially alter the course of world development.

Embracing global education means that multiple perspectives are taught and valued. Subedi (2010) argued that the inclusion of "subaltern knowledge," knowledge that has been historically marginalized, is a crucial component of teaching from a global perspective. Case (1993) concurred, explaining that promoting global education "involves nurturing perspectives that are empathic, free of stereotypes, not predicated on naive or simplistic assumptions, and not colored by prejudicial statements" (p. 319). Many researchers, such as Loewen (1995), have documented a lack of the inclusion of multiple perspectives and alternative worldviews in traditional classroom instruction and textbooks.

There is a general consensus in the education literature that integrating global education into America's educational system must be a priority (Anderson & Anderson, 1977; Hong & Halvorsen, 2010; Merryfield, 2012; Nganga, Kambutu, & Russell, 2013; Rapoport, 2009; Ukpokodu, 2010). Ukpokodu (2010) explained that "global education is not only essential today but should be an integral part of school curriculum on every grade level" (p. 139). Hong and Halvorsen (2010) concurred, stating that "students need to have global knowledge and multicultural awareness to be socially and economically successful in a rapidly changing world" (p. 371). Merryfield (2012) also emphasized the need for American students, who live in a very multicultural society, to develop intercultural competence.

Numerous specific recommendations on how to promote global perspectives in American k-16 education exist in the literature. Recommendations include requiring more multicultural, foreign language, or global issues courses (Braskamp & Engberg, 2011), globalizing the content of already existing courses (Case, 1996; Eslami, 2005; Frederickson, 2010; Heimonen, 2012; Martin, Smolen, Oswald, & Milam, 2012; McNulty, Davies, & Maddoux, 2010), encouraging participation in study abroad programs (Braskamp, Braskamp, & Merrill, 2009; Braskamp & Engberg, 2011; Talbert-Johnson, 2009), and increasing student involvement in cross-cultural activities (Braskamp & Engberg, 2011).

Importance of the Teacher

Despite the standards-driven nature of modern American education, teachers in most school districts possess a considerable amount of autonomy over instructional decision-making (Barton, 2012). Thornton (1991) described the teacher's role as that of a curricular-instructional gatekeeper, responsible at the individual classroom level for choosing the exact content to be covered and the pedagogical strategies employed. Thus, the extent to which global perspectives are integrated into the classroom rests to a considerable extent on teacher decision-making. Taylor (1969) summarized this concept eloquently: "education is only as good or as bad as the teachers who plan it and carry it on" (p. viii). Researchers agree on the need for extensive teacher preparation in global education in order to develop teachers who regularly incorporate global perspectives into their instructional repertoire (Browett, 2003; Merryfield, 1997; O'Connor & Zeichner, 2011; Ukpokodu, 2010; Wilson, 1993).

Merryfield (1994a) found that when global education is skillfully integrated into teacher education programs the teachers who graduate from those programs are likely to globalize their own teaching through the addition of multiple perspectives, a comparative instructional approach, and interdisciplinary studies. Carano (2013) found that many of the global educators in his case study specifically attribute their development of a global perspective to the global education courses they had taken during their teacher preparation. Gaudelli (2003) similarly argued that teachers tend to emphasize content areas within which they have the most background knowledge and suggested that becoming informed about other content areas, while potentially time-consuming, would increase teacher comfort in leading instruction of these areas. Conversely, Rapoport (2010) concluded that the lack of global citizenship education in secondary social studies classes was directly attributable to a lack of focus on global citizenship in undergraduate teacher preparation courses.

Globalizing Teacher Education

Multiple frameworks for incorporating global education into teacher preparation have been promoted in the last 40 years. Klassen (1975) felt that globalizing teacher education would require building partnerships with other academic departments to infuse global curriculum content, securing administrative support, expanding the education curriculum, including cross-cultural experiences, recruiting more diverse faculty members, utilizing foreign students, and gaining the support of the state and federal authorities. The AACTE Guidelines for International Teacher Education (1989) emphasized the importance of administrative leadership, global curriculum development, faculty development, building student awareness of the importance of cross-cultural experiences, and the accessibility of appropriate resources. Merryfield's (1997) global teacher education framework included four elements: conceptualizing global education, acquiring global content, experiencing cross-cultural learning, and teaching for a global perspective. Roberts (2007) supported the integration of an interdisciplinary international knowledge base, global networking, and cross-cultural activities, such as study abroad. The essential elements that all these frameworks have in common are the inclusion of global content courses and participation in cross-cultural activities. Thus, these factors will be examined in this study.

To what extent have these elements been incorporated into American teacher education programs? A 1994 American Association of Colleges of Teacher Education study concluded that schools of education were not doing enough to prepare future educators to meet the demands of global education, finding that "only about 4% of the nation's K-12 teachers have had any academic preparation in global or international studies" (Merryfield, 1994b, p. 4). However, while many conceptual articles recommending an increased global perspective in teacher preparation exist (Crocco, 2010; Ochoa, 2010; Talbert-Johnson, 2009; Ukpokodu, 2010) a thorough ERIC search yielded no empirical studies of the global education requirements in teacher education programs completed in the past 20 years.

METHODS

Participants

The participants in this study were all elementary school teachers currently employed by public school districts across the U.S. Potential participants were selected through a multistage, random sampling method (Fraenkel & Wallen, 2006). First, ten states were selected using a random number generator. Then, a list of public elementary (K-5 or PK-5) schools in that state was accessed through the NCES database. A random number generator was used to select ten elementary schools from each state. Ten teachers were randomly selected from each selected school's website and contacted via e-mail with requests to complete the online survey. The Tailored Design Method was used in an attempt to maximize response rate (Dillman, Smyth, & Christian, 2009).

One hundred and twelve teachers completed the online survey. The survey respondents were a diverse group in every respect except for gender. Ninety-two percent of respondents were female, while only 8 percent were male. This is most likely due to the large gender discrepancy commonly found within the field of elementary education. Eight percent of respondents indicated that they were 25 years of age or younger, 30 percent were between 26 and 35, 19 percent were between 36 and 45, 25 percent were between 46 and 55, and 18 percent were aged 56 or older. Forty-four percent indicated that they had earned a bachelor's degree, 51 percent had earned a master's degree, and 3 percent had earned an educational specialist degree. Only one respondent had earned a doctoral degree. Eighty-one percent of participants graduated from a traditional bachelors-level teacher preparation program. Additionally, 21 percent indicated that they could speak at least one language other than English.

Materials

This study utilized the Global Perspectives Inventory (GPI) questionnaire, which was created by Larry Braskamp, Kelly Carter Merrill, David Braskamp, and Mark Engberg (2010). The researchers obtained written permission to utilize the survey. The GPI was designed to measure individuals' development along three interrelated domains—cognitive, intrapersonal, and interpersonal—identified by Braskamp and colleagues as the three main aspects of global perspectives (Braskamp, Braskamp, Merrill, & Engberg, 2012; King & Magolda, 2005). The cognitive domain relates to the knowledge and understandings one has about the world, what knowledge one judges to be important, and the way in which knowledge is gained. The intrapersonal domain focuses on one's personal values and self-image. The interpersonal domain measures one's ability and comfort in relating to others and acceptance of cultural differences. Braskamp, Braskamp, Merrill, and Engberg (2012) indicated that the questionnaire is appropriately taken by people of any age or cultural or national heritage.

The bulk of the survey is a 40-question Likert-type questionnaire regarding the global perspectives of the participants. This questionnaire is broken down for analysis purposes into six subscales: Cognitive-Knowing, Cognitive-Knowledge, Intrapersonal-Identity, Intrapersonal-Affect, Interpersonal-Social Responsibility, and Interpersonal-Social Interaction. The Cognitive-Knowing subscale focuses on the way participants approach thinking and knowing, while the Cognitive-Knowledge subscale focuses more on the actual knowledge that participants have acquired about the world. The Intrapersonal-Identity subscale measures the participants' knowledge about themselves and their unique identity and purpose in life, while the Intrapersonal-Affect subscale measures participants' level of respect for and acceptance of cultural differences. The Interpersonal-Social Responsibility subscale measures participants' feelings of concern for members of other cultural groups, while Interpersonal-Social Interaction measures participants' degree of interaction with members of other cultural groups (Merrill, Braskamp, & Braskamp, 2012). The GPI also includes a demographic questionnaire, which contains questions about the global content courses and cross-cultural activities in which participants may have taken part.

The authors of the GPI have used several measures to verify the reliability and validity of the instrument. Test-retest reliabilities of each of the subscales were measured and resulted in correlation coefficients between .59 and .81 (Braskamp, Braskamp, & Engberg, 2014). Cronbach's alpha was used to measure the internal consistency of each subscale. Braskamp et al. (2014) reported alpha coefficients for the six subscales ranging from .657 to .773. Glass (2012) used the GPI in his study of international college students currently studying at American universities. He reported subscale alpha coefficients ranging from .687 to .724. These scores indicate an acceptable level of reliability (Glass & Hopkins, 1996).

Limitations

One limitation of this study is the sample size. It is possible that a larger and statistically representative sample size might have generated different results, and may have been generalizable to the actual population of elementary school teachers in the U.S. Additionally, the study relied on self-reported data only, which may be skewed by the perceptions of the participants or participant concerns about the social desirability of their answers. Due to the sample size, the results of this study are not intended to be generalized. Instead, this survey presents a national snapshot of elementary teachers and is intended to convey a general picture of these participants and their teacher education experiences.

RESULTS

We will first report descriptive statistics from the survey, and then answer the research questions.

Descriptive Statistics

Global perspectives questionnaire. The first analysis completed was of the Likert-style questionnaire. Teachers rated themselves highly on several aspects of the intrapersonal and interpersonal domains. Ninety-six percent responded that they take into account different perspectives before drawing conclusions about the world. Ninety-three percent responded that they were accepting of people with different religious or spiritual traditions. Additionally, 95 percent of participants indicated that they enjoyed learning about cultural differences, while only 6 percent indicated that working with people from diverse cultural backgrounds felt threatening to them.

From a global perspectives approach, a few of the results were troubling. For example, 36 percent of respondents agreed or strongly agreed that when cultural differences occur, their culture has the better approach. Fifty-two percent agreed or strongly agreed that most of their friends were from the same racial or ethnic group as themselves. Only 68 percent agreed or strongly agreed that they could discuss cultural differences from an informed perspective. Similarly, only 59 percent agreed or strongly agreed that they were informed about current issues that impact international relations. Additionally, only 47 percent agreed or strongly agreed that they intentionally involve people from different cultural backgrounds in their lives.

Global content courses. An analysis of college courses taken by the participants during their teacher preparation program revealed an overall lack of global education-related courses. The results of this analysis are shown in Table 8.1. Almost half (40%) of participants reported that they had taken no foreign language courses. Nearly one-fifth (16%) of respondents recalled taking no multicultural courses. More than half of the respondents (52%) reported that they had taken no courses that required participation in multicultural service learning. Additionally, 52 percent indicated that they had taken no college classes that focused on significant global issues or problems, while 46 percent indicated that they had taken no classes that provided time for intensive cross-cultural dialogue.

Cross-cultural activities. Cross-cultural activities also had mixed results. Seventy-seven percent of participants stated that they watch news programs on television often or very often, while 76 percent often or very often read

Table 8.1 Number of Global Content Courses Taken

Class	0	1–2	3–4	5+
Multicultural courses	16%	66%	14%	4%
Foreign language courses	40%	40%	13%	7%
World history courses	12.5%	70%	11%	7%
Multicultural service learning	52%	31%	14%	3%
Global/international issue courses	52%	41%	7%	0%
Intercultural dialogue courses	46%	34%	9%	11%

Table 8.2 Frequency of Participation in Cross-Cultural Activities

Activity	Never	Rarely	Sometimes	Often	Very often
Events from own culture	9%	19%	41%	21%	10%
Events from other cultures	8%	29%	48%	10%	4%
Leadership activities	4%	9%	27%	41%	20%
Community service	4%	16%	38%	28%	14%
Global/international lecture	38%	30%	24%	5%	3%
Read a newspaper	0%	8%	16%	23%	53%
Watched TV news	4%	4%	15%	23%	54%
Followed international event	.9%	3%	22%	28%	46%
Discussed current events in class	3%	16%	36%	24%	21%
Interacted with students/coworkers from other countries	5%	11%	13%	29%	41%
Interacted with students/coworkers from other ethnic groups	3%	3%	16%	26%	53%

newspapers or news magazines. Seventy-four percent indicated that they often or very often follow international events or crises through media sources. Sixty-one percent reported that they often or very often participate in leadership programs that stress collaboration and teamwork. Eighty percent of respondents at least sometimes participate in community service activities.

However, 28 percent of participants indicated that they never or rarely attend cultural events reflecting their own cultural heritage, while 37 percent indicated that they never or rarely attend cultural events reflecting a different cultural heritage than their own. Also, 68 percent of respondents indicated that they never or rarely attend lectures, workshops, or discussions on global or international issues. Please see Table 8.2 for a breakdown of frequency of participation in cross-cultural activities.

Research Questions

Each individual research question was investigated using a one-way analysis of variance ANOVA. The results of each analysis are discussed ahead.

Research question 1. Is there a significant difference between the number of global education courses taken by American elementary teachers when compared by graduation year?

An ANOVA was conducted to compare the total number of global content courses taken by survey participants when grouped by graduation year. The total number of global education courses taken was found to be significantly higher for teachers who graduated from their initial teacher preparation program in the year 2000 or later (n = 55) (M = 14.33, sd = 4.13) than for teachers who graduated before 2000 (n = 54) (M = 12.15, sd = 3.77) ($F_{1,107}$ = 8.266, p <. 01). A significant difference also existed in specific types of global education courses taken. Teachers who graduated in 2000 or later took significantly more world history (M = 2.87, sd =. 91) courses than those who graduated before 2000 (M = 2.41, sd=1.12) ($F_{1,106}$ = 5.52, p <. 05). More recent graduates also reported taking more multicultural service-learning courses (M = 2.30, sd = 1.31) than those who graduated longer ago (M = 1.56, sd =. 90) ($F_{1,106}$ = 11.668, p <. 01). Lastly, as noted in Table 8.3, a significant difference was also found in regards to the number of courses that focused on current global or international issues ($F_{1,106}$ = 4.077, p <. 05) taken by participants who graduated in 2000 or after (M = 1.93, sd = 1.03) and those taken by participants who graduated before 2000 (M = 1.57, sd =. 77).

Research question 2. Is there a significant difference between American elementary teachers' year of graduation from their teacher preparation program and rate of participation in cross-cultural activities?

An ANOVA was conducted to compare overall rate of participation in cross-cultural activities of teachers when grouped by year of graduation. A significant difference was found in overall participation in cross-cultural

Table 8.3 Mean Global Content Courses Taken by Graduation Year

Course type	Graduation		Sig
	Pre-2000	2000 or later	
Multicultural courses	2.37	2.68	
Foreign language courses	2.24	2.43	
World History courses	2.41	2.87	$p <. 05$
Service learning courses	1.56	2.30	$p <. 01$
Global issue courses	1.57	1.93	$p <. 05$
Cross-cultural dialogue courses	2.00	2.39	
Total global content courses	12.148	14.327	$p <. 01$

activities ($F_{1,107} = 7.621$, $p <. 01$). Teachers who graduated before 2000 reported participating in more cross-cultural activities (M = 43.69, sd = 5.9) than those who graduated more recently (M = 39.78, sd = 8.59). A significant difference was found on 2 out of 11 individual activities: discussing current events with students ($F_{1,106} = 4.339$. $p <. 05$) and following international events or crises ($F_{1,106} = 6.551$, $p <. 05$). On both of these questions, teachers who graduated before 2000 indicated a higher rate of participation than those who graduated more recently.

Another avenue through which college students frequently gain cross-cultural experience is study abroad programs. However, 77 percent of survey respondents indicated that they had not participated in a study abroad program during college. Respondents who did participate in study abroad were equally split between those who graduated in 2000 or later and those graduated before the year 2000. Twenty-three percent of study abroad participants indicated that their study abroad experience lasted for two weeks or shorter, while 77 percent indicated their program was longer than two weeks.

Research question 3. Is there a significant difference between American elementary teachers' year of graduation from their teacher preparation program and their degree of global perspectives as measured by the GPI?

An ANOVA was used to compare mean total GPI scores to determine if there was a significant difference based on teachers' year of graduation from their primary certification program. There was no statistically significant difference in the mean total GPI score based on the teachers' year of graduation ($F_{1,107} =. 307$ $p >. 05$). However, teachers who graduated before the year 2000 actually had a slightly higher mean total GPI score (M = 150.15, sd = 12.59) than those who graduated in 2000 or later (M = 148.95, sd = 9.96).

Additional Findings

The questionnaire was divided into subscales, and each subscale was analyzed separately and compared to the established national mean using a one-sample t-test. As noted in Table 8.4, the respondents scored highest on the Intrapersonal-Identity (M = 4.16) and Intrapersonal-Affect (M = 3.98) subscales. The lowest score was obtained on the Interpersonal-Social Interaction subscale (M = 3.44). Mean scores on these subscales were also compared to the established national norms. The means of all subscales except Intrapersonal-Affect and Cognitive-Knowledge were at least slightly higher in our sample than the established norms. A significant difference was found between the established norms and the means found in this study on the Interpersonal-Social Responsibility (t = 3.968, df = 109, p <. 01), Intrapersonal-Affect (t = 3.853, df = 109, p <. 01), Cognitive-Knowledge (t = 2.025, df = 109, p <. 05), and Interpersonal-Social Interaction (t = 2.557, df = 109, p <. 05) subscales. The teachers in this sample scored significantly higher (M = 3.89) than the national norm (M = 3.72) on the Interpersonal-Social Responsibility subscale. Participants also scored

Table 8.4 Mean Scores by Subscale

Subscale	Mean	Standard deviation	National norm	Sig
Intrapersonal-Identity (self-knowledge)	4.16	.384	4.09	
Intrapersonal-Affect (intercultural respect and acceptance)	3.98	.437	4.14	p <. 01
Interpersonal-Social Responsibility (concern for others)	3.89	.448	3.72	p <. 01
Cognitive-Knowing (approach to thinking and knowing)	3.65	.429	3.63	
Cognitive-Knowledge (accumulated world knowledge)	3.49	.536	3.60	p <. 05
Interpersonal-Social Interaction (degree of intercultural interaction)	3.44	.429	3.34	p <. 05

significantly higher (M = 3.44) than the national norm (M = 3.34) in Interpersonal-Social Interaction. However, the teachers in this sample scored significantly lower (M = 3.49) than the national norm (M = 3.6) on the Cognitive-Knowledge subscale. Participants also scored significantly lower (M = 3.97) than the national norm (M = 4.14) on the Intrapersonal-Affect subscale. When participants were divided into groups based on year of graduation, no significant differences were found in mean subscale scores.

DISCUSSION

The results of this research indicate that overall, the global perspectives found among the elementary school teachers who participated in this study were very similar to the established national norms. Teachers scored slightly higher on most of the survey subscales, while scoring slightly lower on the Cognitive-Knowledge and Intrapersonal-Affect subscales. The only subscale on which the teachers scored significantly higher than the norm was Interpersonal-Social Responsibility. It is possible that this is due to the nature of the profession of education itself, as many people who feel called to become educators may already have a heightened sense of social responsibility (Liu, 2010; Sanatullova-Allison, 2009; Su, 1993; Zimpher, 1989). The Cognitive-Knowledge and Intrapersonal-Affect subscales were found to be significantly lower than the national norm. It is slightly problematic for teachers to score lower on accumulated world knowledge than average, because teachers are entrusted with imparting world knowledge to their students. A low mean score in Intrapersonal-Affect suggests that teacher participants are not as developed in intercultural tolerance and respect as other members of society. This is troubling because teachers are called to interact successfully with students from a variety of cultural backgrounds. In fact, 29 percent of the teachers who participated in this study indicated that their school was "very diverse," while an additional 45 percent indicated that their school was "somewhat diverse." Both of these issues relate directly to the multiple frameworks for global education discussed previously in this paper, all of which emphasized the acquisition of global content knowledge and cross-cultural experiences. The results suggest that more must be done to develop global content knowledge and cross-cultural competency in teacher candidates.

Our data indicated that elementary teachers who have graduated since the year 2000 reported having taken significantly more global content courses. However, this course-taking did not correspond to a significant difference on the Cognitive-Knowledge subscale based on year of graduation. The researchers anticipated that because the group of teachers who graduated in 2000 or later reported taking more global content courses, they would have scored higher on the Cognitive-Knowledge subscale than the other teachers. Similarly, more recent graduates from teacher education programs reported taking significantly more multicultural service learning courses than other teachers. However, as evident in Table 8.5, they did not score significantly higher on the Interpersonal-Social Responsibility or Interpersonal-Social Interaction than the other teachers did. Further research may be needed to determine why an increase in these types of college courses does not seem to be related to an increased score in these areas.

A significant difference was also found in the amount of cross-cultural experiences in which teachers participate. Surprisingly, teachers who graduated before 2000 were more likely to participate in cross-cultural activities than those who graduated more recently. It was expected that more recent graduates would have participated in cross-cultural activities more frequently due to an increase in these types of activities on campuses and in local communities as well as the increased availability of study abroad programs. This finding suggests that colleges of education should encourage their teacher candidates to participate in as many cross-cultural activities as possible.

Due to the increase in global content courses documented in this study, it was expected that teachers who graduated more recently would have scored higher on the global perspective inventory than older or more experienced teachers. However, no significant differences could be found on the total

Table 8.5 Mean GPI and Subscale Scores by Graduation Year

Scale type	Graduation*	
	Pre-2000	2000 or later
Intrapersonal-Identity (self-knowledge)	4.19	4.13
Intrapersonal-Affect (intercultural respect and acceptance)	4.00	3.96
Interpersonal-Social Responsibility (concern for others)	3.92	3.87
Cognitive-Knowing (approach to thinking and knowing)	3.69	3.62
Cognitive-Knowledge (accumulated world knowledge)	3.49	3.51
Interpersonal-Social Interaction (intercultural interaction)	3.44	3.46
Total GPI Score	150.15	148.95

* None of these means were found to be statistically significant.

mean score or on the individual subscale scores based on graduation year. This suggests that more recent graduates of American teacher education programs are not any more likely to have a global perspective than those who graduated 15 or more years ago. It is possible that the effect of newer teachers having taken more global content courses is roughly equivalent to the increased life experience and increase in cross-cultural activities of more experienced teachers, yielding similar global perspectives. Another possible explanation is that global content courses offered by American schools of education are currently not meeting global education goals, a conclusion that coincides with other researchers' claims (Merryfield, 1994a; Ukpokodu, 2010).

Another interesting finding of this study relates to study abroad programs. Study abroad programs are typically seen as a powerful means to increase college students' global perspectives. Despite the suggestion by multiple researchers that study abroad experiences are of the utmost importance in creating globally minded individuals (Braskamp, Braskamp, & Merrill, 2009; Braskamp & Engberg, 2011; Talbert-Johnson, 2009), only 23 percent of teachers in this study participated in a study abroad program. Because the literature suggests that well-planned and well-implemented study abroad programs can be transformative experiences in the lives of college students, colleges of education should increase their emphasis on the value of these experiences to their students. Additionally, teacher preparation programs can attempt to mitigate the factors that discourage teacher candidates from participating in study abroad programs, such as the cost of study abroad and credit requirements of their teacher education programs.

CONCLUSION

This study compared the global perspectives of American elementary school teachers who graduated from their teacher education program before and after the year 2000. Our findings provided evidence to support the belief that teacher preparation programs have taken steps to increase the globalization of their teacher candidates, especially in the area of increased global content course requirements. However, no significant difference was found in the global perspectives of teachers based on graduation year. This suggests that despite the increase in global content courses taken by elementary preservice teachers since 2000, recent graduates are not actually more globally aware than older or more experienced teachers. In fact, the discovery that teachers who graduated before the year 2000 were more likely to participate in cross-cultural activities may provide evidence that newer graduates are actually less cross-culturally competent. Further research may elucidate the reasons that the increased global content courses are not as successful in globalizing teacher candidates as the conceptual literature would suggest.

Perhaps an investigation of the exact nature and content of specific global content courses would provide more information.

Teachers are responsible for providing an inclusive and culturally relevant education for all students. Because 70 percent of respondents reported that they often or very often interact with students or coworkers from other countries, it is clear that cross-cultural communication skills are a required part of their work. This is especially relevant because research suggests that the vast majority of teachers in the U.S. are female, Caucasian, and middle class, yet they will be educating a student population that is expected to be made up of up to 70 percent from diverse backgrounds (Ochoa, 2010). More must be done to ensure that our future teachers are ready, willing, and able to provide culturally relevant pedagogy to all students.

Elementary school teachers are charged with providing the first exposure most students have to global perspectives. If the goals of globalizing teacher education programs were realized, teachers would graduate more prepared to integrate these important concepts into their daily instruction. The results of this study suggest that while some recommendations from the global education frameworks have been implemented, more needs to be done to further globalize American teacher preparation programs. The four global education frameworks examined in this study all concurred that two essential components of globalizing teacher preparation are increasing the number of global content courses that preservice teachers take, such as international comparative courses and multicultural courses, and encouraging preservice teachers to participate in cocurricular cross-cultural experiences, such as study abroad and multicultural community service (AACTE, 1989; Klassen, 1975; Merryfield, 1997; Roberts, 2007). The number of global content courses that teacher candidates completed while enrolled in their teacher preparation program, as well as the specific content of those courses, is within the control of the university administration and faculty. This study found that an increase in global content courses by itself is not correlated with increased global perspectives in teachers. Perhaps teacher preparation programs should explore the content of the global courses they offer to look for areas for improvement. Similarly, low rates of participation in some types of cocurricular cross-cultural activities were reported by many teachers. Offering more of these types of experiences on campus or through partners in the community may help teacher candidates to value their importance. Intentional recruitment of a more diverse teacher candidate pool and education faculty members may also help encourage teacher candidates to spend time with people from other ethnic, cultural, and religious backgrounds and discuss global or international topics outside of class. Active participation in these kinds of cross-cultural activities during teacher preparation will also help prepare our future teachers to communicate effectively with diverse students, families, and coworkers in their future role as K-12 educators, and may encourage them to make participation in these activities a habit they will continue once they become teachers. In order to help increase the global perspectives of elementary school teachers, in-service professional developments that provide global content and/or emphasize participation in cross-cultural activities should also be provided.

REFERENCES

American Association of Colleges for Teacher Education. (1989). *Guidelines for international teacher education.* Washington, DC: AACTE.

Anderson, C., & Anderson, L. (1977). Global education in elementary schools: An overview. *Social Education, 41*(1), 34–37.

Au, W. (2007). High stakes testing and curricular control: A qualitative metasynthesis. *Educational Researcher, 36*(5), 258–267.

Au, W. (2009). Social studies, social justice: W(h)ither the social studies in high-stakes testing? *Teacher Education Quarterly, 36*(1), 43–58.

Barton, K. (2012). Wars and rumors of war. In T. Taylor & R. Guyver (Eds.), *History wars and the classroom: Global perspectives* (pp. 187–202). Charlotte, NC: Information Age.

Braskamp, L. A., Braskamp, D. C., & Engberg, M. E. (2014). *Global perspective inventory (GPI): Its purpose, construction, potential uses, and psychometric characteristics.* Chicago, IL: Global Perspectives Institute. Retrieved from http://gpi.central.edu/supportDocs/manual.pdf

Braskamp, L. A., Braskamp, D. C., & Merrill, K. C. (2009). Assessing progress in global learning and development of students with education abroad experiences. *Frontiers: The Interdisciplinary Journal of Study Abroad, 18*, 101–118.

Braskamp, L. A., Braskamp, D. C., Merrill, K. C., & Engberg, M. E. (2010). *Global perspective inventory (GPI).* Retrieved from http://gpi.central.edu

Braskamp, L. A., Braskamp, D. C., Merrill, K. C., & Engberg, M. E. (2012). *The global perspectives inventory (GPI): Its purpose, construction, potential uses, and psychometric characteristics.* Chicago: Global Perspectives Institute.

Braskamp, L. A., & Engberg, M. E. (2011). How colleges can influence the development of a global perspective. *Liberal Education, 97*(3–4), 34–39.

Browett, J. (2003). Culture—Are we speaking the same language? Teachers' conceptual frameworks of culture. *Babel, 38*(2), 18–25.

Carano, K. T. (2013). Global educators' personal attribution of a global perspective. *Journal of International Social Studies, 3*(1), 4–18.

Case, R. (1993). Key elements of a global perspective. *Social Education, 57*(6), 318–325.

Case, R. (1996). Promoting "global" attitudes. *Canadian Social Studies, 30*(4), 174–177.

Common Core State Standards Initiative. (2012). Mission statement. Retrieved from www.corestandards.org

Crocco, M. (2010). [How] do we teach about women of the world in teacher education? In B. Subedi (Ed.), *Critical global perspectives: Rethinking knowledge about global societies* (pp. 19–38). Charlotte, NC: Information Age.

Crose, B. (2011). Internationalization of the higher education classroom: Strategies to facilitate intercultural learning and academic success. *International Journal of Teaching & Learning in Higher Education, 23*(3), 388–395.

Dillman, D. A., Smyth, J. D., & Christian, L. M. (2009). *Internet, mail, and mixed-mode surveys: The tailored-design method.* Hoboken, NJ: Wiley & Sons.

Engberg, M. E., & Fox, K. (2011). Exploring the relationship between undergraduate service-learning experiences and global perspective-taking. *Journal of Student Affairs Research and Practice, 48*(1), 85–105.

Eslami, Z. R. (2005). Global education: Instructional strategies used and challenges faced by in-service teachers. *Teacher Education and Practice, 18*(4), 400–415.

Fraenkel, J. R., & Wallen, N. E. (2006). *How to design and evaluate research in education.* New York: McGraw-Hill.

Frederickson, M. E. (2010). Going global: New trajectories in U.S. women's history. *History Teacher, 43*(2), 169–189.

Gaudelli, W. (2003). *World class: Teaching and learning in global times.* Mahwah, NJ: Lawrence Erlbaum Associates.

Glass, C. R. (2012). Educational experiences associated with international students' learning, development, and positive perceptions of classroom climate. *Journal of Studies in International Education, 16*(3), 228–251.

Glass, G. V., & Hopkins, K. D. (1996). *Statistical methods in education and psychology.* Boston, MA: Allyn and Bacon.

Gragert, E. H. (2012). The role of the teacher and technology innovations in professional development: Toward a scalable and sustained global education. In B. M. Maguth (Ed.), *New directions in social education research: The influence of technology and globalization on the lives of students* (pp. 155–175). Charlotte, NC: Information Age.

Hanvey, R. G. (1976). *An attainable global perspective.* Denver, CO: Center for Teaching International Relations, University of Denver.

Heafner, T. L., & Fitchett, P. G. (2012). Tipping the scales: National trends of declining social studies instructional time in elementary schools. *Journal of Social Studies Research, 36*(2), 190–215.

Heimonen, M. (2012). Music education and global ethics: Educating citizens for the world. *Action, Criticism, and Theory for Music Education, 11*(1), 62–80.

Hong, W. P., & Halvorsen, A. (2010). Teaching Asia in United States secondary school classrooms: A curriculum of othering. *Journal of Curriculum Studies, 42*(3), 371–393.

King, P., & Magolda, B. M. (2005). A developmental model of intercultural maturity. *Journal of College Student Development, 46*(6), 571–592.

Klassen, F. H. (1975). The international dimension of American teacher education. In C. M. Anderson & J. C. Willmon (Eds.), *Teacher education and world awareness* (pp. 13–26). Birmingham: University of Alabama.

Landorf, H. (2009). Toward a philosophy of global education. In T. F. Kirkwood-Tucker (Ed.), *Visions in global education* (pp. 47–67). New York: Peter Lang.

Liu, P. (2010). Examining perspectives of entry-level teacher candidates: A comparative study. *Australian Journal of Teacher Education, 35*(5), 53–78.

Loewen, J. W. (1995). *Lies my teacher told me: Everything your American history textbook got wrong.* New York: W. W. Norton.

Martin, L. A., Smolen, L. A., Oswald, R. A., & Milam, J. L. (2012). Preparing students for global citizenship in the twenty-first century: Integrating social justice through global literature. *Social Studies, 103*(4), 158–164.

McNulty, C. P., Davies, M., & Maddoux, M. (2010). Living in the global village: Strategies for teaching mental flexibility. *Social Studies and the Young Learner, 23*(2), 21–24.

Merrill, K. C., Braskamp, D. C., & Braskamp, L. A. (2012). Assessing individuals' global perspective. *Journal of College Student Development, 53*(2), 356–360.

Merryfield, M. M. (1994a). *From teacher education to the classroom: Reflections of teachers upon their teacher education experiences in global education.* Retrieved from http://files.eric.ed.gov/fulltext/ED392724.pdf

Merryfield, M. M. (1994b). *Teacher education in global and international education.* Washington, DC: American Association of Colleges of Teacher Education.

Merryfield, M. M. (1997). A framework for teacher education in global perspectives. In M. M. Merryfield, E. Jarchow, & S. Pickert (Eds.), *Preparing teachers to teach global perspectives: A handbook for teacher educators* (pp. 1–24). Thousand Oaks, CA: SAGE.

Merryfield, M. M. (2012). Global education: Responding to a changing world. In W. B. Russell (Ed.), *Contemporary social studies: An essential reader* (pp. 57–76). Charlotte, NC: Information Age.

Muirhead, P. (2009). Rethinking culture: Toward a pedagogy of possibility in world language education. *Critical Inquiry in Language Studies, 6*(4), 243–268.

National Council for the Social Studies. (2005). *Position statement on global education.* Silver Spring, MD: National Council for the Social Studies.

National Council for the Social Studies. (2010). National curriculum standards for social studies. Retrieved from www.socialstudies.org/standards/strands

Nganga, L., Kambutu, J., & Russell, W. (Eds.). (2013). *Exploring globalization opportunities and challenges in social studies: Effective instructional approaches.* New York: Peter Lang.

Ochoa, A. M. (2010). International education in higher education: A developing process of engagement in teacher preparation programs. *Teaching Education, 21*(1), 103–112.

O'Connor, K., & Zeichner, K. (2011). Preparing U.S. teachers for critical global education. *Globalisation, Societies, and Education, 9*(3–4), 521–536.

Organization for Economic Cooperation and Development. (2010). *Education at a glance: OECD indicators.* Paris: OECD.

Partnership for 21st Century Skills. (2009). *Framework for 21st century learning.* Retrieved from www.p21.org/storage/documents/P21_Framework_Definitions.pdf

Rapoport, A. (2009). A forgotten concept: Global citizenship education and state social studies standards. *Journal of Social Studies Research, 33*(1), 91–112.

Rapoport, A. (2010). We cannot teach what we do not know: Indiana teachers talk about global citizenship education. *Education, Citizenship, and Social Justice, 5*(3), 179–190.

Roberts, A. (2007). Global dimensions of schooling: Implications for internationalizing teacher education. *Teacher Education Quarterly, 34*(1), 9–26.

Russell, W. (2009). Social studies, the lost curriculum: A research study of elementary teachers and the forces impacting the time spent on social studies. *Curriculum and Teaching, 24*(2), 75–86.

Sanatullova-Allison, E. (2009). Why men become elementary school teachers: Insights from an elementary teacher education program. *Action in Teacher Education, 31*(4), 28–40.

Su, Z. (1993). The study of the education of educators: A profile of teacher education students. *Journal of Research and Development in Education, 26*(3), 125–132.

Subedi, B. (2010). Introduction: Reading the world through critical global perspectives. In B. Subedi (Ed.), *Critical global perspectives: Rethinking knowledge about global societies* (pp. 1–18). Charlotte, NC: Information Age.

Talbert-Johnson, C. (2009). Establishing internationally competent leaders for the future: Promoting an agenda for social justice, equity, and intercultural sensitivity. *International Journal of Educational Reform, 18*(3), 174–184.

Taylor, H. (1969). *The world as teacher.* New York: Doubleday.

Thornton, S. J. (1991). Teacher as curricular-instructional gatekeeper in social studies. In J. P. Shaver (Ed.), *Handbook of research on social studies teaching and learning* (pp. 237–248). New York: Macmillan.

Turner, T. N., Russell, W. B, & Waters, S. (2012). *Essentials of elementary social studies.* New York: Routledge.

Tye, B. B., & Tye, K. A. (1992). *Global education: A study of school change*. Albany: State University of New York Press.

Tye, K. A. (2009). A history of the global education movement in the United States. In T. F. Kirkwood-Tucker (Ed.), *Visions in global education* (pp. 3–24). New York: Peter Lang.

Ukpokodu, O. N. (2010). Teacher preparation for global perspectives pedagogy. In B. Subedi (Ed.), *Critical global perspectives: Rethinking knowledge about global societies* (pp. 121–142). Charlotte, NC: Information Age.

United Nations Educational, Social, and Cultural Organization. (2006). *UNESCO guidelines on intercultural education*. Retrieved from http://unesdoc.unesco.org/images/0014/001478/147878e.pdf

VanFossen, P. J., & McGrew, C. (2008). Is the sky really falling?: An update on the status of social studies in the K-5 classroom in Indiana. *International Journal of Social Education, 23*(1), 139–182.

Vogler, K. E., & Virtue, D. (2007). "Just the facts, ma'am": Teaching social studies in the era of standards and high-stakes testing. *Social Studies, 98*(2), 54–58.

Wilson, A. (1993). Conversation partners: Helping students gain a global perspective through cross-cultural experiences. *Theory into Practice, 32*(1), 22–26.

Zimpher, N. (1989). The RATE Project: A profile of teacher education students. *Journal of Teacher Education, 12*, 27–31.

9 Discussions within Online Learning Formats
Are Meaningful Encounters with Difference Possible?

Sarah A. Mathews and Hilary Landorf

Conversations throughout institutions of higher education often center on how to effectively prepare graduates with the knowledge, skills, and dispositions 21st-century learners need to develop in order to succeed in a globally interdependent world. At a minimum, university graduates need critical reasoning, information literacy, intercultural competency, and ethical, social, and professional understanding. However, critics suggest that institutions of higher education inadequately prepare American students for these attributes (Spring, 2013; Suárez-Orozco & Qin-Hillard, 2004; Suárez-Orozco, Suárez-Orozco, & Todorova, 2008). Global learning, defined in this chapter as the process by which students are prepared to fulfill their civic responsibilities in an increasingly diverse and interconnected world, provides the conditions for students to gain these attributes by explicitly focusing on diversity, interconnectedness, and collaborative problem-solving.

Given changing student demographics, economic challenges, and directives to ensure that *all* students are prepared to live and work in a globalized world, institutions of higher education are recognizing the need to deliver global learning via the core student learning experience: the curriculum. Data from the American Council on Education's *Mapping Internationalization on U.S. Campuses* (2012) study indicate that global learning is a priority for many colleges and universities. While the global learning curriculum differs based on institution type and mission, locale, student demographics, and availability of resources, its focus is always on the advancement of students' achievement of specified global learning outcomes.

Global learning outcomes may vary according to institutional goals, context, and student needs, but they cluster around three competencies: (1) an understanding of the interconnectedness of global trends and issues; (2) an appreciation of diverse perspectives; and (3) a willingness to take part in problem-solving on the local, national, global, and/or international levels.

With the wealth of information from around the world that can be found online, as well as the recent increase in the use of social media sites, it stands to reason that technology has increased the opportunities for students to interact with global issues. For example, students may acquire an understanding of the interconnectedness of the world by analyzing global issues through online news sources, electronic journals, and websites. They may develop *global awareness* by conducting a comparative analysis of a current issue covered by online newspapers from different parts of the world. Students can become *globally engaged* when they contribute online to a non-government organization, sign a petition via the Internet, or create and publish media to bring awareness to a specific cause (Baildon & Damico, 2012; Jenkins, Ito, Davidson, & Benkler, 2006; Mathews, 2012). However, research on the potential for online platforms to facilitate increases in *global perspective* is still emerging. Are online formats effective means of helping individuals learn to respect diverse worldviews, facilitate civic deliberation, and empathize with others who hold different cultural, religious, and disciplinary perspectives?

This chapter builds on recent research (Braskamp, Braskamp, Merrill, & Engberg, 2012; Glass & Braskamp, 2012) that concludes that meaningful "encounters with difference" contribute significantly to students' development of a global perspective. The first section of this chapter outlines a conceptual framework informing the definition and characteristics of a global perspective. This section includes results from a large-scale research project that used the Global Perspective Inventory (GPI), a survey that measures the connection between educational experiences and university students' global perspective development (Braskamp & Engberg, 2011; Glass & Braskamp, 2012). The GPI indicated that encounters with difference, through class face-to-face discussions and on-campus interactions, resulted in the greatest gains in global perspective. In particular, we examine the potential gains in, and obstacles to, global perspective development through asynchronous online discussion formats.

If experiences with difference make the difference, can these encounters take place in fully online spaces? In an era when many colleges and universities are facing pressures to offer more classes online, develop fully online programs, and create and accept credit for massive open online courses (MOOCS), is it possible for students to have meaningful conversations with difference in cyberspace? In the second half of the chapter we outline the potential successes and obstacles to creating and maintaining meaningful online discussions in these formats. This chapter seeks to advance this conversation, examining research on practice, in order to determine if there are successful approaches that foster meaningful dialogue with difference in virtual environments.

CONCEPTUAL FRAMEWORK OF GLOBAL PERSPECTIVE DEVELOPMENT

Scholars have theorized the need for, and content of, a global perspective since Diogenes claimed to be a "cosmopolites" or "citizen of the world" in the 300s B.C. (Appiah, 2006). Since the 1960s, when global education had its curricular beginnings in the U.S. (Tye, 2009), several scholars have articulated the development of a global perspective as essential for responsible, active citizenship in an increasingly complex and interconnected world (Case, 1993; Hanvey, 1976; Merryfield, Jarchow, & Pickert, 1997; Pike & Selby, 1995). Professor of education and senior fellow at the American Council of Colleges and Universities Larry Braskamp, with colleagues Braskamp, Merrill, and Engberg (2012), is interested in *holistic* student development and theorized global perspective in terms of three domains of student learning.

The three domains influencing Braskamp et al.'s (2012) work are based on Robert Kegan's (1994) three domains of human development: cognitive, interpersonal, and intrapersonal. Braskamp et al. (2012) explain that the cognitive domain answers the question "How do I know?" In this domain individuals realize that knowledge is never neutral and that it is valuable to examine information from multiple sources and perspectives. The intrapersonal domain answers the question "Who am I?" In this domain, individuals examine their own identity, sense of self, and individual values. The third domain, the interpersonal domain, involves the ability to interact with other geographically and culturally diverse people. Braskamp et al. (2012) define global perspective as the capacity for a person to think with complexity, take into account multiple perspectives to form a unique and authentic sense of self, and to relate to others with respect and openness.

Braskamp et al. (2012) developed an instrument, the Global Perspective Inventory (GPI), to measure respondents' global perspective by asking them to rank 64 statements on a five-point Likert scale (Strongly Agree, Agree, Neutral, Disagree, and Strongly Disagree). Using this instrument, Braskamp et al. (2012) examined over 48,000 undergraduate students in 140 public and private four-year colleges in the U.S. who completed the GPI from 2008 to 2012. Results indicated that students' direct engagement with issues that create cognitive dissonance can force them to turn the mirror on their own values, perspectives, and cultural practices. This allows students to examine these issues as others might (Glass & Braskamp, 2012). These encounters must include interactions that question, provide something new, problematize previous perspectives, and require one to readjust, adapt, or alter ideas and views (Braskamp & Engberg, 2011).

From these survey results, Braskamp et al. (2012) determined that "encounters with difference" had the biggest impact on an individual's global perspective.

> Encounters are more than exposure, observation, or touring. They require direct engagement that questions, provides something new, creates a cognitive dissonance, requires one to readjust, adapt, and alter existing ideas, views, relationships and sense of self, through interactions with others.
>
> (Braskamp et al., 2012, p. 41)

While universities provide a variety of meaningful experiences for their students, one of the most prevalent methods involves the incorporation of discussion or deliberation over complex or controversial issues. Braskamp and Chickering (2009) suggested that individuals need to recognize the importance of reciprocity and consensus-building within local, national, and global arenas. This requires skills to communicate and empathize with people "who differ dramatically in national origin, ethnicity, religious, and spiritual orientations, as well as in race and gender" (p. 27). We draw on these same perspectives when arguing that encounters with difference are crucial for helping students develop a global perspective.

Colleges and universities throughout the world are facing increasing pressure to incorporate distance education into their academic programs. Many state legislators, trustee boards, and university presidents suggest that distance education will help make learning accessible to more students, decrease overhead costs while increasing profits, and allow their institutions to remain competitive. Options include single courses delivered through online formats, entire online degree programs, and the promotion of massive open online courses (MOOCs). We examine research on using online formats to incorporate opportunities for students to develop a global perspective. We ask the following research question: what instructional strategies, if any, foster online asynchronous discussions in which students engage in meaningful encounters with difference?

METHODS

Procedures

To address our inquiry we entered a combination of the following key terms into prominent education search engines: MOOCs, global education, online discussions, and asynchronous discussions. As we continued to engage with the research, the following additional terms emerged: Technological Pedagogical Content Knowledge (TPCK), computer-mediated discussions/communication, social presence, and transactional distance. We engaged in an iterative process of reviewing research and redefining our search. We used all identified key words to search through the following journals: *Journal of Asynchronous Learning Networks, Distance Education, Journal of Interactive Media in Education, The American Journal of Distance Education, Internet and Higher Education, Contemporary Issues in Technology and Teacher Education, Journal of Computer-Mediated Communication, Journal of Research on Computing in Education,* and *Educational Technology Review.*

Results from empirical studies conducted on the effectiveness of MOOCs are limited as the MOOC movement is relatively new—circa 2008. However, the value of the MOOC is a relevant and highly debated conversation in education today. Therefore, these same key words were used to search through editorials and articles in news outlets such as the *Chronicle of Higher Education*, the *New York Times*, and the *Huffington Post*. After reading through the literature that resulted from our search, we identified research that indicated the obstacles to, and recommendations for, promoting each domain of global perspective within online, asynchronous discussion formats.

CAN ONLINE DISCUSSIONS MAKE A DIFFERENCE?

One of the first studies in education concerning the use of an online format for diversity education was conducted by Merry Merryfield. In 1998, Merryfield incorporated an online threaded discussion to supplement a face-to-face course on multicultural education. In doing so she was able to connect 50 educators from nine different countries in an online, asynchronous learning environment (Merryfield, 2000, 2001). Using this format, students created individual autobiographies that examined their construction of knowledge, discussed readings on privilege, inequity, and imperialism, and reflected on course issues as manifested in their local contexts. Threaded discussions allowed participants the opportunity to read about issues from multiple perspectives. Individuals reported feeling that they could communicate without the risk of observing others' reactions (Merryfield, 2001). However, participants also reported feeling constrained by being limited to the written word as their only means of communication. Participants in this course were well aware that what they said in an online format was permanent and that there is the potential for others to read and analyze responses beyond the scope of one class session or semester. They concluded that technology served as a barrier to truly knowing those with whom they interacted.

Although Merryfield's (2000, 2001) study occurred more than a dozen years ago, the results highlight contradictions that currently result from online discussions. While online discussions provide a safe space to communicate, free of traditional norms of interaction, participants often feel pressured to revise their postings to control how they are represented online. Although there is an immediate connection with the technology, cyberspace creates a physical distance between individuals interacting within these online formats.

Moore (2005) described this as transactional distance, or a perceived pedagogical distance that leads to a communication and psychological gap. This phenomenon makes it easier to leave or ignore conversations in online formats that are messy or uncomfortable, precisely the conversations that are vital for global perspective development. Social norms often force individuals to listen to uncomfortable conversations in face-to-face formats, preventing one from physically leaving the room; however, individuals are able to tune out, turn off, silence, or downplay uncomfortable conversations in online formats (Mason & Metzger, 2012; Voithofer & Henry, 2012). As a result individuals may feel less inhibited to share their points of view, opinions, and perspectives (Larson & Keiper, 2002; Warschauer, 1996; Zutshi, O'Hare, & Rodafinos, 2013).

Cognitive, Social, and Teacher Presence

Research on distance learning has expanded significantly since the early 2000s as individuals seek to find effective strategies for engaging learners in online formats. Much of this research stems from online educators' need to determine more productive ways to deliver material online. Garrison, Anderson, and Archer (2000) outlined a model for facilitating computer-mediated communication, which they refer to as the Community of Inquiry (CoI) model. Through this model, the researchers posit three core elements that are necessary for successful online communication: cognitive presence, social presence, and teaching presence (Garrison, Anderson, & Archer, 2000, 2001). An increase in each core element should decrease transactional distance.

Cognitive presence refers to the extent to which "learners are able to construct knowledge through reflected discourse in a critical community of inquiry" (Wang & Chen, 2008, p. 159). In terms of developing a global perspective, it makes sense that students would need a cognitive presence that addresses an individual's understanding of the state-of-the planet or knowledge of global dynamics (Hanvey, 1976). Online formats might provide opportunities for students to gain access to a wealth of new knowledge, forcing them to reflect on the notion that knowledge is not neutral (Braskamp et al., 2012). This dimension requires the process of exploration and resolution that is embedded in inquiry, critical thinking, and problem-solving.

Social presence refers to the extent to which an individual feels a sense of belonging, a sense of togetherness, and mutual awareness of members within the online community (Wang & Chen, 2008). Garrison et al. (2000) describe social presence "as the ability of participants in the Community of Inquiry to project their personal characteristics into the community, thereby presenting themselves to the other participants as 'real people'" (p. 90). Social presence is an essential element of the development of a global perspective online. It necessitates instruction that meets the needs of a variety of cultures, provides multiple forms of communication, and facilitates connection-building in small and large cross-cultural groups (Hill, Song, & West, 2009; Kim & Bonk, 2002; Olesova, Yang, & Richardson, 2011).

Meaningful discussion with difference can help individuals develop cross-cultural awareness and the interpersonal domains of social responsibility and social interactions. These conversations must go beyond occasional contact or superficial chatting with geographically or culturally diverse others. Activities must provide direct engagement that questions, provides something new, creates a cognitive dissonance, requires one to readjust, adapt, and alter existing ideas, views, relationships, and sense of self, through interactions with others (Braskamp, 2012).

Individuals that have high levels of perspective consciousness, a range of skills that promote cross-cultural awareness and interaction, and a disposition toward embracing social responsibility may be able to transcend transactional distance and be socially present in the online format. However, if the goal for an online course is to help individuals develop a global perspective, the teacher then becomes responsible for triggering, scaffolding, and sustaining these conversations. Researchers agree that the onus often rests on the facilitator or instructor to develop social, as well as cognitive, presence in computer-mediated dialogue (Darabi, Liang, & Yurekli, 2013). Garrison et al. (2000) refers to this element as teaching presence. The authors suggest that teaching presence requires the ability to define and initiate discussion topics and build understanding among students.

Much attention in the literature on asynchronous forums in distance education has been directed toward the need to structure effective discussion sessions. This supports the notion that a tremendous amount of modeling, coaching, and scaffolding is required for effective online discussions (Boling & Beatty, 2010). Dynamic discussions in a face-to-face forum often require the facilitator to initiate the conversation with open-ended and engaging critical thinking questions. Discussion leaders are advised to then gradually withdraw from the conversation, allowing the students or participants to control and shape the discussion with limited teacher interaction (Trufant, 2003). In contrast, the online discussion facilitator must take an active and participatory role in order to coordinate the dialogue.

The Strengths and Obstacles of Asynchronous Discussions

One frequently cited benefit with regard to online discussion formats is the ability for individuals to access discussions at various different times and from unlimited locations all over the world. Online discussions may also allow a wider range of students to engage in a dialogue than in face-to-face instruction alone, as individuals may feel they have more uninterrupted time to reflect and craft responses. This may also allow for a deeper analysis of course concepts and issues (Meyer, 2007; Ruday, 2011). Peters (2012) recommends the use of online discussion as a way to help individuals interact, communicate, and empathize with culturally and geographically diverse others. Trufant (2003) suggests that Socratic discussions are perfect in an online format because they provide a risk-free environment that encourages a frank exchange and minimizes the potential for confrontation. She also suggests that these dialogues are ideal in this format because they neutralize status indicators and social distracters. This may decrease a person's perceived tension over racial, socioeconomic, gender, or cultural differences (for a discussion on how White privilege, race, and social hierarchy are enacted in online spaces, see Voithofer & Henry, 2012).

Yet not every online discussion proves successful. Distance educators "expect that students cannot benefit from online learning unless they fully engage in it; however this does not mean that all students will be equally active or influential" (Waters, 2012, p. 12). Wang and Chen's (2008) review of the literature on online discussions found that non-participation, low interaction among users, and topic digression often hindered student learning (p. 162). Student participation in discussions may be influenced by an individual's leadership style (Waters, 2012), language fluency or proficiency (Kim & Bonk, 2002), or perception that participation is or is not a priority for the course or assessed for a grade (Oliver & Shaw, 2003). Oliver and Shaw (2003) noticed that students in their study were often "just 'playing the game' of assessment, making postings that earned marks but rarely contributing otherwise" (p. 56).

Postsecondary Instruction Offered Online: The Pressure for MOOCs Mounts

Over the past 25 years, interest in online or distance education has increased in postsecondary institutions, with 31 percent of college students reporting they have enrolled in at least one online course (Ruth, 2012). Universities have recently promoted MOOCs as a way to reach thousands of potential students around the world. In this section we outline the history behind the MOOC movement and situate the limited research on the effectiveness of MOOCs within contemporary conversations surrounding the pros and cons for adopting this approach. In particular, we examine whether the MOOC format is compatible with global perspective development. Can MOOCs facilitate meaningful dialogues with difference?

The History of MOOCs

In 2008 George Siemens and Stephen Downes of the University of Manitoba developed the first experiment in open courseware by offering a course they had previously facilitated in a face-to-face format to thousands of online viewers. The instructors based this on the following idea:

> We learn best when we learn collaboratively, in networks, because the process of learning is less about acquiring new knowledge, and much more about building the social and neural connections that will allow knowledge to circulate, be used, evolve, and grow.
> (Bady, 2013, para. 32)

They wanted to create a space that fostered exploration, creativity, and collaboration, and provide individuals the opportunity to develop social networks. In 2011 professors at Stanford University utilized a similar approach, drawing thousands of students into their online computer science courses. These innovations launched the current MOOC movement (Kolowich, 2013).

Harvard and MIT quickly followed this trend, creating nonprofit MOOCs over concerns about the commercialization of online education. The difference was that the Harvard and MIT versions of open courseware were designed to provide individuals with access to experts and content rather than focus on the social networking potential of open access to information. The momentum grew as 2012 was designated the year of the MOOC (Pappano, 2012). While most MOOCs were usually free and credit-less, university presidents and boards of trustees interpreted the rapid increase in participation as a sign that MOOCs would provide a profitable means of enrolling massive amounts of students into online programs. Universities turned toward for-profit companies, such as Coursera and Udacity, to build, support, and market these courses (Big Three, 2012). Stakeholders also began to discuss the potential to provide certification for the completion of MOOCs.

Welsh and Dragusin (2013) suggest that there are two generations of MOOCs that have different formats and different implications for learners. The authors described the first generation, cMOOCs, as the group of courses that developed around 2008 and focused on knowledge generation, creativity, autonomy, and networking (p. 54). In this version of the MOOC, there are no required assignments and individuals are not required to follow a simple or singular path to obtain information. The second generation of MOOCs, xMOOCs, refers to the period that started in 2012 and includes courses that are based on traditional instructional formats, fixed content, and centralized discussion forums (Welsh & Dragusin, 2013). The xMOOC design is often driven by the desire to market each MOOC to hundreds or thousands of students around the world, all at one time. The market-driven motivations behind the xMOOC format are often in opposition to the egalitarian goals—that is, unrestricted access and mutual collaboration—which propelled the original cMOOC framework.

Resistance toward MOOCs

While it seems that many are embracing MOOCs, the movement has received considerable resistance, notably from the academic community. Critics point to the fact that online courses have lower completion rates, well under 10 percent, and higher levels of plagiarism and cheating than face-to-face courses (Herman, 2014; North, Richardson, & North, 2014; Zutshi, O'Hare, & Rodafinos, 2013). University faculty members suggest the market-driven interest in MOOCs comes at the risk of sound pedagogy. For some, MOOCs have become synonymous with the colonization and commodification of knowledge and the passive transfer of content from expert to student (Bady, 2013). Many scholars see MOOCs as a threat to their productivity and intellectual property, or fear the elimination of their position as a result of the offering of MOOCs (Berrett, 2013; Peralta, 2012). Many courses designated as MOOCs are massive but not open, or open but not massive, thus complicating the MOOC classification (Bagley, 2013, p. 371). Overall MOOCs are often critiqued along three lines: creators rely too much on business models to focus solely on making money; MOOCs do not incorporate effective pedagogical practices; and MOOCs have high attrition rates and low completion rates (Daniel, 2012). Yet even with a sizeable resistance, experts suggest MOOCs are here to stay.

Can MOOCs Facilitate Encounters with Difference for Global Perspective Development?

Many scholars and institutions of higher education feel the pressure to embrace MOOCs in order to compete with other colleges and universities. In fact, 43 percent of universities reported they plan to offer MOOCs by 2016 (Afshar, 2013). Although MOOCs are the latest trend in postsecondary education, we believe it is important to critically examine the pedagogical practices used in these formats to determine if this medium is consistent with sound educational goals. What role do MOOCs play in holistic learning? Is global perspective development compatible with the asynchronous format utilized by MOOC creators? In terms of the potential for higher education to use MOOCs for global perspective development, after examining the research, we recognized two areas that are simultaneously empowering and problematic.

Access. Many view the MOOC platform as a way to connect thousands of people around the world in collaborative and knowledge-generating online spaces. In fact, proponents of MOOCs claim that the format serves as an extension of democratic education. Carver and Harrison (2013) suggest,

> MOOCs have the benefit of a global reach. A transnational educational model carries with it many of the benefits of study abroad programs. In particular, the MOOC's collaborative design incorporates ample opportunities to encourage cultural exchange and reinforce diverse approaches to problem solving.
>
> (para. 8)

There is also growing evidence of partnerships between the business and education sectors to bring MOOCs to developing nations, such as recent partnerships in Rwanda and Tanzania (Facebook, 2014; Trucano, 2014).

Yet, critics of the MOOC movement suggest that advances in technology still do not adequately address the global digital divide. Carver and Harrison (2013) acknowledge there are large gaps in technological infrastructure between the developed and developing world. This divide is illustrated when examining the geographic distribution of MOOC users. Coursera, one of the leading producers of MOOC courses, reported high to medium participation in North and Central America, Western and Eastern Europe, East Asia, and the Indian subcontinent. There was only intermittent participation in parts of South America, and no recognizable participation on the continent of Africa, West and Central Asia, and the post-Soviet states (Coursera, 2013). Gaps in participation may result from inadequate technological infrastructure or governmental interference with the open access of information, and there are still conflicting perspectives on the role and validity of MOOC courses.

Social presence. As depicted in the section on distance education, transactional distance often limits the impact of social interactions in online spaces. Much of the literature on MOOCs indicates that individuals are choosing to participate in these formats for two reasons: interest in the content and access to well-known professors (Zutshi, O'Hare, & Rodafinos, 2013). This means that MOOCs have the potential to satisfy the cognitive and teaching presence components of online instruction. However, many MOOC participants report they never have direct access to, or interact with, the professor of record. Instead participants report having gained the most valuable information from watching videos and taped lectures and reading the posted materials (Liu, Kang, Coa, Lim, & Ko, 2013).

The original cMOOC generation of courses was geared toward helping individuals collaborate in order to generate new knowledge accessible to all. However, much of the limited research on xMOOCs suggests that social presence, or interaction between peers or colleagues, is missing in these formats. For example, Liu, Kang, Coa, Lim, and Ko (2013) surveyed 5,000 students from 138 countries who had registered for a MOOC. Participants in this study reported feeling disconnected from the student community, overwhelmed by the number of students in the course, and dissatisfied with the little peer-to-peer interaction they experienced. Discussion posts decreased dramatically from the first week (4,153) to the last week (1,918), providing obstacles to forming smaller discussion or collaborative groups. Others note that while MOOCs have the potential to bring geographically distant and culturally diverse audiences together for study, institutions of higher education, as well as MOOC instructors, have yet to fully utilize the cultural and geographic diversity of the students in these online courses (Olds & Robertson, 2014).

IMPLICATIONS FOR GLOBAL EDUCATION

While there is an abundance of research on distance education, there is still limited research on the effectiveness of asynchronous discussion to facilitate the development of a global perspective and no research on the development of a global perspective using the MOOC format. The cultural and geographical diversity *of* MOOC classrooms have not been used to sufficiently advance the development of a global perspective *in* MOOC classrooms.

After reviewing the research on asynchronous learning, in particular learning that occurs in MOOCs, we are not convinced this is a promising format for global perspective development. We acknowledge that MOOCs can introduce students to global issues and information from a variety of online sources. This satisfies the global learning outcome, global awareness, and helps to develop the cognitive domain. However, from our review of the current research on MOOCs, we conclude that the asynchronous format is problematic in terms of helping students develop a global perspective. While asynchronous learning can introduce individuals to consider content from multiple perspectives—that is, the cognitive domain—and may ask individuals to reflect on their own identity formation—that is, the intrapersonal domain—these formats do not necessarily build the social presence necessary for developing the interpersonal domain. Without attending to social presence MOOCs are not facilitating either social interaction or social responsibility. Transactional distance creates a barrier that prevents encounters with difference that make a difference. This barrier also hinders the development of a complex sense of self.

From our review of research we think that *hybrid* courses offer the most effective online format to facilitate meaningful cross-cultural dialogue by combining online and face-to-face components. A hybrid course is one in which in which some face-to-face course time is replaced by online learning activities. The online component of a hybrid course may allow individuals to take risks when discussing controversial and sensitive topics, while the face-to-face component may reinforce social presence and authenticity (e.g., Merryfield, 2000, 2001; Voithofer & Henry, 2012). The MOOC format seems inconsistent with global perspective development and should be used only as a massive open online *resource* (MOOR) (Olds & Robertson, 2014), similar to the original goals of the cMOOC model.

While the research on asynchronous discussions for the purposes of facilitating global perspective development is inconclusive, informative examples of practice emerged from our review of literature. We offer these strategies to advance the conversation about the use of asynchronous discussion in online formats that promote global learning. These recommendations are organized according to the three domains of global perspective used by Braskamp et al. (2012).

Recommendations to Facilitate the Intrapersonal Domain

The intrapersonal domain asks students to reflect on the question "Who am I?" This process allows individuals to examine how their identity is shaped by factors such as ethnicity and gender, and how these factors in turn shape their values and perspectives.

1. Trufact (2003) suggests all participants must acknowledge their assumptions in order for critical thought to take place. Instructors should design initial discussions or assignments geared to providing a

space for individual and intrapersonal reflection on their own values and perspectives as related to course content.
2. Instructors should provide an opportunity for students to write a personal reflection, personal autobiography, or narrative of their learning as a way to introduce themselves to others. Merryfield (2000, 2001) asked students to reflect on their own knowledge construction. Others have asked students to create digital or photonarratives to explore issues of identity and perception (see Community Center for Media Arts, 2010; Croghan, Griffin, Hunter, & Phoenix, 2008, Janzen, Perry, & Edwards, 2011).
3. Video, digital images, and auditory clips often have the ability to invoke an emotional reaction that might increase motivation (Dillion & Gabbard, 1998; Hartsell & Yuen, 2006; Schank, 1993). These formats can be used to help individuals construct their online identities and communicate this identity to others.

Recommendations to Facilitate the Cognitive Domain

The cognitive domain of global perspective requires that students ask themselves, "How do I know?" This includes metacognitive processes that allow one to differentiate between what she or he knows and what she or he does not know, as well as the recognition that knowledge is not neutral.

1. Instructors should include clear instructions pertaining to the quantity and quality of online postings. Instructors may ask students to respond multiple times and to spread these discussions throughout the week or module (Anderson, 2008). Some authors recommend a "bookend" approach, in which students might answer questions at the beginning of a reading or module and then return to this discussion after a reading or toward the end of a particular module.
2. Dabbagh (2000) recommends developing a rubric to evaluate student discussion posts, including criteria such as timely discussion contributions and adherence to online protocols.
3. To foster global awareness instructors can ask students to include links to related articles or websites from reputable sources within discussion posts. Students could be required to visit their peers' suggested websites and write a review about the source.
4. The cognitive domain requires that individuals question knowledge sources. Instructors should model and reinforce information literacy and critical media literacy skills. This can help students gain the skills necessary to examine how various sources, as well as the media, cover global issues. This could be done by asking students to consider why certain sources are considered more reputable than others, identify whose voice is missing from these sources, and practice methods of crowdsourcing to improve the dissemination of knowledge.

Recommendations to Facilitate the Interpersonal Domain

This domain focuses on the question "How do I relate to others?" Development in the interpersonal domain requires interdependence with, and a social concern for, other individuals, as well as the ability to interact with culturally and geographically diverse others.

1. In order to promote social presence instructors should require students to read and possibly respond to their peers' autobiographical sketches or introductory reflections. Some suggest that digital media should be used for autobiographical assignments because these formats provide a powerful introduction to people and ideas. "Video or digital autobiographical sketches can serve as a mechanism for students to actively engage with other cultures and build bridges of understanding that force students to move from their set of beliefs" (Hartsell & Yuen, 2006, p. 179). It is important to recognize that experienced online learners often skip the introduction sections of online modules and are reluctant to break the ice with novice online learners (Vonderwell, 2003). Therefore these activities should be made explicit assignments or components of the learning process.
2. Many distance educators recommend assigning roles to students. For example, divide large sections into smaller discussion groups and assign each student the responsibility to lead at least one discussion session. Poole (2000) has shown moderated discussions received more responses and more lines per response when compared with non-moderated discussions. Students can also serve as judges responsible for making sure everyone in the group is contributing to the discussion. Likewise, the judge is evaluated based on his or her efforts at maintaining, encouraging, or appraising the discussion.
3. Instructors should discuss the importance of maintaining civility within these discussions and may offer examples of civil and uncivil discussion threads to model the distinction. Discussions about civility should also take into consideration that online conversations lack some of the social cues and intonations incorporated in face-to-face conversations. A reader could misinterpret the authors' tone or neglect cues that indicate different cultural contexts.
4. Some of the same techniques used in face-to-face discussions can be used in online formats. For example, individuals can be forced to defend an unfavorable or unconventional position. Students can interact with diverse perspectives about an issue by analyzing case studies.

Finally, as determined earlier, teacher presence is an essential component for facilitating effective online discussions. Gunter (2007) found that some "easy-to-implement strategies—such as frequent and specific feedback, addressing students by name, praise and use of supporting tone—impacted students' intrinsic motivation and self-efficacy, thus leading to better learning discussion experiences" (p. 229).

CONCLUSION

The literature describing asynchronous online discussions is not conclusive. For every author who outlines a great idea to facilitate classroom discussion, there is another who describes the obstacles she or he encountered in implementing effective computer-mediated dialogue. Many educators who use online formats for instruction acknowledge the drawbacks alongside benefits when reflecting on their practice. The recommendations offered in this chapter emerged as prevalent themes or unique pedagogical approaches. Yet, we are not convinced that fully online, asynchronous discussions can foster the global perspective development necessary for 21st-century learners. Current research suggests that the MOOC format reinforces isolated and independent learning and the commodification and transfer of content rather than facilitating the collaborative and creative social networks that inspired the original models.

Therefore, we caution colleges and universities that are quick to adopt fully online and MOOC formats blindly, without examining the potential obstacles this may pose to global learning. Instead we call for additional research in this area. How can fully online programs and MOOCs foster the social presence necessary to help participants develop the three domains of global perspective development? If MOOCs are the inevitable transformation of learning platforms, how can educators use the cultural and geographical diversity *of* MOOC classrooms to advance the development of a global perspective *in* MOOC classrooms? Finally, many isolated MOOC courses, devoid of global perspective development, are used for credentialing or substitute course credit. If this remains the trend, how can programs within postsecondary education supplement these courses with face-to-face and hybrid courses in which global learning is infused in order to prepare citizens for 21st-century learning?

REFERENCES

Afshar, V. (2013, May 20). Adoption of massive open online courses. Retrieved from www.huffingtonpost.com/vala-afshar/infographic-adoption-of-m_b_3303789.html

American Council on Education. (2012). *Mapping internationalization on U.S. campuses, 2012 edition.* Washington, DC: American Council on Education.

Anderson, T. (2008). Teaching in an online learning context. In T. Anderson (Ed.), *The theory and practice of online learning* (pp. 343–366). Edmonton: Athabasca University.

Appiah, K. A. (2006). *Cosmopolitanism: Ethics in a world of strangers.* New York: W. W. Norton.

Bady, A. (2013). The MOOC moment and the end of reform. *Liberal Education,* 99(4). Retrieved from www.aacu.org/liberaleducation/le-fa13/bady.cfm

Baggley, J. (2013). Reflection: MOOC rampant. *Distance Education, 34*(3), 368–378.

Baildon, M., & Damico, J. (2012). Using technology to support relational cosmopolitanism for social education. In B. Maguth (Ed.), *New directions in social education research: The influence of technology and globalization in the lives of students* (pp. 21–40). Charlotte, NC: Information Age.

Berrett, D. (2013, May 10). Debate over MOOCs reaches Harvard. *Chronicle of Higher Education.* Retrieved from http://chronicle.com/article/Debate-Over-MOOCs-Reaches/139179/

The big three, at a glance. (2012, November 2). *New York Times.* Retrieved from www.nytimes.com/2012/11/04/education/edlife/the-big-three-mooc-providers.html?adxnnl=1&ref=edlife&adxnnlx=1385996734-fLxv0EoWsekb75qpPQfvfw

Boling, E. C., & Beatty, J. (2010). Cognitive apprenticeship in computer-mediated feedback: Creating a classroom environment to increase feedback and learning. *Journal of Educational Computing Research, 43*(1), 47–65.

Braskamp, L. (2012). Creating encounters with difference that make a difference. Retrieved from www.geneseo.edu/webfm_send/7155

Braskamp, L. A., Braskamp, D. C., Merrill, K. C., & Engberg, M. (2012). *The global perspective inventory (GPI): Its purpose, construction, potential uses, and psychometric characteristics.* Chicago: Global Perspective Institute.

Braskamp, L. A., & Chickering, A. (2009). Developing a global perspective for personal social responsibility. *Peer Review, 11*(4), 27–30.

Braskamp, L. A., & Engberg, M. E. (2011). How colleges can influence the development of a global perspective. *Liberal Education, 97*(3–4), 34–39.

Carver, L., & Harrison, L. M. (2013). MOOCs and democratic education. *Liberal Education, 99*(4). Retrieved from www.aacu.org/liberaleducation/le-fa13/carver_harrison.cfm

Case, R. (1993). Key elements of a global perspective. *Social Education, 57*(6), 318–325.

Community Center for Media Arts. (2010). *About Photovoice.* Retrieved from http://photovoice.ca

Coursera. (2013). Coursera MOOC participation. Cartography Lab, University of Wisconsin-Madison. Retrieved from https://class.coursera.org/globalhighered-001/wiki/week1

Croghan, R., Griffin, C., Hunter, J., & Phoenix, A. (2008). Young people's constructions of self: Notes on the use and analysis of the photo-elicitation methods. *International Journal of Social Research Methodology, 11*(4), 345–356.

Dabbagh, N. (2000). Online discussion protocols and rubrics. Retrieved from http://mason.gmu.edu/~ndabbagh/wblg/online-protocol.html

Daniel, J. (2012). Making sense of MOOCs: Musings in a maze of myth, paradox and possibility. *Journal of Interactive Media in Education.* Retrieved from https://oerknowledgecloud.org/content/making-sense-moocs-musings-maze-myth-paradox-and-possibility

Darabi, A., Liang, X., Suryavanshi, R., & Yurekli, H. (2013). Effectiveness of online discussion strategies: A meta-analysis. *American Journal of Distance Education, 27*(4), 228–241.

Dillon, A., & Gabbard, R. (1998). Hypermedia as an educational technology: A review of the quantitative research literature on learner comprehension, control, and style. *Review of Educational Research, 68*(3), 322–349.

Facebook. (2014, February 24). Internet.org announces SocialEDU. *Facebook Newsroom.* Retrieved from http://newsroom.fb.com/news/2014/02/internet-org-announces-socialedu

Garrison, D. R., Anderson, T., & Archer, W. (2000). Critical inquiry in a text-based environments. Computer conferencing in higher education. *Internet and Higher Education, 2*(2–3), 87–105.
Garrison, D. R., Anderson, T., & Archer, W. (2001). Critical thinking, cognitive presence, and computer conferencing in distance education. *American Journal of Distance Education, 15*(1), 7–23.
Glass, C. R., & Braskamp, L. A. (2012, October 26). Foreign students and tolerance. *Inside Higher Ed.* Retrieved from www.insidehighered.com/views/2012/10/26/essay-how-colleges-should-respond-racism-against-international-students
Gunter, G. A. (2007). The effects of the impact of instructional immediacy on cognition and learning in online classes. *International Journal of Social Sciences, 2*(3), 87–105.
Hanvey, R. G. (1976). *An attainable global perspective.* Denver, CO: American Forum for Global Education.
Hartsell, T., & Yuen, S. C. (2006). Video streaming in online learning. *AACE Journal, 14*(1), 31–43.
Herman, R. L. (2014). Letter from the editor-in-chief: MOOCs—How are they doing? *Journal of Effective Teaching, 14*(1), 1–4.
Hill, J. R., Song, L., & West, R. E. (2009). Social learning theory and web-based learning environments: A review of research and discussion of implications. *American Journal of Distance Education, 23*(2), 88–103.
Janzen, K. J., Perry, B. A., & Edwards, M. (2011). Becoming real: Using the artistic pedagogical technology of photovoice as a medium to becoming real to one another in the online educative environment. *International Journal of Nursing Education Scholarship, 8*(1), 1–16.
Jenkins, H., Ito, M., Davidson, C., & Benkler, H. (2006). *MacArthur online discussion sources on civic engagement 2006.* Retrieved from http://ccce.com.washington.edu/about/assets/Civic_Engagement-Online_Discussions06.pdf
Kegan, R. (1994). *In over our heads: The mental demands of modern life.* Cambridge, MA: Harvard University Press.
Kim, K. J., & Bonk, C. J. (2002). Cross-cultural comparisons of online collaboration. *Journal of Computer-Mediated Communication, 8*(1). Retrieved from http://onlinelibrary.wiley.com/doi/10.1111/j.1083-6101.2002.tb00163.x/full
Kolowich, S. (2013). The professors who make the MOOCs. *Chronicle of Higher Education,* 18. Retrieved from http://chronicle.com/article/The-Professors-Behind-the-MOOC/137905/?cid=wb&utm_source=wb&utm_medium=en#id=overview
Larson, B. E., & Keiper, T. A. (2002). Classroom discussion and threaded electronic discussion: Learning in two arenas. *Contemporary Issues in Technology and Teacher Education, 2*(1), 45–62.
Liu, M., Kang, J., Coa, M., Lim, M., & Ko, Y. (2013, October). *Understanding MOOCs as an emerging online perspectives from the students.* Paper presented at the World Conference on E-Learning. Las Vegas, NV.
Mason, L., & Metzger, S. A. (2012). Reconceptualizing media literacy in the social studies: A pragmatic critique of the NCSS position statement on media literacy. *Theory and Research in Social Education, 40*(4), 436–455.
Mathews, S. A. (2012). Using photovoice to promote global advocacy: A review of projects with the potential to connect local and global civic engagement. In B. Maguth (Ed.), *New directions in social education research: The influence of technology and globalization in the lives of students* (pp. 135–152). Charlotte, NC: Information Age.
Merryfield, M. M. (2000). Using electronic technologies to promote equity and cultural diversity in social studies and global education. *Theory and Research in Social Education, 28*(4), 502–526.

Merryfield, M. M. (2001). The paradoxes of teaching a multicultural education course online. *Journal of Teacher Education, 52*(4), 283–299.

Merryfield, M. M., Jarchow, E., & Pickert, S. (1997). *Preparing teachers to teach global perspectives: A handbook for teacher educators.* Thousand Oaks, CA: Corwin Press.

Moore, M. G. (2005). Theory of transactional distance. In D. Keegan (Ed.), *Theoretical principles of distance education* (pp. 20–35). Taylor & Francis e-Library.

Myers, K. A. (2007). Student perceptions of face-to-face and online discussions: The advantage goes to . . . *Journal of Asynchronous Learning Networks, 11*(4), 53–69.

North, S. M., Richardson, R., & North, M. M. (2014). To adapt MOOCS, or not? That is no longer the question. *Universal Journal of Educational Research, 2*(1), 69–72.

Olds, K., & Robertson, S. (2014). A MOOC on globalising higher education and research. *IAU Horizons, 20*(1–2), 41–42. Retrieved from www.iau-aiu.net/sites/all/files/IAU%20Horizons%20Vol.20.1%20%5bEN_web%5d.pdf

Olesova, L., Yang, D., & Richardson, J. C. (2011). Cross-cultural undergraduate students' perceptions of online barriers. *Journal of Asynchronous Learning Networks, 15*(3), 68–80.

Oliver, M., & Shaw, G. P. (2003). Asynchronous discussion in support of medical education. *Journal of Asynchronous Learning Networks, 7*(1), 56–67.

Pappano, L. (2012, November 2). The year of the MOOC. *New York Times.* Retrieved from www.nytimes.com/2012/11/04/education/edlife/massive-open-online-courses-are-multiplying-at-a-rapid-pace.html?_r=1&

Peralta, C. (2012, November 1). Online courses raise intellectual property concerns. *Stanford Daily.* Retrieved from www.stanforddaily.com/2012/11/01/intellectual-property-concerns-for-moocs-persist

Peters, L. (2012). Exploring the relationships between global connectivity and the development of student empathy. In B. Maguth (Ed.), *New directions in social education research: The influence of technology and globalization in the lives of students* (pp. 177–187). Charlotte, NC: Information Age.

Pike, G., & Selby, D. (1995). *Reconnecting from national to global curriculum.* Toronto: International Institute for Global Education, University of Toronto.

Poole, M. D. (2000). Student participation in a discussion-oriented online course: A case study. *Journal of Research on Computing in Education, 33*(2), 162–177.

Ruday, S. (2011). Expanding the possibilities of discussion: A strategic approach to using online discussion boards in the middle and high school English classroom. *Contemporary Issues in Technology and Teacher Education, 11*(4), 350–361.

Ruth, S. (2012). Can MOOC's and existing e-learning paradigms help reduce college costs? *International Journal of Technology in Teaching and Learning, 8*(1), 21–32.

Schank, R. C. (1993). Learning via multimedia computers. *Commun.ACM, 36*(5), 54–56.

Spring, J. (2013). *American education* (16th ed.). New York: McGraw-Hill.

Suárez-Orozco, C., Suárez-Orozco, M. M., & Todorova, I. (2008). *Learning a new land: Immigrant students in American society.* Cambridge, MA: Belknap Press.

Suárez-Orozco, M. M., & Qin-Hilliard, D.B. (2004). *Globalization: Culture and education in the new millennium.* London: University of California Press.

Trucano, M. (2014). MOOCs in Africa. *EducTech: A World Bank blog on ICT use in education.* Retrieved from http://blogs.worldbank.org/edutech/moocs-in-Africa

Trufant, L. W. (2003). *Move over Socrates: Online discussion is here.* Retrieved from http://net.educause.edu/ir/library/pdf/ncp0330.pdf

Tye, K. A. (2009). A history of the global education movement in the United States. In T. F. Kirkwood-Tucker (Ed.), *Visions in global education: The globalization of curriculum and pedagogy in teacher education and schools* (pp. 3–24). New York: Peter Lang.

Voithofer, R., & Henry, B. A. (2012). "Great, they're gonna invade second life now": Technology, bias, and global education. In B. Maguth (Ed.), *New directions in social education research: The influence of technology and globalization in the lives of students* (pp. 187–205). Charlotte, NC: Information Age.

Vonderwell, S. (2003). An examination of asynchronous communication experiences and perspectives of students in an online course: A case study. *Internet and Higher Education, 6*(1), 77–90.

Wang, Y., & Chen, V. (2008). Essential elements in designing online discussions to promote cognitive presence—A practical experience. *Journal of Asynchronous Learning Networks, 12*(3–4), 157–177.

Warschauer, M. (1996). Comparing face-to-face and electronic communication in the second language classroom. *CALICO Journal, 13*(2), 7–26.

Waters, J. (2012). Thought-leaders in asynchronous online learning environments. *Journal of Asynchronous Learning Networks, 16*(1), 19–31.

Welsh, D., & Dragusin, M. (2013). The new generation of massive open online course (MOOCS) and entrepreneurship education. *Small Business Institute Journal, 9*(1), 51–65.

Zutshi, S., O'Hare, S., & Rodafinos, A. (2013). Experiences in MOOCs: The perspectives of students. *American Journal of Distance Education, 27*(4), 218–227.

Section 3: Conceptual Approaches to Teaching and Learning

10 Learning from 21st-Century International Schools
Global Education That Is Action-Oriented, Globally Connected, and Inclusive

Adrienne Michetti, Rebekah Madrid, and Kimberly Cofino

When considering 21st-century global education, one model schools can look toward is that of international schools. Edna Murphy defines international schools as

> [those that] serve the children of those international organizations and multinational companies whose parents are called upon to work in many different countries and to change their assignment at frequent intervals; the schools also educate the children of the diplomatic corps, and offer educational opportunities to children of host country nationals who want their children to learn English or who prefer the greater flexibility which an international school offers over the national system.
> (cited in Hayden, 2006, p. 11)

Because international schools are often not bound by national, state, or local policy, they can take risks in ways that national public schools often cannot. Successful international school practices can be strong starting points for national schools looking to implement the qualities of global education.

Many foreign families sending children to international schools are raising *third-culture kids*, a term used to describe children raised in a culture different than the home culture of their parents (Hill Useem, 1999). Third-culture kids, also called global nomads, are defined by McGaig and Schaettie as

> individuals of any age or nationality who have spent a significant part of their developmental years living in one or more countries outside their passport country because of a parent's occupations. Global Nomads are member of a worldwide community of persons who share a unique cultural heritage. While developing some sense of belonging to both their host(s) cultures and passport culture(s), they do not have a sense of total ownership in any. Elements from each culture and from the experiences

of international mobility are blended, creating a commonality with others of similar experience.

(cited in Langford, 1998, p. 30)

Killiham notes that these third-culture kids speak several languages, have cross-cultural skills and have "three-dimensional worldviews" (cited in Langford, 1998, p. 30). Moreover, third-culture kids and their parents report benefits such as open-minded views of the world, greater understanding of diversity and communication with people from varied backgrounds, and willingness to take risks (Pollack & Van Reken, 2009). International schools actively work to create, by design, environments to cultivate these benefits.

There are many types of international schools, with various curricula and governance. For the purposes of this study, we confined ourselves to international schools that are private, coeducational, board-governed, English-language, nonprofit institutions. Historically, international schools' primary function was to educate children of diplomats and other expatriates in a manner similar to that of their home countries. The concept of international schooling has changed over the past 50 years in ways that mirror global development. While international schools were once temporary educational clusters for children until they returned to their home countries, 21st-century international schools have evolved into distinct and integrated communities within a third culture. Corporations, NGOs, and even governments have become more mobile, and international schools reflect this change by becoming interconnected and global, yet still learning from and serving local communities. A new breed of international schools is emerging—schools not tied to a specific national culture, and where families stay for more than a few years. These schools must meet the needs of their new, interconnected, highly global, and outward-thinking communities (Hayden & Thompson, 2008). International schools equip students with mind-sets and tools to emerge as globally aware stewards of their planet.

Our goal in this chapter is to provide examples and adaptable strategies for school leaders to work toward changing traditional school culture in order to advance the key qualities of a 21st-century global education, which include being action-oriented, globally connected, and inclusive.

In this study, we draw from international schools that have adopted one of the International Baccalaureate (IB) programmes. While other models exist, our experiences have primarily been in IB programme schools and we feel schools can look to the IB for a foundation. IB programme curriculum frameworks are increasingly popular in both national-system and international schools (International Baccalaureate Organization, 2014a). Since 2008, the IB programme of Primary Years Programme (PYP), Middle Years Programme (MYP), and Diploma Programme (DP) have shown remarkable growth, with compound annual growth rates of 21 percent, 13 percent, and

8 percent respectively, indicating substantial uptake worldwide (International Baccalaureate Organization, 2014a).

The IB curriculum framework is organized into three stages: ages 4–10 (PYP), ages 11–15 (MYP), and ages 16–18 (DP). While the curriculum in each IB school is developed by teachers locally, all schools must meet common standards, including philosophy, terminology, curriculum structure, assessment practices, and more (International Baccalaureate 2014b). Frameworks consist of a selection of disciplines and conceptual understandings; external assessments exist in final years of MYP and DP.

As experienced international school teachers primarily working in IB framework schools, we feel the frameworks provide a strong foundation for schools to build upon. The mission of the International Baccalaureate (2014a) states,

> The International Baccalaureate aims to develop inquiring, knowledgeable and caring young people who help to create a better and more peaceful world through intercultural understanding and respect. To this end the organization works with schools, governments and international organizations to develop challenging programmes of international education and rigorous assessment. These programmes encourage students across the world to become active, compassionate and lifelong learners who understand that other people, with their differences, can also be right.

It is from this mission that we derive the ideal characteristics of global education: action-oriented, globally connected, and inclusive. When we speak of an "ideal school," it is an amalgamation of best practices we have witnessed or experienced in our careers at international schools. Our diverse experiences have exposed us to many different ways schools can use IB frameworks, and how nearly any school—IB or not, international or national—can adopt the three most promising qualities of 21st-century global education—*action-oriented, globally connected, and inclusive*. In the following space, we will describe the ideal of each quality in order to provide a goal for which school leaders can strive. Then, we will offer what we feel are key elements and strategies to implement each quality. Table 10.1 summarizes our approach.

ACTION-ORIENTED

In an ideal school, all learning directly leads to action. An action-oriented school empowers students and creates opportunities for them to be change-agents in the world. An ideal school allows students to develop solutions to problems and act on those solutions, knowing they will be supported in their efforts.

Table 10.1 Promising Qualities of 21st-Century Global Education

Quality	Key elements	Strategies
Action-oriented	Action and curricula	Consider concept-based learning
		Build action into the curriculum
	Service learning	Move from counting hours to reflection-based service learning
Globally connected	Cocurricular and extracurricular activities	Develop sports and arts networks
		Offer student leadership opportunities
	Globally connected	Use social media for global connection
		Use third-party network organizations
		Leverage mobile device use
	Networks	Tap into existing networks, conferences, and professional membership organizations
Inclusive	Mission-derived foundational statements	Create mission-derived foundational statements
	A learner profile	Develop a school-specific learner profile
	Diverse and globally connected curricula	Develop an inclusive and diverse curriculum
	Community learning	Invite parents into schools

Students feel what they learn will impact their lives and feel connected to their learning. Students feel learning is relevant in an ideal action-oriented school because the school encourages students to use skills and knowledge to make social change at local, national, or international levels. An ideal action-oriented school responds to student interests and allows students to take action in areas of personal passion. Inquiry-based and concept-based curricula allow students to connect learning to what is happening in their own lives (Erickson, 2007). The curriculum encourages students to take ownership of learning, while supporting students' development.

An ideal school presents numerous opportunities for students to take action outside the classroom. The emphasis is on creating opportunities for student action through service learning or extracurricular activities.

Moreover, an ideal school ensures students reflect on outside learning and how it impacts their action. As such, service is not reduced to counting hours, nor does club participation exist for résumé-building. Students feel empowered.

A school that does not encourage student action risks developing students who believe learning happens to them, rather than being something they actively participate in. It further risks developing students who believe that what they learn has no real-world application and implementing content-driven and inflexible learning.

Key Elements: Action and Curricula

All three IB frameworks include obligatory service and action components. PYP uses an Action Cycle (Choose—Act—Reflect), which encourages learners to see other perspectives and engage locally and globally (International Baccalaureate Organization, 2008c, p. 33). MYP currently contains a component called Community and Service, wherein learners participate in, act in, and reflect on service activities, preferably with academic links (International Baccalaureate Organization, 2008b, pp. 25–27). DP's Creativity, Action, Service requirement of the program requires students be involved in activities in both local and global contexts (International Baccalaureate Organization, 2008a).

Although all IB frameworks include service requirements, service is not explicitly addressed in subject learning outcomes, and as a result many schools link service to written curricula through a conceptual lens. For instance, math students might be asked to identify an issue of importance, collect and present data related to the issue, and then carry out action based on the data. Theory of Knowledge, a required cross-curricular core component of DP, focuses on the guiding question "How do we know?" (International Baccalaureate Organization, n.d.-b). Such a question prompts further questions, which helps students to achieve the course's primary goals, which are for students to be aware of themselves as thinkers and to recognize the need to act responsibly in an increasingly interconnected but uncertain world. Founded on the philosophy that "learning how to learn" is key to meaningful education, and that students must use what they learn to make up their own minds, the IB invites students to take ownership of learning and use it in developmentally appropriate ways (Fox, 1998, p. 66).

Interdisciplinary learning allows students to engage in curriculum-related action. At its best, the curriculum encourages students to make connections between subjects; this leads to finding connections elsewhere, which empowers students. In MYP, intentional opportunities exist for interdisciplinary links. For instance, following the triple disaster of March 11, 2011, nuclear power and energy sustainability became a major issue for students at Yokohama International School (YIS) in Japan. Grade 10 science students now study energy sources and take the information they learn to humanities class, where they create a real-life campaign advocating for sustainable energy sources for Yokohama. Students create an action plan—for example, a community awareness campaign, inviting experts to speak, or writing letters to newspapers. The IB challenges schools to create deep relationships between disciplinary learning, service, and action.

Strategy

Schools are often required to follow a state or national mandated curriculum. However, teaching any content through a conceptual lens helps students see how learning can be used to impact a community. We recommend schools shift toward a concept-based learning mind-set. Interdisciplinary links can help students understand the importance of required learning (Erickson, 2007). Moreover, linking community needs to a written curriculum can help students see relevance in learning.

Moving any school to action via a curriculum is an involved process. Students do not automatically begin saving the world once a global perspectives or IB course is implemented. Any school beginning this journey should start to create awareness of global issues and communities in both the explicit and implicit curriculum. This will lead to developing skills needed to act—when learning is truly authentic and applied. The final stage is to build the action component *into* the curriculum. The key strategy for school leaders adopting an action-oriented approach is to start small. For example, schools could build action into stand-alone courses or through project-based learning. Ambitious school leaders could even revamp the entire curriculum map with an emphasis on implementing action at different levels of the curriculum. In short, action-oriented schools make these skills, knowledge, and concepts part of instruction and assessment—not just a "thing we learn about" but a "thing we do" (M. Johnston, personal communication, November 20, 2013).

Key Element: Service Learning

International schools have a long tradition of providing service to local communities. In a 2008 survey of 64 international schools, 28.4 percent of schools mentioned civic engagement as part of their mission (Hayden, 2008, p. 55). Nine percent of schools in the same survey mentioned service as part of their mission. Some school models, such as that offered by the United World Colleges (UWC), have made service an intrinsic part of their mission and identity (UWC, 2014). Other schools that have adopted IB must commit to students doing service. Based on the UWC model, service in IB schools is not a "box-ticking" but seen as a sustained commitment to service learning (Jenkins, 1998, p. 99). While there is no single definition of service learning, Furco (1996) states,

21st-Century International Schools 161

> Service learning programs are distinguished from other approaches to experiential education by their intention to equally benefit the provider and the recipient of the service as well as to ensure equal focus on both the service being provided and the learning that is occurring.
>
> (p. 5)

Students become involved in reflective and experiential learning processes when service benefits both the community being served *and* the students engaged in the service.

IB programme schools find service learning central to the curriculum. For example, in DP's Creativity, Action, Service component, students reflect on experiential learning through the lenses of eight learning outcomes. Having completed service activities (e.g., a week-long house-building trip to Cambodia, or hosting a party for a local orphanage), students must show evidence they have met requirements such as increase awareness of their own strengths and areas for growth, and consider the ethical implications of their actions (International Baccalaureate, 2008a). Counting service hours does not demonstrate engagement. Likewise, fundraising is not the best use of student time and energy. Students cannot simply write letters on behalf of Amnesty International; they must show commitment to the cause. Students cannot raise funds for disaster relief without showing they have considered ethical implications. Students are prompted to think about how they are challenged as individuals.

All schools face challenges when introducing service learning. Schools in economically developed nations may recognize fewer opportunities for hands-on, sustained service. While students can benefit from foreign travel, short trips to provide service to an at-need population can often take on aspects of voluntourism (Raymond & Hall, 2008). Schools also must consider the host country's understanding of service. For instance, the English word *service*, サービス, connotes "complimentary" or "free" in Japanese; as such, it is imperative that schools and the local community understand international school students are not free labor (Jungnitsch, 2013).

Strategy

Service is commonly required for graduation or school completion. Schools can shift away from counting hours and move toward more reflective, action-oriented service learning. In our experience, prompting students to be reflective about their service leads them to be more thoughtful about costs and benefits of service. Introducing holistic assessments of the service benefits both students and service recipients.

Students do not need to travel to find service opportunities. Opportunities often exist for students to work in the local or school community; ask students to think about how these opportunities allow for change. If a school wants students to think globally, it may be important to help develop empathy for those in less developed nations. Schools should allow students to initiate their own service learning opportunities and should develop strategies for supporting them.

GLOBALLY CONNECTED

In an ideal globally connected school, students, parents, and teachers feel connected to learning, and recognize the student as an individual through selected sharing. An authentic audience engages with student work, providing feedback and growth opportunities. To be truly authentic, this includes collaborations with others around the world to learn from different perspectives and to build communication skills that transcend countries and cultures.

Ideally, connections also happen outside the classroom. Athletic and artistic events allow students in an ideal school to compete or collaborate within a regional network of like-sized schools, offering the experience of travel and forming bonds through interests with those who may not be an everyday part of their lives. Ideally, when moving from school to school, students feel connected to previous learning experiences via similar curricula and educational philosophies. Teachers also feel connected both within the community and beyond it, through face-to-face and electronic, distance learning opportunities.

Each aspect of this globally connected learning environment supports a deep understanding of the ways in which we communicate, collaborate, and create in today's society. Without these elements, we deprive students of opportunities to explore connected learning in ways that are developmentally appropriate and that enhance face-to-face experiences. Transferrable skills learned in a globally connected learning environment not only augment students' abilities to learn from a variety of experiences, but also prepare them for success in diverse future working environments.

A school that is not globally connected risks:

- Developing superficial relationships between teachers and students, rather than deep and guided relationships around students' interests and needs extending beyond school walls.
- Prioritizing a content-heavy curriculum rather than skills required for students to be leaders in local and global communities.
- Inadequately preparing students for inevitable diverse and connected environments of the future.

Key Element: Cocurricular and Extracurricular Activities

As with any school, many learning experiences happen outside the classroom. One of the three aims of the IB is "to improve and extend international education and so promote international understanding" (IBO, cited in McKenzie, 1998, p. 243). International schools capitalize on beyond-classroom learning opportunities via clubs, sports, and other extracurricular activities because students benefit from exposure to new cultures. One of the most commonly agreed upon characteristics of international school populations is "the strong probability that the cultural development of their pupils will be influenced by the culture of the host country as well as by the various cultures that they collectively represent" (Langford, 1998, p. 29).

One example of an international student community is the Global Issues Network (GIN) (http://global-issues-network.org), founded by teachers at the International School of Luxembourg. Secondary school teams empower students to solve problems facing local and global communities. Students meet at GIN conferences in places such as Kenya, Quito, Jakarta, and Singapore. Model United Nations (www.nmun.org) connects students to debate real and current global issues to learn conflict resolution, communication, problem-solving, and research skills. Students involved in GIN and Model United Nations have opportunities to travel and meet other like-minded, globally aware students, so as to authentically connect on current and future world issues. While Model United Nations is common in many national school systems, those participating in international schools often travel to different countries to participate in conferences, thus bringing the international element of the activity to life through travel and personal experience.

Athletics offer other ways to connect. Many third-culture kids use sports to quickly become part of a new community, as language is not a requisite for success on a playing field. Moreover, most student athletes travel. Munich International School sports teams, for instance, travel to other schools within Europe for weekend exchanges. All leagues place importance on experiencing the event's host country culture, so learning extends off the playing field. Some leagues, such as Interscholastic Association of Southeast Asian Schools, offer cultural exchanges where students share music, art, and writing inspired by their home nation. Another opportunity exists when international schools play local host country teams. For instance, Munich International School teams participate weekly in local league games (Sportverein), allowing students to engage with the local community and improve their foreign language skills.

Strategy

Sports and arts can advance student-student global connections in any school. Connections may start small, with students playing or performing with students at other schools. The essential element is the opportunity to connect beyond the immediate community; smaller successes can lead to development of larger networks over time.

Furthermore, any school can develop authentic student leadership opportunities. We strongly suggest all schools develop and implement traditional student council programs at all levels of primary and secondary school. These should be overseen by a teacher, but must be authentically organized and run by students. Moreover, we recommend additional student leadership opportunities. External organizations can also help facilitate student leadership opportunities. Organizations such as MOUSEsquad (www.mousesquad.org) and GlobalKids (www.globalkids.org) offer structures for activities in public American schools. In the UK, similar programs exist—for example, UK Youth (www.ukyouth.org) and the ever-popular Duke of Edinburgh's International Award (www.intaward.org).

Key Element: Globally Connected Infrastructure

One high-priority aspect of international schools is connecting to share learning. As a result, several international schools have developed 1:1 device programs, placing emphasis on connected learning. These device programs include high-quality network infrastructure, technological availability of equipment (e.g., one laptop per student), and a school-wide focus on sharing learning with wider audiences. Connected infrastructure is an essential element outlined in the IB Programme Standards and Practices (International Baccalaureate Organization, 2014b).

Yokohama International School (YIS) is an example of a globally connected school, as evident in its Connected Learning Community vision statement:

> Our Connected Learning Community leverages advanced technologies and progressive teaching approaches to enhance student learning, promote collaboration and facilitate the creation and sharing of knowledge locally and globally.
>
> (Yokohama International School, n.d.)

This vision is abundantly evident at YIS, from publicly accessible student and teacher blogs school-wide to Web 2.0 platforms where teachers connect with students—Facebook, Google+, and more. From this network, students and teachers also make global connections through collaborative blogging, partnering for exhibition reflections, collaborative book authoring in primary school, and Skyping with authors in DP language and literature classes.

From hardware to curricula, many international schools make learning a globally connected experience, taking advantage of student diversity and highlighting connections with peers and others worldwide.

Strategy

We recommend schools place value on using social media to connect with people globally, regardless of school location. Students and teachers can develop relationships in multiple contexts and participate in global conversations about learning.

Schools might consider utilizing programs like iEARN (www.iearn.org), which began long before digital technology became ubiquitous, and continues to connect schools with those in areas without technology access:

> In just twelve years of operation, iEARN has linked schools from Tucson, Arizona, to Paramaribo, Suriname, to Novosibirsk, Russia. iEARN works with approximately 350,000 students at 4,000 schools in more than ninety countries; twenty-nine languages are represented. Global projects are based on interactive discussions, in which students and teachers debate, research, and share opinions.
> (Gragert, 2007, para. 6)

Technology does not need to be a limiting factor; the idea is to connect with others. Examples of iEARN-facilitated collaborations between American and local schools around the world can be found on the Chris Stevens Youth Network (About, n.d.). One such example is a collection of projects featuring student female empowerment, under the umbrella of Girls Rising to the Challenge of Collaborative Action (see http://iearnusa.wordpress.com/2013/06/12/girls-rising-to-the-challenge-of-collaborative-action/ for more on this particular project).

We recommend schools allow and encourage students to use mobile devices for learning. Schools can work with nonprofit organizations to leverage available devices, and take advantage of free, cloud-based tools rather than pay licensing fees (e.g., Google Apps for Education). This approach requires a shift in mind-set about technology in schools, particularly regarding filters, blocking, and restricting content. While we understand the limitation and challenges associated with using technology to build global connections, we advise schools to devise media and access policies that allow students and teachers the opportunities to use technology when available to learn about the world, its people, and issues.

Again, we advise school leaders to start small. Being globally connected need not begin with a global collaboration project. It begins with simple connections, such as students and teachers in the same school benefiting from using collaborative tools together. Connecting at the class level is the first step.

Key Element: Networks

International school teachers tend to be a connected network of individuals, despite geographic separation. Educators might work in several countries together over their careers or meet at conferences in different regions with former colleagues. This often creates close-knit (even if physically distant) networks that connect educators throughout their careers. The network transfers to each school, creating globally minded physical and mental spaces for learning where even a standard faculty meeting is an opportunity to learn new perspectives about pedagogy.

Regional organizations on most continents further connect international school communities. For example, the East Asia Regional Council of Overseas Schools (EARCOS) connects schools in East Asia. These organizations provide professional development, like annual conferences, weekend workshops, and organizational support for projects like action research. From specialized events, like the intimate YIS-hosted #beyondlaptops conference, to rotational conferences, like Asia's Learning 2.0, to regional events, like the annual EARCOS Teachers Conference, educators regularly gather to share ideas, learn, and stretch their thinking. The international school community is a professional learning network.

Even with these regular opportunities, international educators' professional growth does not begin and end with conferences. Well-connected local communities, like Tech Pilots at YIS or Tech Mentors at UWCSEA, allow teachers to connect regularly in person and via social media. Shared Twitter and Flickr hashtags help educators share year-round, along with school- and event-specific hashtags representing distinct learning communities, like #yispd, #uwcsea_east, and #learning2.

Strategy

Schools can implement networked learning for students and teachers by having students collaborate with peer reviews, comment on blog posts, or create multimedia with students from partner schools. Teachers in any school can utilize available technologies—for example, Twitter hashtags like #mathchat, #sschat, and #kinderchat. Teachers can take advantage of organizations like the National Council of Teachers of Mathematics and National Board Certification to connect with like-minded teachers. Conferences, particularly those more personal like EdCamp, Ignite, and TEDx, are also opportunities to connect in a local region.

INCLUSIVE

In an ideal inclusive school, all members are welcome, regardless of ethnicity, race, creed, orientation, or socioeconomic background, and the school meets all student needs via whatever means necessary. Social isolation and bullying are relatively rare in an ideal inclusive school, as new community members become part of the fabric of the school in very short time frames. To achieve such an environment, a school needs to meet as many student—and human—needs as possible. Maslow's (1943) hierarchy of needs lists five levels of human needs that drive motivation. If we assume that a child's parents or guardians provide the most basic level (physiological), then a school should aim to provide the next three—safety, love and belonging, and esteem—as well as laying the groundwork for students to reach the final level, that of self-actualization. A truly inclusive school will actively aim to meet all of these needs within the context of learning and growth. How does a school cultivate a culture of sweeping acceptance and inclusivity—one where every community member is equal, equitable, and valued—despite societal norms, pressures, and hierarchies? Although we acknowledge that many potential obstacles exist, our experiences in international schools indicate that implementing the following key elements *can* make a significant change in how a school culture moves to become more inclusive. Further, we believe any school can become more inclusive by giving value to these elements, and we advocate that even the smallest growth in this direction is positive growth. Most importantly, an ideal inclusive school truly exists only when all community members believe in the value of creating such a place.

A school not committed to being inclusive risks:

- Choosing a content-based curriculum rather than a curriculum supporting the whole child (ASCD, 2012; Forbes, 1996).
- Becoming a community with no common beliefs to guide behavior and action.
- Instruction without differentiation based on readiness, interests, and learning profiles (Tomlinson, 1999).
- Disconnected parent-teacher relationships.

Key Element: Mission-Derived Foundational Statements

A common thread in the most effective international schools we have encountered is that they have mission-derived values and attitudes built into the core of their learning programs. The school community, guided through a process by a leadership team or committee, has developed school mission, vision, and values statements—sometimes referred to as *foundational statements*—directing the ethos of the school. Foundational statements guide decisions, actions, and initiatives for all parts of the school, and are consciously referenced in activities such as department meetings, athletic ceremonies, and newsletters. Focusing on foundational statements, schools can hire people who fit the community. Further, the mission shapes the curriculum and assessment, and students entering the school know the vision.

The IB's mission statement can be a starting place for schools because it encapsulates what many idealistic educators aspire to: "to develop inquiring, knowledgeable and caring young people who help to create a better and more peaceful world through intercultural understanding and respect" (International Baccalaureate Organization, 2014a). Schools running any IB programme must have IB-aligned mission and philosophy statements (International Baccalaureate Organization, 2014b, p. 3).

Strategy

Any school can create inclusive, mission-derived foundational statements. The first step is for leaders to ask: *Does our mission allow all students to access curricular and other programs? Does our mission communicate what we believe about learning? Does our mission welcome and encourage differentiated experiences?* These questions will guide the community through a process of (re)shaping the school's mission and developing foundational statements—representing vision, values, and attitudes—which will further articulate how the school's mission will live and breathe.

The process of developing a mission and foundational statements is arduous work. From experience, we estimate such a process takes between 2–4 years to authentically complete in any sized school. Leaders may find useful resources regarding this particular element in our bibliography; in particular we recommend John Adair's (2011) work on strategic leadership, Robert Evan's chapter on vision building (1996, pp. 206–228), and Zmuda, Kuklis, and Kline's chapter on establishing shared vision (2004, pp. 57–86).

Key Element: A Learner Profile

Once a school has foundational statements, it should ask: *What kinds of people do we want our students to be?* This question assumes the school subscribes to a community-of-learners philosophy (Rogoff, 1994) rather than viewing learning as transmission or acquisition. Thus, answers to the foregoing question will invariably include descriptors and outcomes aimed to unite a community, and will lead to a learner profile. A learner profile serves as a guide and a motivator, and helps focus all learning and behaviors within the school.

The IB offers a learner profile to help schools answer the foregoing question, and to help teachers frame learning experiences for students (International Baccalaureate, n.d.-c). The IB Learner Profile lists attributes students aim to embody: inquirers, knowledgeable, thinkers, communicators, principled, open-minded, caring, risk-takers, balanced, and reflective. Because these attributes grow out of the IB's mission, they should be reflected in all aspects of a school, including students' contributions. For example, students may be asked to reflect on how to cultivate these attributes while participating in school trips. Teachers also create opportunities for Learner Profile attribute development in subject areas, such as a YIS project involving the creation of anti-bullying ads in a Design Technology class. While the project addresses curriculum needs, teachers designed it to cultivate student habits of being caring, principled communicators.

Strategy

Any school can develop its own learner profile with mission-derived attributes. Doing so supports student development where all adults are stakeholders in developing learners as people. When a school develops a learner profile including attributes such as "caring" or "empathy," it reinforces inclusivity of the learning community. Other attributes might indicate that a school values critical or innovative thinking, two types of non-traditional thinking. Such descriptors are also curriculum indicators, pointing toward ways to authentically cultivate these attributes.

Key Element: A Diverse and Globally Focused Curriculum

The most responsive international schools recognize that they serve a diverse community and foster inclusivity via a curriculum. To serve a diverse school community, a curriculum must address values such as service, multiculturalism, collaboration, problem-solving, and creativity. Embedding these values into learning outcomes is ideal, although challenging. However, to *not* embed inclusive values into a curriculum is a disservice to such a school community.

IB frameworks offer much for an inclusive curriculum, as they require schools to develop an inherently inclusive curriculum. Firstly, all IB frameworks are holistic; they address traditional disciplines and give equal value to each. Further, as teachers in all programmes develop a written curriculum, they must include content and skills that address a variety of cultural contexts. For example, DP students are required to study language and literature, which includes literature in translation. In DP Individuals and Societies, a syllabus must include content on global development and/or non-Western countries. Lastly, language acquisition and development for both mother-tongue and additional languages are a high priority in IB programmes. In MYP and DP, additional language study is required, resulting in learning that reflects cultural and language-systems diversity.

Regarding special educational needs, PYP and MYP commend inclusion and actively advocate equal access via differentiated instruction and assessment (International Baccalaureate, 2008c). However, within DP, special educational needs become challenging. In theory, many needs can be accommodated, even in exams (International Baccalaureate, 2007). In practice we have seen few schools go through the onerous process of applying for arrangements for students with special needs. Indeed, international schools can learn from national schools regarding special educational needs and inclusion. Publicly funded schools in many countries are required to accept every child within a certain catchment area; international schools are not.

The new IB career-related certificate (www.ibo.org/ibcc) may address access issues in grades 11 and 12, but currently few international schools offer it. As such, the issue remains that inclusion of all learning needs is a prickly one at the DP level.

Strategy

Any school can create an inclusive curriculum. While IB frameworks can assist, they are not the only means to make learning accessible to all. Some international schools have chosen to step outside national and IB frameworks in order to develop their own curriculum. UWCSEA has done this at primary and middle school levels to accommodate heavy growth in service learning and outdoor education, and the International School of Brussels in Belgium has developed its own conceptual curriculum (International School of Brussels, n.d.). At minimum, we suggest schools include the following:

- A broad, well-balanced, and holistic curriculum.
- Curriculum content from a variety of cultural backgrounds, contexts, and experiences.
- Required language learning as part of the curriculum, including equal support for both mother-tongue and additional languages; we further recommend schools develop inclusive language policies.
- Differentiation policies and practices that give all learners access to a taught and assessed curriculum.

These items affirm student identity, and indicate value of all community members' experiences.

Key Element: Community Learning

A school as a community-of-learners (Rogoff, 1994) is more than a knowledge institution. International schools are often "community-of-learners" schools, which include students, teachers, and parents as learners and contributors, because

> it is a community working together with all serving as resources to the others, with varying roles according to their understanding of the activity at hand and differing responsibilities in the system.
> (Rogoff, 1994, p. 214)

It is this kind of reciprocal relationship that defines a school's community learning. Because international schools are often the sole community for expatriate families, they become hubs for community events. This often leads to high parent engagement, allowing community growth around service, the curriculum, and the host country culture. Moreover, parents regularly participate in learning opportunities, including events to help understand the curriculum, learning environments, or school structure. For example, YIS and UWCSEA regularly offer Parent Technology and Learning Coffee Mornings to help parents understand the nature of learning in a connected learning community or 1:1 laptop environment.

Parents also often collaborate on school-wide decisions. For example, parents and students at YIS helped develop the Vision and Mission Statement, as well as the Responsible Use Agreement for technology, as part of its Connected Learning Community vision statement. Community members value giving input about important issues where they can share ideas. International school parents are often members of the Board of Directors, responsible for managing the school, particularly the budget and the head of the school. These parent involvement examples add value to the school when it is open-minded enough to include all stakeholders in decision-making.

Strategy

We strongly recommend inviting parents into schools often, with the goal of creating a learning community. First, extend invitations for information sessions on the curriculum, extracurricular activities, or assessment. Once a "parents-as-learners" culture is established, take the next step: invite parent feedback on school decisions. Start small; collecting feedback on canteen lunch options invites less conflict than collecting feedback on school technology policies. Communication is key in these interactions—it must be respectful, professional, and empathetic. School leaders and teachers must genuinely want to build bridges, as parents must feel the school is taking active steps toward making them valuable contributors. We suggest this be a dedicated part of a 2–4-year strategic plan. The end result is a school functioning as a truly inclusive learning space for the entire community.

CONCLUSION

We have shown how international schools embody qualities essential to global education in the 21st century: being action-oriented, globally connected, and inclusive. The IB provides a starting place for cultivating many of these qualities. However, international schools often customize IB provisions for their own settings and needs; we strongly recommend national schools do this too.

An important ingredient of all of these systems is the willingness to be flexible when and where needed. Due to the constant influx of new families in their communities, international schools are typically understanding and appreciative of the need to stay open-minded about systems that no longer positively influence learning. All schools, regardless of location, can benefit from open-minded approaches to learning, particularly in our rapidly changing world. We have offered examples from various international school contexts that we believe have wide application. We hope our suggested tools and structures might be adapted and developed for use in *any* school context in order to influence school culture to be more inclusive, globally minded, and, ultimately, more action-oriented.

REFERENCES

About the Chris Stevens Youth Network. (n.d.). Retrieved June 4, 2014, from http://exchange.csyn.org/about/

Adair, J. (2011). *Strategic leadership: How to think and plan strategically and provide direction*. London: Kogan Page.

ASCD. (2012). *Making the case for educating the whole child.* Alexandria, VA: ASCD.
Erickson, H. L. (2007). *Concept-based curriculum and instruction for the thinking classroom.* Thousand Oaks, CA: Corwin Press.
Evans, R. (1996). *The human side of school change: Reform, resistance, and the real-life problems of innovation.* San Francisco: Jossey-Bass.
Forbes, S. H. (1996). Values in holistic education. Paper presented at the Third Annual Conference on Education, Spirituality, and the Whole Child. Roehampton Institute, London.
Fox, E. (1998). The IB as an impetus for curriculum reform. In M. Hayden & J. Thompson (Eds.), *International education: Principles and practice* (pp. 65–76). London: Kogan Page.
Furco, A. (1996). Service-learning: A balanced approach to experiential education. In J. Raybuck (Ed.), *Expanding boundaries: Serving and learning* (pp. 1–6). Washington, DC: Corporation for National Service.
Gragert, E. H. (2007). It takes many villages to make a world: The international education and resource network (iEARN). Retrieved June 4, 2014, from www.edutopia.org/international-education-resource-network
Hayden, M. (2006). *Introduction to international education.* London: SAGE.
Hayden, M., & Thompson, J. (2008). *International schools: Growth and influence.* (Fundamentals of Educational Planning Booklet). Paris: United Nations Education, Scientific, and Cultural Organization.
Hayden, M. J. (2008). *Mission statement possible: What do international schools' mission statements reveal about their cosmopolitan education tendencies?* Unpublished MA thesis. Columbia University.
Hill Useem, R. (1999). Third culture kids: Focus of major study—TCK "mother" pens history of field. Retrieved from www.tckworld.com/useem/art1.html
International Baccalaureate Organization. (n.d.-a). Diploma programme curriculum—Core requirements. Retrieved from www.ibo.org/diploma/curriculum/core/
International Baccalaureate Organization. (n.d.-b). Diploma programme curriculum—Core requirements: Theory of knowledge. Retrieved from www.ibo.org/diploma/curriculum/core/knowledge/
International Baccalaureate Organization. (n.d.-c). IB learner profile. Retrieved from www.ibo.org/programmes/profile/
International Baccalaureate Organization. (2007). *Diploma programme: Candidates with special assessment needs.* Cardiff, UK: International Baccalaureate.
International Baccalaureate Organization. (2008a). *Creativity, action, service guide.* Cardiff, UK: International Baccalaureate.
International Baccalaureate Organization. (2008b). *MYP: From principles into practice.* Cardiff, UK: International Baccalaureate.
International Baccalaureate Organization. (2008c). *Towards a continuum of international education.* Cardiff, UK: International Baccalaureate.
International Baccalaureate Organization. (2014a). IB fast facts. Retrieved from www.ibo.org/facts/fastfacts/index.cfm
International Baccalaureate Organization. (2014b). *Programme standards and practices.* Cardiff, UK: International Baccalaureate.
The International School of Brussels. (n.d.). Curriculum: Where did the curriculum at ISB "come from"? Retrieved from www.isb.be/page.cfm?p=429
Jenkins, C. (1998). Global issues: A necessary component of a balanced curriculum for the 21st century. In M. Hayden, & J. Thompson (Eds.), *International education: Principles and practice* (pp. 92–102). London: Kogan Page.
Jungnitsch, M. (2013). Service learning sinks in. Retrieved from www.coetail.com/jungnitschm/2013/11/19/service-learning-sinks-in/

Langford, M. (1998). Global nomads, third culture kids, and international schools. In M. Hayden & J. Thompson (Eds.), *International education: Principles and practice.* (pp. 28–43). London: Kogan Page.
Maslow, A. H. (1943). A theory of human motivation. *Psychological Review, 50*(4), 370–396.
McKenzie, M. (1998). Going, going, gone ... global! In M. Hayden, & J. Thompson (Eds.), *International education: Principles and practice* (pp. 242–252). London: Kogan Page.
Pollack, D. C., & Van Reken, R. E. (2009). *Third culture kids: Growing up among worlds.* Boston: Nicholas Brealey.
Raymond, E. M., & Hall, C. M. (2008). The development of cross-cultural (mis)understanding through volunteer tourism. *Journal of Sustainable Tourism, 16*(5), 530–543.
Rogoff, B. (1994). Developing understanding of the idea of communities of learners. *Mind, Culture, and Activity, 1,* 209–229.
Tomlinson, C. A. (1999). *The differentiated classroom: Responding to the needs of all learners.* Alexandria, VA: ASCD.
UWC. (2014). Community service. Retrieved from www.uwc.org/uwc_education/community_service.aspx
Yokohama International School. (n.d.). Connected learning community vision. Retrieved from www.yis.ac.jp/page.cfm?p=1824
Zmuda, A., Kuklis, R., & Kline, E. (2004). *Transforming schools: Creating a culture of continuous improvement.* Alexandria, VA: ASCD.

11 A Values-Based Pedagogical Stance
Teaching Teachers for Global Education in Australia

Ruth Reynolds, Debbie Bradbery, Joanna Brown, Debra Donnelly, Kate Ferguson-Patrick, Suzanne Macqueen, and Anne Ross

This chapter builds on and contributes to the scholarship addressing global education pedagogies across a range of contexts. Although many others have provided definitions of global education and acknowledge the confusions around this notion (Carano, 2013; Cogan & Grossman, 2009; Kirkwood-Tucker, 2009; Oxfam, 2006; Tye, 2009) we moved from being transfixed by problems of definition to refocus on implementation of global education. By analyzing teacher educators' and preservice teachers' perspectives on effective global education instruction, we developed a model of values-based global education pedagogy. Besides providing a practice-based roadmap for global education teaching, this approach provided insight into how practitioners define global education and helped resolve some of the tensions in the field by clarifying the importance of *stance* in this area of study.

GLOBAL EDUCATION REDEFINED

There are a myriad of ideas about what global education (GE) should be and what purpose it serves (Wang, Lin, Spalding, Odell, & Klecka, 2011; Zong, Wilson, & Quashiga, 2008). A key division in thinking about GE is between globally competitive education and education for living in a global world. The first definition alludes to how we educate students to be globally mobile, to compete with others on a global scale, to consider how education is a global imperative economically, culturally, ecologically, and politically, enabling nations and corporations to exploit others and take advantage of these global opportunities (Apple, Kenway, & Singh, 2005; Ball, 2012). As Zhao (2012) argues, this can homogenize and narrow the curriculum to a set of standards able to be tested and compared internationally. The second definition stresses that 21st-century students need to be interconnected and interdependent to address global issues that have arisen particularly as a result of global capitalism and globalization, such as human rights abuses

(Abdullahi, 2011; Cogan & Grossman, 2009). It focuses on grappling with issues of learning to live together (Starkey, 2012). This latter focus can lead to a critical global curriculum and a reflective ethical pedagogy that deals with issues beyond the nation-state, examines power and privilege, and values marginalized knowledge, such as third-world and Indigenous traditions and perspectives (Merryfield, 2002, 2009; Myers, 2010). Both conceptions can operate in a global education program—it is the associated values that direct the learning.

METHODOLOGY

The Global Education Research and Teaching (GERT) team is a collective of like-minded teacher educators at a regional university in Australia who formed GERT as a mutually supportive research and teaching group. We were drawn to work together by shared values around the ideals of global education (Bradbery et al., 2013), aligning with the second definition of GE, with hope of affecting the first, thus collaborating to advance a form of global education with inclusivity, humanitarianism, and global-mindedness at its core. The aim was to further our own knowledge and skills related to global education through discussion, professional learning, and research, and to concurrently inspire our university students (all future teachers) in promoting GE values and practices. As such, we recognized the need to document and research our emerging practices and understandings, as well as their effectiveness for our preservice teachers. We developed a research program in 2010 that is still ongoing.

This chapter reports results from the qualitative portion of a larger research study. Our larger study followed an action-research design to study the process of incorporating global education (GE) into our university teaching. The present study incorporated two sources of qualitative data: researchers' reflective diary comments and preservice teachers' survey comments and attitudes scale data. We used the collected data to reflect upon and influence our teaching practices (Elliott, 1991). Twice yearly for the first two years of the project, GERT members (n=7) recorded diary entries that reflected on our developing understandings and changing practices related to GE. The research and teaching agenda became an integral part of our collaborative team. Details of courses incorporating GE, *which* GE perspectives were included in each course, and *how* those perspectives were incorporated into each course were documented to ensure continuity of the student learning experience over time.

For our second data source, we surveyed preservice teachers in GE-focused courses. These courses represented a cross-section of key learning areas in the preservice teacher education program in which particular values were being explicitly taught and integrated with the content of the course. These courses included the following: elementary courses in social studies pedagogy, English pedagogy, mathematics pedagogy, integrated curriculum studies, behavior management, and secondary school history, geography, and general social studies education; and professional experience/school-based practicum courses for both elementary and secondary students. The survey was completed by 939 students in 12 courses on four occasions over a two-year period. The survey was designed to ascertain the following: students' developing knowledge about and attitudes toward GE, their definitions of GE, how they rated the importance of GE to their teacher education programs, which strategies were effective in promoting GE in their classes, and which aspects of GE they wanted to learn more about. Students' rating of the importance of GE according to a series of Likert scales was analyzed using the Statistics Package for the Social Sciences (SPSS) statistical analysis program. Students rated the importance of GE to their course/program using a scale where 1 = very little, through to 5 = very high. Means for each course were calculated. Qualitative responses in the surveys and reflective diaries were coded according to evident themes using NVivo. A preliminary exploratory analysis (Creswell, 2012) enabled us to consider the general sense of the data and consider how to organize this initial examination. Themes around education *for*, *in*, and *with* GE were identified. Two researchers worked separately and then together to identify the themes in the qualitative data, and then compared and negotiated interpretations until a mutual understanding around the parameters of the themes was reached.

A VALUES-BASED PEDAGOGY

Global education implies certain values; these values imply certain pedagogies and these pedagogies and values become what we call a "global stance." Teachers of global education help students find ways of living together satisfactorily in a world more varied and less certain than our own or previous generations have known. GE teachers usually have a passion and strong beliefs about what they are doing, and a futures orientation. It is obvious by the manner in which the GERT members approach their teaching that we are taking a particular GE stance, one that emphasizes living with others in a global world. Taking a global stance can be understood in terms of Rosenblatt's (2004) transactional theory, which is when "the reader adopts a selective attitude or stance, bringing certain aspects into the center of attention and pushing others into the fringes of consciousness" (p. 1372). As we became more conversant with GE, we took a stance—we viewed the curriculum through the lens of this stance, choosing particular pedagogies to support our values and promote global education to our preservice teachers; we have a view reflected in "ways we stand, the ways we see, and the lenses we see through" (Cochran-Smith & Lytle, 1999, p. 288). We could say that *stance* guides "the 'choosing activity' in the stream of consciousness" (Rosenblatt, 2004, p. 1372). Vinterek (2010) refers to this in relation to her notion of a "democracy stance" in classroom pedagogy, noting that "different stances also call for different actions. In practice, different stances will be revealed in different actions" (p. 369). It can thus be asserted that taking a global stance means the GERT team views the world through a particular global lens and we assume particular values (and enact particular strategies) as both a cause and a result of this lens.

There is a considerable body of research that demonstrates a strong correlation between teachers' knowledge, beliefs, and attitudes and their classroom practices, even if the precise mechanisms of such linkages are unclear (Sato & Kleinsasser, 2004). Current issues of schooling, such as bullying and racism (Applebaum, 2005), teaching diverse groups, exploring spirituality, and simply engaging in collaborative conversations, are all related to the teaching of values in some way. Debate continues about how to teach values (sometimes called character education; Lickona, 1997) and even whether the task should be undertaken by teachers (Department of Education, Science and Training [DEST], 2005; Lovat, Dally, Clement, & Toomey, 2011), but in GERT we have identified values as strong driving forces to our pedagogy and they could not be ignored.

The National Framework for Values in Australian Schools (DEST, 2005) gave GERT a framework, sanctioned by the government, to which we could relate our GE-focused teachings. The need for a common language to identify, examine, and encourage values such as caring, tolerance, and understanding (Anders, Moni, & Gitsaki, 2008) is apparent when teaching students to learn *for* a global world, where they will need to learn to live *with* others. In the Australian context there has been an upsurge of interest in exploring the teaching of values, with the *National Framework for Values Education in Australian Schools* (DEST, 2005) and *Global Perspectives: A Framework for Global Education in Australian Schools* (Curriculum Corporation, 2008) focusing on values such as "fair go" (a very Australian value, meaning social justice and equal opportunity); care and compassion; responsibility; understanding, tolerance, and inclusion; and respect for freedom, rights, and justice.

Internationally there has emerged a commonality of language surrounding key values for schooling and a commonality of best strategies to teach global values (Bliss, 2005; Merryfield & Wilson, 2005). These common best teaching strategies are: explicit teaching of key values and key values terminology; establishing a caring classroom and school community; modeling key globally acknowledged values; developing skills to discern different perspectives and values associated with key societal issues, often controversial (Holden, 2007); and clarifying and discussing them (Reynolds, 2012). Global education teaching can elicit traits, often referred to as character strengths or core values, including hope, happiness, optimism, and persistence (Peterson & Seligman, 2004). Lombardo (2007) argued that optimism and wisdom are primary traits that need to be nurtured so that individuals feel empowered to act in positive ways. However, it can also be argued that other traits, such as curiosity, initiative, persistence, and resilience, are equally important. Teaching through global education gives educators the opportunity to explicitly teach these global ways of acting, being, and feeling. As Noddings (2002) asserted, assisting people to act in caring and compassionate ways is the moral imperative of educators if the values of responsibility and respect for the earth and its people are to be encouraged. A GE stance implies the teaching and the living of particular values, and these values include teaching *about*, *for*, and *with* the world and its people.

OUR CONCEPTION OF A GLOBAL STANCE

All GERT members held firm beliefs on the importance of GE in teacher education, as evidenced by comments from early diary entries. GERT members had joined the group because of their passion for "peace and human rights education, a. . . commitment to human rights, education, and world peace," and a belief "that it's important to all, and that it is. . . good for students to consider the big picture rather than being totally egocentric." In early group discussions around GE values, it became clear that GERT members all subscribed to values related to equality, social justice, diversity, cooperation, care for others and the environment, diversity and difference, tolerance and inclusion, and respect for all people.

These values were then reflected in the pedagogies we employed when incorporating GE in our teacher education courses, and this in turn affected preservice teacher application in school classrooms, which in turn influenced the teacher educators. We conceived of a process that seemed to represent the impact of global education values and pedagogy on each other in the teaching cycle (Figure 11.1).

We thus acknowledged that global education is an evolving and conceptually complex phenomenon, deserving of multiple iterations. The GERT understanding is one where GE is couched in a culture of respectful dialogue and cooperation. This involves facilitating the development of critical, reflective thinking, problem solving, and communication skills—tools for effective global citizenry. This dialogic cooperative approach incorporates cultural, ethical, racial, and linguistic diversity in conversations between people as they engage meaningfully and inclusively to create sustainable futures at societal, cultural, environmental, and community levels. GERT is concerned that inclusive practices, alongside personal values and attributes such as honesty, resilience, and respect for others (Ministerial Council on Education Employment Training & Youth Affairs [MCEETYA], 2008), underpin our work. The intention of our work is from the perspective of open-minded learners and teachers personally transforming (Mimoun-Sorel, 2009) as we focus on teaching and learning *about*, *for*, and *with* a global world. Our definition thus comes from the stance of our day-to-day practice in teaching global education, a stance centered on values.

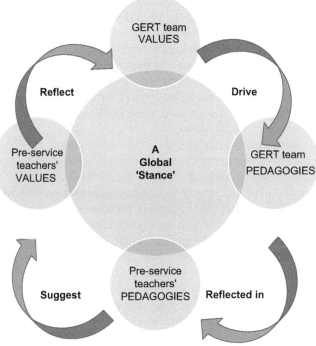

Figure 11.1 Interactive Process of Developing a Global Stance

One of the earliest definitive models of environmental education (EE), that of Lucas (1972), who proposed that we teach *about, for,* and *in,* is a useful conceptual frame for understanding best practice pedagogies for global education. This GERT-modified conceptual frame has sustainable futures embedded within it, in addition to other emphases dependent on sustainability, such as social justice and conflict resolution. Teaching and learning *about* involve the teaching of concepts—the provision of information and the teaching of appropriate technical and intellectual skills (Linke, 1980). Teaching and learning *for* involve the development of an interest in and concern for the concepts and ideas that engender positive attitudes and values (Linke, 1980) coupled with behavioral changes. Focusing teaching and learning *for* a global world encourages teachers to use pedagogies of inquiry (Crick, 2009), where students are encouraged to develop feelings of curiosity, initiative, persistence, and resilience. Lucas also proposed teaching and learning *in* as a way of describing education conducted outside the confines of the traditional educational setting. Teaching and learning *in* characterize a particular pedagogical technique that can lead to action learning, which in itself engenders a focus on values education. Actions and reflection on these actions enhance and challenge prior attitudes to ideas and concepts, such as those evident in environmental education and sustainability

(Kusmawan, O'Toole, Reynolds, & Bourke, 2009). While *in* seems appropriate for environmental education, the GERT team came to consider that an action learning approach enacting a strong values component would be teaching and learning *with*. Dialoguing *with* others in a cooperative manner and sharing *with* other peoples or experiences are a stronger pedagogy for global education. Thus teaching and learning *about, for*, and *with* a global world are aimed at changing behavior through a holistic approach connected with a futures dimension, using both the cognitive and affective domains of learning (Hicks, 2006).

Global education as a relatively new, non-academic outcome within schooling systems (like environment education in the second half of the 20th century) shares many "fringe dweller" commonalities with environmental education, particularly its strong values-based component (Ladwig, 2010). Although some argue that the slogan-like positioning of *about, in*, and particularly *for* environmental education has not captured the full range of possible educational approaches, the empowerment and sociopolitical inquiry generated by the use of such simple refrains has been acknowledged (Jickling & Spork, 1998) and gives confidence in the transference of a similar stance to global education. This values-based pedagogy, focusing on teacher educators' and their students' personal and collective values, attitudes, and beliefs, affects change at the cognitive, attitudinal, and behavioral level as they learn *about, for*, and *with* a global world—it elucidates a global stance.

LEARNING *ABOUT* GLOBAL EDUCATION

It is important that society develops understandings about global education and its associated pedagogies—that we *learn about* GE. This is about learning to know and learning to do in a global world (Delors et al., 1999). Quantitative data analysis reported in an earlier GERT-authored paper established that preservice teachers saw GE as important, and their ratings of this importance increased as they were exposed over time to GE ideas as they progressed through their various teacher education programs (Ferguson-Patrick, Macqueen, & Reynolds, 2014). A student summarized her understandings of the importance of learning about GE: "Global education builds awareness and tolerance that would enable students to cooperate and share and communicate about global issues from different perspectives."

Differences in ratings of importance of GE varied significantly among students enrolled in different specialist courses and courses positioned early or late in the degree program, signifying varied emphasis and exposure to GE concepts (Ferguson-Patrick, Macqueen, & Reynolds, 2012). For example, secondary (high school) geography students rated the importance of GE significantly higher (mean=4.84 [rating on scale of 1–5]) than students in first- or second-year primary (elementary) courses (mean=3.65, 3.72). Students in a third-year primary course about inclusive practices also rated the importance of GE significantly higher (mean=4.46) than students in first- and second-year primary English (mean=3.65) and classroom management courses (mean=3.72).

For learning *about* a global world, teacher educators saw links to particular pedagogical strategies. For example, the inquiry process—when students take a great deal of control over their own learning and construct their own knowledge, incorporating new knowledge into preestablished constructs (Reynolds, 2012)—is seen as crucial when teaching children topics related to other cultures/countries and diversity, sustainability, global issues, human rights, and social justice. This inquiry process allows students the freedom to pursue a variety of issues, problems, or themes, with the values guiding the topic choice. Thus there are a number of topics associated with global education that can illustrate positive and negative examples of a "fair go," for example. In the current Australian context, refugee rights feature largely as illustrative of perspectives on this value. GERT members report having used strategies such as inquiry-based instruction, visual literacy, jigsaw groups, role play, hands-on learning, such as artifact examination and games, simulation, ICT, and the inclusion of big-picture and often controversial issues. These strategies reflect values of tolerance, understanding, social justice (fair go), democracy, diversity, and difference.

When analyzing data *about* GE, preservice teacher education students noted the importance of particular pedagogical strategies. They favored strategies that will facilitate inclusive classrooms, where "we include all people and cultures to create a greater understanding of each other, that teachers and students should... be respectful and inclusive of all cultures," in classrooms "that promote risk taking and are judgement-free."

LEARNING *FOR* GLOBAL EDUCATION

Learning *for* GE requires developing skills and knowledge to help us learn to live together. The GERT team listed global education pedagogical approaches that encourage participation *for* all and student-centered learning to help us learn *for* GE. Reflecting this, GERT members report using pedagogies where communication and thinking skills were fundamental. Examples include: cooperative learning and other group work, critical literacy, Thinkers' Keys (Ryan, 1990), De Bono's Six Thinking Hats (De Bono, 1992), Multiple Intelligences (Gardner & Hatch, 1989) activities, and debates. In these strategies, values of inclusion, care, understanding, freedom, and respect are evident.

When asked about how they used participation *for* all in their classrooms on professional experience (PE), preservice teachers mentioned "adapting lessons to enhance participation" and that they had employed "differentiation [by using] varied activities—tried to integrate MI [Multiple Intelligences] and Bloom's [Revised Bloom's Taxonomy] to all PBL [problem-based activities]." In addition, preservice teachers mentioned that they used student-centered practices in the following ways: "[planning] based on students' ideas and interest in their learning;. . . allow[ing] students to choose their own activities from a list of choices [through use of contracts]."

It was observed by examining their professional experience diaries that many of the preservice teachers were incorporating global education perspectives and mirroring the pedagogies modeled by the GERT team in its teaching of GE. *For* involves the development of an interest in and concern for the GE concepts and ideas engendering positive attitudes and values (Linke, 1980), coupled with behavioral changes. Focusing teaching and learning *for* a global world encourages teachers to use pedagogies of inquiry (Crick, 2009). Pedagogical approaches of inquiry related to learning *for* GE should encourage the development of social skills, such as working in groups, questioning, listening to others, and following directions. Students develop these skills as they interact effectively in class using pedagogical strategies such as cooperative learning. Our preservice teachers recognized the value of such pedagogical approaches during professional experience:

> Used talking chips so everyone got a chance to talk and participate;. . . [encouraged] students to work together to develop cooperative skills, where students were. . . learning to work together to achieve a desired goal; an important skill on a global scale due to the world becoming more connected globally.

A preservice teacher's comment about using cooperative learning sums up the importance of this pedagogical approach well: "It. . . creates an atmosphere of sharing, tolerance and understanding which is a common concept in global education."

The values that we saw as important are similar to the ones that preservice teachers also saw as important: tolerance and understanding, caring and compassionate concern for others, and a fair go. They thought it was important that their students "feel safe and secure," and they valued responsibility as they believed that we should teach "cooperative skills for students to use in the future," as well as design "appropriate [class] environments and lesson types to suit all intelligences." This view supports Merryfield's (1998) study, which claimed that the use of cooperative learning is important in order to develop necessary understandings for GE. Most of the teachers in Merryfield's study used cooperative learning and collaborative projects to teach students skills to work with people different from themselves. Understanding, tolerance, and inclusion are important values for preservice teachers who believe "all children have the right to participate and be educated" and in "creating an environment where all students can participate regardless of ethnicity, gender, age, sex, nationality, needs," as well as them having respect for the rights of all to participation and expression, "outlining that every answer or question is welcome."

As preservice teachers used particular pedagogies in their classrooms, particular values were also enacted. So as preservice teachers' own values are developed and enacted, we can assume a change to their pedagogical practices that affirms the importance of and belief in global education.

LEARNING *WITH* GLOBAL EDUCATION

When learning *with* a global world, real-life experiences are key. Our GE teaching strategies included the incorporation of such real-life experiences, including contemporary global issues, going on excursions, interacting and working *with* international students, and creating resources (including ICT resources) of value to and catering for differentiated audiences. A major focus of real-life experiences for our preservice teachers is the professional experience itself, where students interacted *with* a wide variety of different types of secondary, primary, and early childhood students and school communities. Core to these teaching strategies were values of care, respect, responsibility, freedom, and diversity.

Preservice teachers responded well to learning *with* GE in real-world contexts. One preservice teacher reflected on an experience *with* a community/school kitchen garden project: "I feel empowered to make a difference in terms of sustainability. I also now know about a lot of community groups who can help me in my teaching and everyday life."

We invite international students studying a wide range of courses in the university to contribute to teacher education courses, including the kitchen garden project, where they use their own narratives to highlight GE concepts from their lives and their countries, inspiring local students to use other ways of knowing in their teaching. This promotes cross cultural understanding: "I found it so interesting to explain the environmental situation in my country and also compare it with others." The GERT kitchen garden project received mention in the media: "It's inspiring to see this collaborative approach" (www.kitchengardenfoundation.org.au/news/news-item/186/). During professional experience, preservice teachers found that "the students are really responsive when a global perspective has infiltrated our learning." Preservice teachers noted in surveys that they found GE approaches were effective in a variety of classroom contexts, including classrooms with students from different cultures/countries and non-English speaking backgrounds and students with disabilities. The effect appears to persist beyond university too, with a graduate reporting that GE approaches work "incredibly well with my Indigenous students."

It is evident that as teacher educators incorporating GE principles we must wield a double-edged sword. We teach our students *about* while also teaching *with*. Using a values approach we have to use pedagogical practices to teach our students *about* strategies, such as cooperative learning, while simultaneously using such strategies in our own classes *with* our preservice

184 *Ruth Reynolds et al.*

teacher education students. By modeling and immersing our students in these practices the strategies become part of our preservice teachers' tool kit to be used when they are in the role of teacher. For more information on teaching about, with, and for global education, see Tables 11.1 and 11.2.

CONCLUSION

We have developed a values-based pedagogical stance as a central tenet of our GE approach. It is difficult to ascertain what came first, the values we developed individually and as a group, or our pedagogical approaches to teaching preservice teachers, almost certainly predisposed by our values. Undoubtedly, there is a long period of honing both these aspects of our global education involvement, and we are in turn influenced by the response of our students to these ideas and strategies. We came to understand that it is not so much the sequence of the learning that was important, but the respectful dialogic cooperation that continues as we adopt our pedagogic stance—one that ensures values drive us toward living in a sustainable way *with* others. It is a pedagogy based on an action-based approach and so it is the interactions, the crucial *with*, (learning to live together), that lead to our *about* and *for*. Our definition of global education has evolved from our practice and takes us further away from a notion of global competiveness to

Table 11.1 An Overview of Values and Pedagogical Strategies to Teach *about, for,* and *with* Global Education—A Global Stance

	Values	Pedagogical strategies
Teaching *about* global education	Tolerance Understanding Social justice (fair go) Democratic practice Diversity and difference	Inquiry-based instruction Visual literacy Jigsaw groups Role play Hands-on learning Games ICT Big-picture issues Debates
Teaching *for* global education	Inclusion Care Understanding Freedom Respect	Cooperative learning Group work Critical literacy Problem-solving Lateral thinking Activities catering to a variety of learning strengths Debates

a social justice, human rights–based approach. We have no doubt that a collaborative approach—not a competitive approach—to education based on social justice and human rights can enhance "good" education and enable students of the future to better function in a global context. *About, for*, and *with* global education becomes much more than a slogan. It is a useful heuristic to describe our pedagogic stance.

This research sought to explore our own developing practices and beliefs around the notion of GE, along with the developing beliefs of our preservice teachers. It must be acknowledged that the results illuminate GE approaches in a specific context. In this case, our values-based pedagogical stance has no doubt been influenced by the context in which we live and work. Values education has an established place in Australian schooling supported by government policies, and as such it may be more feasible for us to incorporate a values-based global education focus than it is for educators working within other systems and countries. This is an area for future research.

Author's Note: Survey questions can be accessed by e-mailing GERT@newcastle.edu.au or Ruth.Reynolds@newcastle.edu.au

REFERENCES

Abdullahi, S. A. (2011). Rethinking global education in the twenty-first century. *World Studies in Education, 12*(2), 77–91.

Anders, D., Moni, K., & Gitsaki, C. (2008). The classroom teacher: Making a difference through values education. *Social Educator, 26*(2), 11–18.

Apple, M., Kenway, J., & Singh, M. (Eds.). (2005). *Globalising public education: Policies, pedagogies and politics*. New York: Peter Lang.

Applebaum, B. (2005). In the name of morality: Moral responsibility, whiteness and social justice education. *Journal of Moral Education, 34*(3), 277–290.

Ball, S. (2012). *Global Education Inc.: New policy networks and the neo-liberal imaginary*. London: Routledge.

Bliss. (2005). Learning to think by studying global education. *Geography Bulletin, 37*(3), 34–41.

Bradbery, D., Brown, J., Donnelly, D., Ferguson-Patrick, K., Macqueen, S., & Reynolds, R. (2013). Teaching global education: Lessons learned for classroom teachers. *Ethos, 21*(1), 18–22.

Carano, K. (2013). Global educators' personal attribution of a global perspective. *Journal of International Social Studies, 3*(1), 6–19.

Cochran-Smith, M., & Lytle, S. (1999). Relationships of knowledge and practice: Teacher learning in communities. *Review of Research in Education, 24*, 249–305.

Cogan, J., & Grossman, D. (2009). Characteristics of globally minded teachers: A twenty-first century view. In T. Kirkwood-Tucker (Ed.), *Visions in global education*, (pp. 240–255). New York: Peter Lang.

Creswell, J. (2012). *Educational research: planning, conducting and evaluating quantitative and qualitative research* (4th ed.). Boston, MA: Pearson Education.

Crick, R. D. (2009). Inquiry-based learning: Reconciling the personal with the public in a democratic and archaeological pedagogy. *Curriculum Journal, 21*(1), 73–92.

Curriculum Corporation. (2008). *Global perspectives: A framework for global education in Australian schools*. Retrieved from www.asiaeducation.edu.au/verve/_resources/global_perspectives_statement.pdf

De Bono, E. (1992). *Six thinking hats for schools*. Cheltenham, Victoria: Hawker Brownlow Education.
Delors, J., Al Mufti, I., Amagi, I., Carneiro, R., Chung, F., Geremek, B., & Zhou, N. (1999). *Learning the treasure within: Report to UNESCO of the international commission on education for the twenty-first century—Highlights*. Paris: United Nations Educational Scientific and Cultural Organization. Retrieved from www.unesco.org/education/pdf/15_62.pdf
Department of Education, Science and Training [DEET]. (2005). *National framework for values education in Australian schools*. Commonwealth of Australia. Retrieved from www.curriculum.edu.au/verve/_resources/framework_pdf_version_for_the_web.pdf
Dept. Education, Science and Training (DEST). (2005). *National framework for values education in Australian schools*. Canberra: Australian Government.
Elliott, J. (1991). *Action research for educational change*. Milton Keynes: Open University Press.
Ferguson-Patrick, K., Macqueen, S., & Reynolds, R. (2014). Pre-service teacher perspectives on the importance of global education: World and classroom views. *Teachers and Teaching: Theory and Practice*, 20(4), 470–482. doi:10.1080/13540602.2014.881639
Gardner, H., & Hatch, T. (1989). Multiple intelligences go to school: Educational implications of the theory of multiple intelligences. *Educational Researcher*, 18(8), 4–10.
Hicks, D. (2006). *Lessons for the future: The missing dimension in education*. Victoria, BC: Trafford.
Holden, C. (2007). Teaching controversial issues. In D. Hicks & C. Holden (Eds.), *Teaching the global dimension*, (pp. 147–160). London: Routledge, Taylor & Francis.
Jickling, B., & Spork, H. (1998). Education for the environment: A critique. *Environmental Education Research*, 4(3), 309–327.
Kirkwood-Tucker, T. F. (2009). *Visions in global education: The globalization of curriculum and pedagogy in teacher education and schools: Perspectives from Canada, Russia, and the United States*. New York: Peter Lang.
Kusmawan, U., O'Toole, M., Reynolds, R., & Bourke, S. (2009). *International Research in Geographical and Environmental Education*, 18(3), 157–169.
Ladwig, J. G. (2010). Beyond academic outcomes. *Review of Research in Education*, 34(1), 113–141.
Lickona, T. (1997). Educating for character: A comprehensive approach. In A. Molnar (Ed.), *The construction of children's character* (pp. 45–62). Washington DC: Council for Research in Values and Education.
Linke, R. (1980). *Environmental education in Australia*. North Sydney: George Allen & Unwin Australia.
Lombardo, T. (2007). The evolution and psychology of future consciousness. *Journal of Future Studies*, 12, 1–24.
Lovat, T., Dally, K., Clement, N., & Toomey, R. (2011). Values pedagogy and teacher education: Reconceiving the foundations. *Australian Journal of Teacher Education*, 36(7), 31–44.
Lucas, A. M. (1972). *Environment and environmental education: Conceptual issues and curriculum implementation*. Unpublished doctoral dissertation. Columbus, Ohio State University. Retrieved from http://files.eric.ed.gov/fulltext/ED068371.pdf
Merryfield, M. (1998). Pedagogy for global perspectives in education: Studies of teachers' thinking and practice. *Theory & Research in Social Education*, 26(3), 342–379.

Merryfield, M. (2002). The difference a global educator can make. *Educational Leadership, 60*(2), 18–21.
Merryfield, M. (2009). Moving the center of global education. In T. Kirkwood (Ed.), *Leadership and vision in global education: The globalization of curriculum and pedagogy in teacher education and school*, (pp. 215–239). New York: Peter Lang.
Merryfield, M., & Wilson, A. (2005). *Social studies and the world*. Silver Spring, MD: National Council of Social Studies.
Mimoun Sorel, M.-L. (2009). Learning to be in the twenty-first century: Its evolving meaning and implication in the classroom pedagogy. In J. Zajda & H. Daun (Eds.), *Global values education: Teaching democracy and peace. Globalisation, comparative education and policy research*, (pp. 103–113). Dordrecht, Netherlands: Springer.
Ministerial Council on Education Employment Training & Youth Affairs (MCEETYA). (2008). *Melbourne declaration on educational goals for young Australians*. Melbourne: Curriculum Corporation.
Myers, J. (2010). The curriculum of globalisation. In B. Subedi (Ed.), *Critical global perspectives* (pp. 103–120). Charlotte, NC: Information Age.
Nodding, N. (2002). *Educating moral people: A caring alternative to character education*. Williston, VT: Teachers College Press.
Oxfam. (2006). *Education for global citizenship: A guide for schools*. London: Oxfam.
Peterson, C., & Seligman, M. (2004). *Character strengths and virtues: A handbook and classification*. Washington, DC: APA Press and Oxford University Press.
Reynolds, R. (2012). *Teaching history, geography and SOSE in primary schools*. Melbourne: Oxford University Press.
Rosenblatt, L. M. (2004). The transactional theory of reading and writing: Article 48. In R. B. Ruddell & N. J. Unrau (Eds.), *Theoretical models and processes of reading* (5th ed., pp. 1363–1398). Newark, DE: International Reading Association.
Ryan, T. (1990). Thinkers keys for kids. Retrieved November 6, 2013, from www.tonyryan.com.au
Sato, K., & Kleinsasser, R. (2004). Beliefs, practices, and interactions of teachers in a Japanese high school English department. *Teaching and Teacher Education, 20*(8), 797–816.
Starkey, H. (2012). Human rights, cosmopolitanism and utopias: Implications for citizenship education. *Cambridge Journal of Education, 42*(1), 21–35.
Tye, K. (2009). A history of the global education movement in the United States. In T. Kirkwood-Tucker (Ed.), *Visions in global education*, (pp. 3–24). New York: Peter Lang.
Vinterek, M. (2010). How to live democracy in the classroom. *Education Inquiry, 1*(4), 367–380.
Wang, J., Lin, F., Spalding, E., Odell, S., & Klecka, C. (2011). Understanding teacher education in an era of globalization. *Journal of Teacher Education, 62*(2), 115–120.
Zhao, Y. (2012). *World class learners: Educating creative and entrepreneurial students*. Thousand Oaks, CA: Corwin.
Zong, G., Wilson, A., & Quashiga, A. (2008). Global education. In L. Levstick & C. Tyson (Eds.), *Handbook of research on social studies*, (pp. 197–218). New York: Routledge.

Contributors

EDITORS

Brad M. Maguth, PhD, is a program coordinator and assistant professor in social studies education in the Department of Curricular and Instructional Studies, and director of the H.K. Barker Center for Economic Education at the University of Akron. As a former high school social studies teacher, he is passionate about the importance of a meaningful social studies education that helps build an active and informed citizenry in a global, multicultural, and technologically advanced age. His research has appeared in such peer-reviewed journals as *The Social Studies, Social Studies Research and Practice, Social Education*, and *Contemporary Issues in Technology and Teacher Education*. He is editor of *New Directions in Social Education: The Influence of Technology and Globalization on the Lives of Students* (Information Age Press, 2013). He received the 2013 Social Studies Leader of the Year Award from the Ohio Council for the Social Studies, and was recognized as the University of Akron's College of Education Researcher of the Year in 2014. He has conducted research and studied at the London School of Economics & Political Science in London, England, and at the Chinese Academy of Sciences in Beijing, China. Knowing that "you can't be neutral on a moving train," he has been leading a statewide advocacy campaign, Save World History in Ohio's Schools.

Jeremy Hilburn, PhD, is an assistant professor at the University of North Carolina at Wilmington, his alma mater. He taught middle grades social studies for seven years, during which he developed an intense interest in the many aspects of global education. He has two primary research interests: social studies curriculum and pedagogy specific to immigrant students in new gateway states and teacher conceptualizations of spatial citizenship. His recent scholarly work includes manuscripts in *Urban Review, Journal of Social Studies Research, Social Studies Research and Practice, Theory and Research in Social Studies*, and the Asian American education anthology.

Contributors

CHAPTER AUTHORS

Douglas Bourn is the Director of the Development Education Research Centre in the Institute of Education at University College London. Outside of serving as Editor of the *International Journal of Development Education and Global Learning* and author of *Theory and Practice of Development Education: A Pedagogy for Global Social Justice* (2015), Dr. Bourn is a member of the Programme Board for the Global Learning Programme for England.

Debbie Bradbery is the deputy program convenor for the Master of Teaching (Primary) at the University of Newcastle, Australia. Her research interests and publications lie in the areas of classroom applications of global education through literacy and teaching for a sustainable future. She is currently studying for a PhD while teaching full-time at the University of Newcastle. She can be contacted at debbie.bradbery@newcastle.edu.au

Joanna Brown is a member of the Global Education Research & Teaching group, and course coordinator and lecturer at University of Newcastle, New South Wales, Australia. She is coeditor of Reynolds, Bradbery, Brown, Carroll, Donnelly, Ferguson-Patrick, & Macqueen (2014), *Contesting and Constructing International Perspectives in Global Education*, and has authored articles on global education, university-school partnerships, and K-6 mathematics. She is also a New South Wales Board of Studies Teaching & Educational Standards Initial Teacher Education Accreditation panel member. She can be contacted at joanna.brown@newcastle.edu.au

Kimberly Cofino is a technology and learning coach at Yokohama International School, Japan. She is the cofounder of the Certificate of Educational Technology and Information Literacy (COETAIL) postgraduate program offered through SUNY Buffalo State. Kim is an Apple distinguished educator, a member of the K12 Horizon Report Advisory Board (2008–present), and a regular presenter, workshop facilitator, and keynote speaker focused on educational technology and the future of learning. She can be reached at mscofino@gmail.com

Ian Davies is a professor of education at the University of York, UK. He is the author of many publications regarding citizenship and global education. He has extensive international research and development experience. He holds various editorial positions, including an associate editorship of the journal *Citizenship Teaching and Learning*.

Debra Donnelly is a history educator in the School of Education at the University of Newcastle in Australia, working with pre-service teachers in both undergraduate and postgraduate programs. Debra's research interests center on the role of the visual and media in the development of historical and global consciousness in an age of ever-increasing access through modern technology and seek to clarify the relationship between teacher conceptual frameworks of understanding, problematic knowledge and pedagogical practice. Dr Donnelly has been the recipient of numerous teaching awards, including the University of Newcastle's Vice-Chancellor's Award for Outstanding Contribution to Student Learning (2011) and Teaching Excellence Award (2010) and a semi-finalist, with Dr Grushka, in the Adobe Design Achievement Awards in 2011.

Kate Ferguson-Patrick is a lecturer at the University of Newcastle, Australia. She lectures in primary education, with math, social studies, and integrated curriculum as her specialty areas. She has recently completed a long-term study of cooperative learning with early career teachers and how this classroom approach leads to democratic classrooms. She has publications in Australian and international journals about this research, as well as in global education. She can be contacted at kate.fergusonpatrick@newcastle.edu.au

Debora Hinderliter Ortloff is the director of assessment and an assistant professor at Finger Lakes Community College.

Hilary Landorf is an associate professor in the College of Education at Florida International University (FIU). She also serves as the director of FIU's Office of Global Learning Initiatives, as well as the leader of its Master of Science degree program in international and intercultural education. She writes and presents internationally on integrating global learning into education, and on the connection between global learning and liberal education. Among her recent publications is a case study on curriculum internationalization at FIU in M. Green (Ed.), *Improving and Assessing Global Learning*. She can be contacted at landorfh@fiu.edu

Caprice Lantz is a lecturer on the postgraduate course in diversity management at the University of Bradford, UK. Her background includes teaching and supporting teaching innovations in UK higher education, and she is the author of numerous publications in this area. Her PhD, completed in 2014 at the University of York, focused upon the development of intercultural competence in university students. She can be contacted at c.lantz@bradford.ac.uk

Suzanne Macqueen is a lecturer in the School of Education at the University of Newcastle, Australia. She has published a number of journal articles related to equity in education and is involved in a number of research projects focusing on inequity in education. She is currently completing a PhD on the experiences of non-traditional students in teacher education. She can be contacted at suzanne.macqueen@newcastle.edu.au

Contributors

Rebekah Madrid is a middle school and high school humanities teacher at Yokohama International School, in Yokohama, Japan. She has taught the International Baccalaureate Middle Years Programme and Diploma Programme in three countries and is interested in how technology can enhance teaching and learning. She can be reached at madridr@yis.jp

Sarah A. Mathews is an assistant professor and program leader of social studies education at Florida International University in Miami, Florida. Her research and teaching interests are influenced by principles of global education, including pedagogies that develop perspective consciousness and intercultural competence. Her research focuses on critical media literacy, photomethodologies, and popular culture as tools for fostering global and multicultural citizenship and civic engagement. She has written articles for *Theory and Research in Social Education, The History Teacher, The Social Studies,* and *The Journal of Social Studies Research.*

Adrienne Michetti is a Digital Literacy Coach at the United World College of South East Asia in Singapore. Her Master's Degree project (NYU) applied Communities of Practice theory to the practical design of online professional development spaces for teachers new to the International Baccalaureate. For 6 years she was a workshop leader with the International Baccalaureate and contributed to developing subject guides and further IB teacher materials. She can be contacted at amh@uwcsea.edu.sg.

Cyndi Mottola Poole is a former middle and high school social studies teacher. She holds a PhD in social science education from the University of Central Florida. She has taught education and history courses at the University of Central Florida and Valencia College, and currently teaches at the University of Pittsburgh. She has published multiple articles and given numerous conference presentations on global education. She can be contacted at cynthia.poole@ucf.edu

Timothy Patterson is an assistant professor in secondary education in the Department of Teaching and Learning at Temple University.

Anatoli Rapoport is an associate professor in the Department of Curricular and Instruction at Purdue University.

Ruth Reynolds is an associate professor and leader of the Global Education Research and Teaching Centre at School of Education at the University of Newcastle in Australia. She is past president of the Social Educators Association of Australia; author of 18 books for researchers, teacher education students, and schoolteachers; editor of the *International Assembly Journal of International Social Studies*; and the recipient of a tertiary Australian citation for Outstanding Teaching and Learning. Her latest book for Oxford University Press, *Teaching Humanities and Social Sciences in Primary School*, will be available shortly.

Anne Ross has a background in environmental analysis, education, and environmental education/sustainability education/research and lectures on educating for ecological sustainability within the School of Education at the University of Newcastle, Australia. She is currently a PhD candidate analyzing the history of environmental education centers in New South Wales, Australia. She can be contacted at anne.ross@newcastle.edu.au

William B. Russell III is an associate professor of social science education at the University of Central Florida, where he teaches undergraduate and graduate social science education courses and serves as PhD track coordinator for the Social Science Education program. He is the director of the International Society for the Social Studies and is the editor-in-chief of *The Journal of Social Studies Research*. He has published numerous articles and books related to social science education, including *Essentials of Middle and Secondary Social Studies* (2014, Routledge) and *Essentials of Elementary Social Studies* (2013, Routledge). He can be contacted at Russell@ucf.edu

Olga N. Shonia is an assistant professor at Capital University in Columbus, Ohio. There she teaches in the Education Department and coordinates the Intercultural Student Teaching Program as well as TESOL Endorsement Program. She received her PhD in educational policy studies from Indiana University, Bloomington. Her research interests include internationalization of teacher education and global citizenship. She can be contacted at oshonia@capital.edu

Guichun Zong is a professor of curriculum and instruction at Kennesaw State University. She received her BA in social science education (1988), MA in comparative education (1991) from Beijing Normal University, and a doctorate in curriculum and instruction (social studies education, 1999) under the direction of Jan Tucker and Mohammed Farouk at Florida International University. Her publications have appeared in journals such as *Teaching and Teacher Education, Teacher Education Quarterly*, and *Theory and Research in Social Education*, and books such as *Social Education in Asia: Critical Issues and Multiple Perspectives* (Grossman & Lo, 2007), *Handbook of Research in Social Studies Education* (Levstik &Tyson, 2008), *Visions of Global Education* (Kirkwood-Tucker, 2009), and *Bridging Cultures: International Women Faculty Transforming the U.S. Academy* (Robbins, Smith, & Santini, 2011). She can be reached at gzong@kennesaw.edu

Author Index

Adair, J., 168
Adams, J., 92
Afshar, V., 142
Aldrich, R., 44
Alger, C., 2
Alpert, D., 92
American Assn. of Colleges for Teacher Education, 114, 117, 128
American Council on Education, 102, 133
Anderson, C., 115–16
Anderson, L., 2, 41, 115–16
Anderson, T., 138, 145
Ang, G., 46
Appiah, K. A., 42, 134
Apple, M., 34, 174
Archer, W., 138
Arkoudis, S., 51
Armstrong, C., 28
Arnot, M., 42
ASCD, 167
Atkins, R., 87
Au, W., 18, 113

Bady, A., 140–1
Baildon, M., 134
Ball, S., 3, 174
Banks, C., 79, 81, 86, 88
Banks, G., 102
Banks, J., 28, 31, 35, 79, 81, 86, 88
Barner, J. R., 102
Barton, K., 114, 117
Beatty, J., 139
Becker, J., 41
Beltramo, J. L., 33
Benkler, H., 134
Bennett, M., 43, 47, 49, 52–3, 73, 86
Berrett, D., 141
Berry, J., W. 43

Bettez, S. C., 93, 97
Big Three., 131
Blohm, J. M., 52
Bohan, C., 30
Boling, E. C., 139
Bolton, P., 100
Bone, D., 45
Bonk, C. J., 138, 140
Bransford, J., 93
Branson, M., 34
Braskamp, D. C. 116, 119, 127, 134–5, 138, 144
Braskamp, L. A. 115–16, 119, 127, 134–6, 138, 144
Brewer, M. B., 46–7
British Council., 46
Browett, J., 114, 117
Brown, L., 101–2
Byram, M., 49

Campbell, J. 47
Carano, K. T. 117, 174
Carfagna, A., 92
Carspecken, P., 80
Carter, A., 28, 35
Caruana, V., 45
Carver, L., 142
Case, P., 45
Case, R., 64, 70–1, 116, 135
Cavanagh, S., 30
Changnon, G., 43
Charan, R., 92
Chen, V., 138, 140
Chickering, A., 136
Christian, L., 118
Clifford, V., 49
Coa, M., 143
Cobb, J., 99, 102
Cochran-Smith, M., 93, 176

Cogan, J.J., 30, 42, 174–5
Collins, M., 31
Common Core State Standards
    Initiative, 113
Community Center for Media Arts, 145
Corry, O., 28
Council of Chief State School Officers, 78
Council of Europe., 15, 52
Cremin, L., 30
Creswell, J., 80, 176
Crocco, M., 118
Croghan, R., 145
Crose, B., 115
Cunningham, D., 100
Cushner, K., 66, 68, 70, 78

Dabbagh, N., 145
Damico, J., 134
Daniel, J., 142
Darabi, A., 139
Darling-Hammond, L., 93, 102
Davidson, C., 134
Davies, I., 28–9, 41–2
Davies, M., 116
Deardorff, D., 43, 49–50
Delanty, G., 28
Demers, K., 93
DeTemple, J., 102
Devereux, L., 51
De Vita, G., 45
Dillabough, J., 42
Dillman, D., 118
Dolby, N., 78–9
Donaldson, D., 3
Donnelly, T., 87
Dower, N., 28, 35–6
Dragusin, M., 141
Drori, G., 95
Duffy, T., 100
Duncheon, J., 33
Dunn, R., 31

Edwards, M., 145
Egron-Polak, E., 44
Ellington, L., 30
Elliott, E., 175
Engberg, M., 115–16, 119, 127, 134–5
Engle, S.H., 36, 64, 68, 75
Erickson, H, 158, 160
Eslami, Z., 116
European Commission, 45–6
Evans, M., 28–9, 32, 35, 42
Evans, R., 30

Fantini, A., 43
Fernekes, W., 31, 35
Ferriter, W., 92
Fitchett, P., 113
Forbes, S., 167
Fowler, S., 52
Fox, E., 159
Fox, K., 115
Fraenkel, J., 118
Francis, L., 27
Franklin, P., 43
Frederickson, M., 116
Frey, C., 79
Friedman, T., 95, 101
Fujikane, H., 41
Furco, A., 160

Gabbard, R., 145
Gallavan, N., 27, 29, 30
Gardner, H., 98, 100–1, 105, 181
Garrison, D., 138–9
Gaudelli, W., 13, 27, 31–2, 35, 72, 92, 114, 117
Gibson, M., 92–3
Giddens, A., 42
Gill, J., 29, 31
Glass, C., 119, 134–5
Glass, G., 119
Goldblatt, D., 42, 95
Gragert, E., 114, 165
Graham, P., 29
Grainger, N., 45
Green, A., 44
Gregersen-Hermans, J., 52
Griffin, C., 145
Guillen, M., 95
Gunter, G., 146

Haigh, M., 49
Hall, C., 161
Halvorsen, A., 116
Hanvey, R., 1–3, 41, 115, 135, 138
Harber, C., 32–3
Harrison, L., 142
Harrison, N., 47
Hart, D., 87
Hartsell, T., 145–6
Hayden, M., 155–6, 160
Heafner, T., 113
Heater, D., 28–9, 35, 41–2, 44
Heilman, E., 108

Author Index

Heimonen, M., 92
Held, D., 42, 95
Henry, B., 137, 139, 144
Herman, R., 141
Hicks, D., 20, 92, 180
Higher Education Statistics Agency, 46
Hill, J., 138
Hill Useem, R., 155
Holden, C., 20, 92, 177
Hong, W., 116
Hopkins, K., 119
Huberman, M., 81
Hudson, R., 44
Hulme, J., 53
Hunter, J., 145
Hwang, H., 95
Hyslop, J., 42
Hytten, K., 93, 97

Ignatieff, M., 42
Ingram, L., 32
International Baccalaureate Organization, 156–7, 159, 164, 167
International School of Brussels, The, 170
Isin, E., 42
Ito, M., 134

Jackson, J., 49
Janzen, K., 145
Jarchow, E., 135
Jenkins, C., 160
Jenkins, H., 134
Johnson, L., R. 46
Johoda, G., 47
Jungnitsch, M., 161

Kagan, S., 78
Kambutu, J., 73, 116
Kang, J., 143
Kaviani, K., 37
Kearney, A., 96
Keating, A., 78
Kegan, R., 135
Keiper, T., 138
Killick, D., 53
Kim, K., 138, 140
King, P., 49, 52, 119
Kirkwood-Tucker, T., 2, 15, 21, 174
Kiwako Okuma-Nyström, M., 36
Klassen, F., 114, 117, 128
Kline, E., 168

Knight, J., 45
Ko, Y., 143
Kolar, N., 85
Kolowich, S., 140
Koutsantoni, D., 45
Kuklis, R., 168

Larkin, R., 87
Landorf, H., 93, 113
Langford, M., 156, 163
Lantz, C., 41, 52–3
Larson, B., 138
Lederman, D., 46
Leduc, R., 27, 35
Leming, J., 30
Levin Institute, 96
Liang, X., 139
Lim, M., 143
Lipsitz, G., 102
Liu, M., 143
Liu, P., 125
Loewen, J., 34, 116

MacDonald, A., 32
Macedo, E., 30
Maddoux, M., 116
Magolda, B., 49, 52, 119
Maguth, B., 3, 106
Mahoney, A., 87
Maiworm, F., 45
Mandelbaum, M., 3
Mann, S., 49
Mansilla, V., 98, 100–1, 105
Marino, M., 92, 106
Marshall, H., 78
Martin, L., 116
Maslow, A., 166
Mason, L., 137
Mathews, S., 134
Matthews, C., 100, 102
McGre, A., 95
McGrew, A., 42
McGrew, C., 32, 113
McIntyre, J., 93
McKenzie, M., 163
McNulty, C., 116
Merrill, K., 116, 119, 127, 134–5
Merryfield, M., 13, 15, 34–5, 41–2, 63, 66–7, 70, 73, 79, 93, 114–18, 127–8, 135, 137, 144–5, 175, 177, 182
Metzger, S., 137
Meyer, J., 95, 139

Author Index

Middlehurst, R., 45
Milam, J., 116
Miles, M., 81
Mohl, R., 103
Moore, M., 49, 137
Muirhead, P., 115
Murray, M., 102
Murray, W., 95
Myers, J., 27, 29–30, 34, 93, 98, 175

National Council for the Social Studies, 113, 131
Nemeth, C., 47
Nganga, L., 73, 116
Ninimiya, A., 30
Noddings, N., 28, 31, 97, 106, 178
Nolan, R., 49
North, M., 141
North, S., 141
Nussbaum, M., 34, 78

Ochoa, A., 36, 118, 128
O'Connor, K., 114, 117
O'Hare, S., 138, 141, 143
Ohmae, K., 95
Okech, D., 102
Olesova, L., 138
Oliver, M., 140
Openshaw, R., 34
Organization for Economic Cooperation and Development, 113
Ortloff, D., 78, 90
Osler, A., 31, 35, 45
Ostry, S., 95
Oswald, R., 116
Overton, J., 102
Oxfam, 14, 20, 35, 174

Pain, R., 51
Pappano, L., 141
Park, M., 49
Partnership for 21st Century Skills, 113
Peacock, J., 100, 102
Peacock, N., 47
Pedersen, P., 46
Peralta, C., 141
Perraton, J., 42, 95
Perry, B., 145
Perry, W., 43
Peters, L., 139
Phoenix, A., 145
Piaget, J., 43
Pickert, S., 135

Pike, G., 13–14, 42, 44–5, 135
Pinar, W., 30
Pithers, R., 43
Pollack, D., 156
Poole, M., 146
Portera, A., 43
Porter-Magee, K., 30
Pusch, M., 52

Qin-Hillard, D., 79, 133

Rahman, A., 79
Rapoport, A., 27, 29, 30, 33, 35, 113, 116–17
Ravitch, D., 44, 78
Raymond, E., 103, 161
Reddy, P., 53
Reid, A., 28–9, 31, 42
Reimers, F., 29–30, 37
Reuben, J., 29
Richardson, J., 138
Richardson, R., 41–2, 141
Robbins, M., 27, 30, 34
Roberts, A., 114, 117, 128, 143–4
Rodafinos, A., 138, 141, 143
Rogoff, B., 168, 170
Ruday, S., 139
Russell, W., 113, 116
Ruth, S., 140

Sanatullova-Allison, E., 125
Sattin, C., 78
Schank, R., 145
Schattle, H., 78
Scholte, J., 42
Schweisfurth, M., 34
Scruton, R., 48
Sears, A., 29, 31
Segall, M., 43
Selby, D., 14, 135
Sercu, L., 49, 51
Shah, P., 78
Shaw, G., 140
Shiel, C., 49
Shonia, O., 85, 87
Skerrett, A., 87
Sleeter, C., 93–4, 97, 99
Smick, D., 95
Smith, L., 65
Smith, N., 95
Smith, S., 31
Smolen, L., 116
Soden, R., 43
Song, L., 138

Sovic, S., 46
Spencer-Oatey, H., 43
Spitzberg, B., 43
Spring, J., 93, 133
Spurling, N., 45
Stachowski, L., 85, 87
Standish, A., 28
Starkey, H., 31, 35, 45, 175
Staub, E., 34
Stearns, P., 92, 98
Stephan, C., 47, 52–3
Stephan, W., 47, 52–3
Stewart, V., 78
Stiglitz, J., 95
Stueck, W., 99, 102
Suarez-Orozco, C., 133
Suarez-Orozco, M., 35, 78–9, 133
Subedi, B., 93, 116
Sumner, W., 46
Szpara, M., 34

Tajfel, H., 46–7
Takacs, S., 102
Talbert-Johnson, C., 116, 118, 127
Teichler, U., 45
Thom, V., 46
Thompson, J., 156
Thornton, S., 31, 114, 117
Tirmizi, A., 43
Todorova, I., 133
Toh, S., 42
Tomlinson, C., 167
Toyoshima, M., 45
Trucano, M., 142
Trufant, L., 139
Tsolidis, G., 30
Turner, T., 46, 113
Tyack, D., 30
Tye, B., 115
Tye, K., 13–14, 113, 115, 135, 174

UK Higher Education International Unit, 46
Ukpokodu, O., 92–3, 114, 116–18, 127

Vande Berg, M., 46
VanFossen, P., 32, 113
Van Reken, R., 156
Vertovec, S., 46
Virtue, D., 113
Vogler, K., 113
Voithofer, R., 137, 139, 144
Volet, S., 46
Vonderwell, S., 146

Wallen, N., 118
Wang, Y., 138, 140, 174
Warschauer, M., 138
Waters, J., 151
Waters, S., 113, 140
Watson, H., 100, 102
Weber, N., 32
Welsh, D., 141
West, R., 74, 138
White, C., 34
Whitehead, D., 79
Williams, A., 49
Williams, C., 46
Willinsky, L., 2
Wilson, A., 2, 73, 93, 114–15, 117, 174, 177
Wood, P., 28, 42
Woodfield, S., 45
Wylie, S., 92

Yamashita, H., 27, 32, 33
Yang, D., 138
Yokohama International School, 159, 164
Youniss, J., 87
Yuen, S., 145–6
Yurekli, H., 13

Zajda, J., 36
Zeichner, K., 93, 114, 117
Zimpher, N., 125
Zmuda, A., 168
Zong, G., 67, 93, 174
Zutshi, S., 138, 141, 143

Subject Index

Australia, 4, 7, 174–5, 177, 181, 185
awareness of human choices, 1, 115–16

case study, 5–6, 63–5, 67, 69, 71–3, 75, 77, 106, 117
CATS model, 79, 81, 86, 88
classroom practice, 14, 22, 34, 89, 93, 177
Cold War, 1–2, 41
community-based inquiry, 6, 92, 94, 99, 102, 105
controversial issues, 35–6, 136, 181
cosmopolitanism, 78
cross-cultural, 45, 66–70, 73, 114–19, 121–3, 125–9, 138–9; awareness, 74, 115–16, 138–9; experiences, 67, 70, 73, 75, 117, 125–6

development education, 13–14, 16–18, 20–1; Global North, 14, 20; Global South, 14, 20; power, 15, 17–20, 22–4
distance education, 136, 139–40, 143; asynchronous online discussions, 147; community of inquiry, 138; social media, 133, 158, 164, 166; threaded discussion, 137

environmental education, 179–80
European Union, 41–4
experiential learning, 5–6, 70, 86, 94, 99–100, 104–5, 161
extra-curricular activities, 158, 162–3, 171

global citizenship 17–18, 27–37, 78–89; democracy, 28, 36; ethic, 28, 35; institutions, 28, 36; utopian, 28; white noise, 29

global citizenship education, 17–18, 27, 31–6; counter-socialization, 36–7; curriculum integration, 31–2
global citizenship education, obstacles, 27, 35, 37; administrative support, 27, 32, 34–5; conceptual vagueness, 27, 35; disciplinary heritage, 30–2; national citizenship, 29, 35
global content courses, 115, 118–23, 125–8
global education, 13, 19, 41, 50, 61, 115, 143, 155, 158, 174; action oriented, 155; behavior management, 176; computer mediated communication, 63, 67, 138; empathy/threat dialectic, 78; fragmentation, 42; global communication, 3; globally connected, 155, 162, 164; global issues, 19–20, 34–5, 66, 133, 163, 174, 180–1; global learning, 17–18, 22–4, 99–101, 133, 144; global outlook, 19
global education pedagogy, 174; teaching about, 180; teaching for, 181; teaching with, 183
Global Education Research and Teaching (GERT), 7, 175, 192
global education stance, 176–80, 184; inclusive, 155–8, 166–71; perceptual dimension, 70
globalization, 17, 20, 32–5, 92–107, 113; defined, 94–6, 174; critics, 95; proponents, 95
global literacy, 88
global perspective, 92, 113–20, 125–9, 134–40, 142–5; cognitive, 52,

119, 124, 135, 138–9, 145; cognitive dissonance, 135, 138; encounters with difference, 133–6, 142; interpersonal, 119–20, 124–6, 135, 146; intrapersonal, 119–20, 124–6, 135, 144; inventory, 119, 126, 134

higher education, 46, 49, 51, 133, 142–3; career placement, 48; neoliberal, 3, 8, 45

inequality, 5, 15, 18–20, 23–4, 95
instructional gatekeeper, 117
intercultural education, 41–3; competence, 41, 43–4, 48–9, 51; contact, 47, 51–2, 65, 68; critical thinking, 43, 49; developmental model of intercultural sensitivity, 53; educational methods, 52
International Baccalaureate Programme, 156–7, 159, 161, 164, 167–9, 172
international schools, 155–7, 160, 163–4, 167, 169–71
interview, 17, 64, 80, 103, 105, 107

Kennedy, John F. 2
knowledge of global dynamics, 1, 115–16, 138

massive open online courses (MOOCs), 7, 134, 136
mathematics, 89, 101, 113, 159, 166, 176

national citizenship, 29–30, 33, 35–6; patriotism, 29–30, 34–5; schools, 29–33, 35, 37

Peace Corps, 2, 63
perspective consciousness, 1, 115, 139
professional development/learning, International teacher professional development, 6, 64–9, 72–5

service learning, 86–7, 115, 121–3, 126, 158, 160–2, 170
Silk Road, 5, 63–5, 67, 69–71, 73, 75
social justice, 15, 18–23, 87, 93, 177–9, 184–5
social studies, 27, 29–31, 33, 98–9, 113, 117; elementary education, 118; standards, 33, 113; tests, 32, 113
Soviet, 2, 143
state of the planet awareness, 1, 115
state standards, 113
study abroad, 45–6, 49, 68–9, 123, 126–8; overseas student teaching, 91, 63, 66; *see also* global education; travel
survey, 17, 43, 52, 80–1, 118–20, 122, 134–5, 143, 160, 175–6

teacher education, 27, 35–6, 65, 92–4, 97–101, 105–6, 117–18; in-service, 27, 63–4; pre-service, 27, 179
third culture kids, 155–6, 163
travel, 53, 63–72, 84, 161–3

United Kingdom, 5, 41

values education, 177, 179, 185; care, 177–8, 181, 183–4; respect, 177–8, 181–4; rights, 174, 177–8, 181–2, 185